I'd Rather Die!

Public Speaking
Survival Skills

ROBERT SCANLON

What others say ...

Robert Scanlon has the magic dust! He's the Master Trainer that the rest of us go to for development. I've attended many of his programs over the years and always learn something new and important. This book has been many years in the making because Robert has been teaching this content to speakers like me for decades. It's actually thanks to Robert's artful teachings I fell in love with presenting in public in the first place and it's thanks to his gift of incredibly practical content that I have had a very successful career. I have been applying the content included in this very book to my stage presentations for years and now I'm a CSP (Certified Speaking Professional), which is the highest designation for speakers in the world. Seriously, this book is a must if you want to dramatically improve your presentation skills.

Michelle Bowden, Authority on Persuasive Presenting in Business
www.MichelleBowden.com.au

I was fortunate enough to run a Business Consulting business with Robert Scanlon for over five years and during that time I saw Robert's genius in action on countless occasions. Mention Robert's name to clients who have experienced his skill in action and they light up with enthusiasm, respect and awe. Few presenters have Robert's ability to shift an audience from a state of confusion, ambivalence and sometimes hostility, to a state of confidence, clarity and consensus.

Robert is not only one of the best presenters I have seen, he also has the ability to make his magic replicable. Robert teaches you in such a way as to make being a great speaker possible and probable.

Watching Robert in action when presenting, it is hard to believe that he started his speaking career as we all start ... a reluctant, nervous amateur. As such, Robert is living proof that with the right skills, the right mindset and persistence you can become an astonishing presenter.

I have seen the content in this book transform people from self-conscious to engaging, from frozen to fantastic, from unsure to unstoppable.

Rod Matthews, Speaker, Author and Director
www.RodMatthews.com.au

Robert is the trainer's trainer. He is able to help transform people's ability to communicate and present in public from the most nervous to the most practiced. Robert's breadth and depth of knowledge, insight and coaching in public speaking will help anyone have the confidence, and develop the competence to achieve their speaking goals.

Nicole Issaakidis, Head of Organization Development
Foxtel

For someone who is in a permanent state of busy, Robert taught me very early on, what matters and what doesn't when it comes to giving great presentations. It's made me both less and more busy ... but only for all the right reasons. Bravo Robert!

Ruuben van den Heuvel, Head of Music Partnerships, (APAC)
Google Play

In my experience very few are able to transform people through their words, especially in the area of public speaking. Robert is a practitioner, teacher and author who is able to cut through the usual and really leave those that listen to him and no doubt read this book, with great insight and tools to exceed in this area.

Fiona Cottrell, Director Employee and Organization Development
AUSTAR Entertainment (1996—2012)

I first met Robert about 20 years ago and many of the lessons he shared are still fresh in my mind and an important part of my daily work life, so I was delighted to get the opportunity to preview this book.

Whether you are new to public speaking or a seasoned campaigner, this book is a must read! It is packed with great ideas and blinding flashes of the obvious to guarantee the public speaker's success.

I have presented at well over 100 conferences, workshops and events over many years and yet I found just so many great tips and reminders in here. I can't wait to use them to improve my next presentation.

My only regret is that Robert did not write this book years ago — he could have saved me, and no doubt those that read it, a great deal of angst!

Steve Mitchinson, Director
BBB Advisory www.bbbadvisory.com.au

Contents

Chapter 1: How To Be A Confident Speaker And Presenter

1.1 Taming Your Inner Crocodile

YOU ARE STANDING OFF TO one side—out of sight of your prospective audience—while the MC (Master of Ceremonies) whips up the audience in anticipation of your presentation.

In your sweaty and slippery hand, you clutch the wireless slide-clicker ever tighter, as if it were a security blanket.

In the other are your notes.

Your notes! Shouldn't you just read through them one more time? Wasn't there something you had to remember ... wait ... the MC is saying something. The audience bursts out into laughter. How will you follow this? Your presentation style is dry, humorless.

You realize your mouth is dry and lick your lips, feeling the tension in your jawbones. Your chest feels tight and you notice you've been holding your breath, so you try to breathe deep, but the nausea starts again.

You turn away and dry retch. Why did you ever agree to this? Never again. You look around. Maybe you can run away?

It's too late though. There is a minor pause in the MC's patter, then you hear your name ring out over the PA (Public Address) system, and the audience begins the customary round of enthusiastic welcome applause.

Your heart attempts to free itself from its bony cage, and you force a fixed rictus-grin as you stride out under the bright lights and across the stage to the lectern. The MC is beaming at you and clapping, walking backwards off to the side of the stage area. A strange thought flits through your mind: how do MCs do that? So slick and confident.

Panic rises rapidly as you try to refocus on your speech and you turn your fixed grin to the audience, stand behind the lectern and wait for the applause to die down. Feeling strangely separate from your body, you place your notes on the lectern.

You look down at the slide-clicker, then back up at the audience, now quiet. You try to undo the rictus-grin, but it's stuck. You lift the slide-clicker and point it at the screen. Where did they say to point it? Had they told you? You don't remember, and suddenly your thoughts whirl into a blur. You press a button and nothing happens.

You try to flash your grin at the audience, but since your face is already stuck in some idiotic frozen puppet smirk, nothing happens, except that you feel like one of those swiveling clown heads in a carnival sideshow stall.

Your maniacal grin remains immovable as you press the slide-clicker multiple times ... and still nothing is happening. You turn the clicker over to peer at the LED indicator light, and up on the screen, your slides begin to advance at speed. You stare back up at the screen in horror, now pressing the back button, but your hand is now so sweaty that the clicker leaps out of your hand like a pip from an orange, and scoots across the stage. It comes to a halt at the feet of the MC, who has the agape expression of someone watching a car crash.

You rush across the stage to pick up the wayward clicker; on the way knocking your shoulder against the lectern and it rocks and yaws ... and crashes to the ground, spilling the water over some papers.

Your notes.

The gasps from the audience seem distant and echoey as you lock eyes with the MC, knowing he sees your deer-in-the-headlights eyes, and you reach down together in seeming slow motion to collect the offending slide-clicker, which is the last thing you remember before your skulls collide in a sickening crunch, and everything turns black.

***

While the example above might seem like some unlikely train-wreck, or some would-be public speaker's private nightmare, if you relate to *any* of it, then I have good news for you.

If you have experienced *any* of those symptoms, or any of the myriad other negative reactions to public speaking such as light-headedness, grinding teeth, a sudden blank mind, desperately dry mouth, feeling like you are rushing your words (I could go on, but I won't), any time you even *think* about public speaking, or are asked to give a presentation ... then you are in the right place.

Yes, dear reader, there is hope and comfort available. I too, have experienced these symptoms, and learned to overcome and rise above these debilitating problems. So much so, that I ended up with a career in public speaking, training trainers and yes, I have even been that MC. That's right, me, an introvert, training hundreds of folks just like you, in how to become wonderful presenters. (This is not a book about me, although I will give you plenty of real life examples. If you want to know more, you can read my story at the back.)

I *know* what it feels like to have those raging butterflies.

But as a very good mentor of mine once said, "*Almost everyone has those butterflies in their stomach. Your job is to teach them to fly in formation.*"

Which is what you will learn in this book.

It's not all just about overcoming nerves though. You'll learn a thorough method for structuring your talk—honed over years and years of use, and based on tried and tested principles—as well as a myriad of practical techniques for almost any scenario.

Who is this book for?

The methods and techniques I will teach you in this book will benefit anyone who at any time finds him or herself in front of an audience, whether or not you experience the crippling fear that many people will genuinely feel before or during public speaking.

If you have to:

- Talk in front of your team
- Make a speech at a wedding (funeral, bar mitzvah—you name it)
- Present to management
- Give a talk at a conference
- Explain something to a small group of people
- Be more popular at parties (no, I didn't make that up. These techniques can do that too!)

Then no matter where you are on the scale of public speaking, introvert or extrovert, from the "I'd Rather Die" sufferer to the "Just Gimme The Mic": I have the tools, techniques, tips and methods that will help you rise to the highest heights.

What you will learn

I will show you, not just how to fly those butterflies in formation, but how to:

- Be a strong and confident presenter
- How to control and steer your nerves
- How to feel at ease with your audience(s)
- How to get your message across; how to make a point
- How to engage and capture attention, and know that you can woo (and wow) your audience. This technique has a double-whammy benefit: it helps you take your attention off you
- How to effectively answer questions in a way that affects your entire audience
- How to project and "be interesting"
- How to design and structure your presentation and speech for an effective impact and outcome
- How to structure your own speaker's notes so they will work for you
- How to deal with difficult audiences or controversial subjects

And many more practical techniques that will lift your professionalism—and confidence—to a superior level.

How to get the most from this book

Whenever I introduce a key concept, I'll ***embolden and italicize*** it for you to internalize and notice whenever it pops up again. Sometimes I will link back to the key concept for ease of reading (in e-readers).

Each section of this book ends with suggestions for what I have named "***Drills.***" I have good reason for doing this: ***Drills*** are actions that must be learned through practicing over and over until they can be recalled without thinking. The kinds of examples that you've probably learned through drills are: reciting the alphabet, your multiplication tables, stopping at a red light, and even singing your National Anthem.

While I want you to learn these methods and techniques with conscious application, deliberation and precision, I also want you to digest them, practice them and install them in your own body until they are second nature.

That is the secret to becoming a polished and confident presenter.

Now let us begin our journey together ...

Fight, Flight, Freeze—or Ease?

Why is it that perfectly normal people—people such as you or I, who have no difficulty in speaking confidently one-on-one—have these sudden onslaughts of anxiety and panic at the thought of public speaking?

How is it even possible to overcome what feels like a whole body reaction?

And therein lies the problem.

We are fighting our body's own defenses.

Which is why, when you learn to overcome them (and not simply suppress them!), you will find a whole new world at your fingertips.

So what is going on there?

There's little point in delving deep into the theoretical psychology of it all, because that's definitely not going to help you make a better speech. I prefer to help you by teaching you what is useful and practical: techniques you can use right off the bat. I'll expose our automatic responses, and show you how to utilize cutting-edge training techniques (and "drills") to tame those primordial reflexes.

5

Your inbuilt reactions

If you were to walk into a room and suddenly discovered that it was filled with your enemies—what would you do?

Stop in horror? Try to run? Pull out your weapons?

In truth, as a member of the human race, you are pre-programmed to attempt any one of those things. Your instinctive, so-called reptilian brain takes over and all you may be able to do is "Fight, Flight or Freeze."

So when you're confronted by an audience with all eyes trained on you—that your mind may be automatically predisposed to think of as "enemies"—it's no surprise that these instinctive reactions take over.

The first step is to wrest back control of your body. Because if you're drowning in puddles of sweat, or bouncing heartbeats off your rib-cage, it's going to be somewhat of a challenge to appear more confident and in control. You'd probably far rather dash off to the bathroom.

I promise this will be a revelation to you: that you've been fighting your own inner crocodile and trying to logic your way out of it (crocs and alligators are terrible at logic. They're more believers in teeth). I guarantee you that a handful of simple techniques (and yes, drills), will push that bad boy back into the swamp where he belongs.

But before I teach you how to do that, we need to attend to something.

You see, you may have been unknowingly nurturing that crocodile for a few years now. Every time it got you in a barrel-roll and persuaded you that public-speaking just isn't your thing, you backed down. After all, who are we to argue with that many teeth?

As you probably realize, if you hear something about yourself more than a few times, you start to think that maybe it's true.

Like the old joke:

"One day a guy came up to me and said, 'You're a horse, buddy!' I thought to myself, how crazy. Next thing I know, a second dude rocks over and says, 'Hey, guy, you're a horse!' I scratched my head, puzzled at the coincidence. Later that day, a third guy looks at me and says, 'Hey, you're a horse!'. 'Neighhhh', I brayed, and bought a saddle."

Over time, that crocodile has got hold of your psyche and shaken it into submission, and demanded that you believe the lie: that you cannot ever be any good at public speaking, and that all it will amount to is a pool of tears.

I am here to tell you that this is a pack of reptilian obfuscation. I am a living example of someone who will attest to the fact that, yes, that croc had a hold of me, and yes, I fought that thing off.

And so can you.

But first, we must empower and infuse you with croc-fighting essence. Your *true* essence in fact. We must restore your rightful place in the hierarchy, and work with the very thing that makes you walk out onto that stage ten-feet tall and bullet-proof.

Your *IDENTITY.*

1.2 The Most Important Addition To Your List

WHO ARE YOU?

Chances are, if someone asks you this question, you will include in your answer something about what you DO: "I work for a telco and manage a small team," "I'm a nurse in the pediatric ward," or "I'm a CEO of a mining supplies manufacturer."

While these may go some way towards revealing a part of your identity, none offer a complete understanding of who you *are*, and neither should they.

Before I go on, I must confess something more about this book. Some aspects of public speaking are concrete, practical and even technical, for example: How to project your voice; How to remember your notes; How to use your body; and many more. I will address these in great detail throughout, and provide drills for you to practice to your heart's content.

But there is another side to your development as a public speaker and confident presenter. One that I have seen transform hundreds of students in seconds. I was reluctant to include it in this book, purely because it might seem a little "woo-woo" to some, and more philosophical or mindset-based skills don't always translate so well in text form.

But the more I thought about my own journey, and some of the light-bulb moments that arose from this simple—and powerful—concept, I realized I'd be selling myself short if I *didn't* include it. After all, if I knew a super-effective technique to immediately get you on your journey while you learn all the nuts and bolts, you'd want me to teach it to you, wouldn't you?

The best way to introduce this, is to think of it as your "inner game."

I can hear you now, "But all I need are better structured presentations and a way to stop saying 'um' so much!"

Yes, I get it. What you might not realize (yet!), is exactly how much of that can flow *automatically* from making small shifts in your **identity**, especially once you include a couple of tricks I have up my sleeve for you ... later.

So let's resume that conversation about "who you are." Here are some examples:

1. I am a parent
2. I am humorous
3. I am a lover of food
4. I am married
5. I am a whiz on computers
6. I am a non-smoker
7. I am an avid reader of fiction and non-fiction

See how this sample list is building up? Make your own list for me now. And while doing it in your head *might* be okay, I strongly recommend you take the time to write it down. You'll find it far more powerful. Got your pen and paper ready? Great. Go write that list.

Now take a look at that list again. Where is public speaking?

I know. How many people would include, "*I am a motivational speaker*," or "*I am a stand-up comedian*," unless they already have a career as one? Stay with me on this, as it is key to your rapid improvement and to removing unwanted, unneeded and unnecessary unconscious barriers.

Please answer this question: If public speaking was on that list right now, what would it look like? Would it be:

- I am a nervous speaker
- I am not good at presenting
- I can't speak in front of a group
- or worse, "I am SCARED of speaking in public"

Or any number of other limiting statements. Feel free to write them down, taking a few minutes of free association to do so.

There is a very good chance that over time, you have developed a set of beliefs about yourself around your "*public-speaking persona,*" or your **Presenter Identity**. And it is now neatly compartmentalized and holding you back every time you try to improve.

Let me expand a little, because there is a very good chance that your internal resistance is one of the biggest challenges, and fortunately one we can quite easily handle.

One of the most fundamental changes anyone can make is to their *identity*. From your identity, everything else flows. Identity changes don't always stem from something deep either: for example, if you change your hairstyle, or your dress fashion, then others may perceive a "new you," even though they may have been no internal changes ... yet. But because of their reactions to the "new you," you are presented an opportunity to accept an *identity shift*; that you *have* changed; that somehow you *are* different.

However, there are issues with shifting your identity. Have you ever tried on a piece of clothing and despite what others might tell you, inside your head there is still a voice screaming, "*This is not me!*"? That's your current identity, and its supporting beliefs, pushing back.

When it comes to your **Presenter Identity** and making changes, you may feel the same push-back, resisting that other part of you which has a positive intention to improve. There may even be some disbelief and discomfort as you progress through the rest of this section.

This is quite normal—indeed some skepticism might be warranted. But I want you to understand how this works. I'm certainly not going to instantly become a Formula One racing hero simply by stating "*I am a Formula One Champion.*"

But I'm *never* going to be one if all I tell myself is that, "*I am a lousy, slow, racing-driver.*"

So first, together, we must work on your **Identity**. Specifically, your new, improved **Presenter Identity**. We can do this a couple of ways (and preferably use both for extra firepower).

1. You can simply add another statement to your previous list, for example: "***I am a confident and appealing Public Speaker.***" I realize this is not (necessarily) a statement of fact yet, but that's the point. Do the work by following the methods, systems and techniques in this book and it will be true one day. You're already doing this by employing a powerful force known as cognitive dissonance. Briefly, cognitive dissonance is an inbuilt human psychological drive to reduce the gap between what you have and what you desire. You can read more about it here:

http://en.wikipedia.org/wiki/Cognitive_dissonance. Your own cognitive dissonance is almost certainly what drove you to acquire this book.

2. I'd also recommend adding another even stronger statement, which alludes to what you are becoming. For example: "*I am becoming a more powerful and magnetic presenter.*" This is much harder for your inner nay-sayer to dismiss out of hand, because there is a part of you that is reading this material for the purpose (presumably) of becoming a better and more confident speaker. By adding this statement, you make your intentions clear and sidestep resistance. You also appeal to the human mind's insatiable quest for improvement, because it implies a never-ending goal: you can always be more powerful, and more magnetic.

So do this now. Write down at least two statements that reflect the new part of your identity you will be embracing from now on. These are your new *Identity Statements*, specific to your public speaking identity.

Once you've done that, here's what I want you to do.

Every time you come across something in this book that sounds like it is *not* you, or for some reason you think may not work for you, take a moment to reflect that this could be your hidden "old self" rearing its head again, and that all you need is Harry Potter's magic wand to wave it away with a simple utterance of your new *Identity Statement*. This will be your mantra for the rest of the book—and for the "new you": the polished, confident, successful public speaker.

At the end of this Chapter, you will also find *Drills* to help you *automatically incorporate* this *Presenter Identity* into your everyday life.

And yes, it will be fun. (Even if that is hard to believe right now.)

But for now, it's time to revisit that toppled lectern and the pile of notes, where the text ink is now slowly dissolving in the spilled water ...

1.3 The Hidden Skills That Bring You Confidence

SO, YOU THINK, HOW AWESOME (that you are now becoming a fabulously loved public speaker!), but how does that take away your nerves, your sweating, your shaking, your mind that wants to go horribly blank at critical moments?

That's a very good point, and one that demands the detailed responses that fill the rest of this book. From the preparations you make, the skill-sets you will learn, and the transformation you are already undertaking, I will be there, taking you by the hand, every step of the way.

But first, I'd like to expose a myth, and share with you a hidden skill. I want to step back for a moment and take an objective look at that "fabulously confident public speaker" as he or she performs an imaginary presentation in front of us.

They walk assuredly to the lectern, don't they? That's if they even use one. How do they stride the stage without notes like that? How are their eyes? Bright? Eager? Connecting with others? Their stance? Is it not tall and straight? Their speech? Assertive and resonant?

Maybe all of the above, and more. But let me ask you this: how do they feel on the inside?

You have no idea. And neither do I.

Even those case-hardened, polished presenters may look "at-ease," but more often than not there will still be some inner nerves, apprehension and self-talk, not dissimilar to that which "regular folk" might experience at a far higher intensity.

How do I know? Because they tell me. Having coached, mentored and trained presenters who are already polished, already confident, I can tell you this still exists.

With one crucial difference: they are not expecting perfection. They know that if something goes wrong, they can recover.

Blank mind? No problem. Walk to their notes; ask an audience member; take a drink: No panic required.

Equipment malfunction? No problem, refer to Plan B.

Weird feeling from the audience? Focus back on your "Presenter Bubble*" (after checking fly is zipped).

Accomplished presenters make it look so easy, *and not because they do everything right.*

A significant reason that we looked at your **_Presenter Identity_** in the previous section is that it underpins your ability to *recover*.

Recovery Skills carry an equal weight with presentation skills.

They give you *confidence*.

No skillful presentation ever goes to the script you may have written out. I'll go a step further and say that if you are responding to your audience then it should *not* follow your script 100%. Why? Because if you try to stick to it *and* simultaneously respond to your audience in the moment, you might find your attention split.

Split between following your script and the audience's reaction, the things you didn't say or do, the point you forgot to make—and maybe even a pile of soggy notes!

It's a myth to say that some people are simply naturally good at public speaking. Which is why I say: Most public speakers and presenters learn **Recovery Skills** from their years of experience in the school of hard knocks.

You won't have to take the hard knocks, or spend that long, because you'll be using the methods, techniques, systems and tools that I will teach you in this book as powerful shortcuts.

And the real joy is that they are not anywhere near as complex or difficult as you are probably imagining in your head (you *were* doing that, weren't you?).

* "Presenter Bubble" you ask? Coming right up in the next section …

1.4 From Nervous To Confident ... In Seconds. Really?

I'M GOING TO SHARE WITH you one of the most transformative techniques for public speakers I have ever taught.

It has made, and continues to make a huge difference to me and my clients, and even my pre-teen daughter has used it to great effect. Those I've taught who have taken on the development of this skill have seen a major turnaround in their public speaking confidence—and corresponding audience satisfaction.

Over the many years I've spent refining this technique, I've come to refer to it simply as the **"*Presenter Bubble*,"** but this simple name belies the depth of the methodology underpinning it. I suggest avoiding making any assumption that you know exactly what it means until you've fully understood how it works. The good news is it only takes a few minutes to learn, so place any judgment you may have to one side for a while until you witness its power.

First we're going to take a look at an important concept called the "state of flow," and why this is key to confident public speaking, and projecting more of who you are to any audience.

The state of "Flow," as described by Professor Mihaly Csikszentmihalyi (http://en.wikipedia.org/wiki/Mihaly_Csikszentmihalyi) is *"being completely involved in an activity for its own sake. The ego falls away. Time flies. Every action, movement, and thought follows inevitably from the previous one, like playing jazz. Your whole being is involved, and you're using your skills to the utmost."*

The professor suggests that one challenge of entering this state of "flow" is that of juggling the skill level of the performer with the difficulty of the task. He also makes the strong point that we are at our happiest when experiencing "flow states."

So what does this have to do with presentation skills, public speaking, projecting well, feeling confident and appearing confident?

Quite a lot, as it turns out.

By learning to enter a flow-like state, you will be able to place your nerves to one side; you will automatically appear more expressive and assertive (to your audience).

Now I'll show you how easily you can make this work for you, and handle the common objections.

In the late 1980s, John Grinder and Judith DeLozier, researchers in human high-performance, were trying to "decode" states of genius and also described the sensations and states of flow as Professor Mihaly Csikszentmihalyi did. In their book *Turtles All The Way Down*, they describe an attention-shifting exercise which was the basis for learning to access this state. More about that shortly.

What they discovered in their pursuits was that the flow states associated with ultra-high performance often had describable elements:

- Peripheral vision enhanced
- Spatial awareness enhanced
- A state of ultra-awareness
- Expanded attention

We're going to undertake the same exercise. This is one of those things where this might seem a little "woo-woo" at first, but I promise you it will transform your understanding of how to *instantly* be a better presenter. It's also somewhat bizarre, so be prepared to place all your judgment to one side for a moment. If you are willing to experience this for yourself, you may well find it transforms your public speaking all by itself. It's that profound, you'll find yourself using the rest of this book to soar to skill levels you'd never dreamed of.

For now, we'll focus on unbiased discovery. I will list the typical effects afterward.

You will need a light stick (or cane), just over one meter long (one and-a-bit yards).

Ask for help from a good friend, or work colleague.

Find a large open space, with level ground. A park, an empty car park, a large empty dance studio or similar space. (It is important there are no obstacles.) If none of the above is available, then a quiet street will do. In fact, my first experience of this was with a whole group of us performing this exercise in pairs on a main street of a red-light area, fortunately in the morning. We attracted a few funny looks, and shortly you will realize why.

The exercise

You will close your eyes and use the stick in front of you, in the same fashion a blind person might.

To begin, ask your partner to take care of your safety without ever touching you (unless an emergency situation arises). They are to say nothing (for the moment), but just ensure that when you begin walking with your eyes closed, you will not step off a curb, or down a hole. I suggest you ask your partner to note their own silent observations during the exercise. Later you can discuss how they match up with your experience. Often your partner will see things that you have no idea are occurring, simply because you will have had your eyes closed, but your partner will have had theirs trained on you and your physical environment.

Now here comes the seemingly odd, but well worthwhile part. Remember this is a discovery exercise, so place your assumptions to one side.

With your eyes closed, place your *Attention* on where the stick connects with the palm of your hand and your fingers. Maintaining your *Attention* exactly there, begin to walk forward (with your eyes closed of course).

Once you have the sense of how this *Feels*, usually after walking a few meters or yards, I'd like you to test *Shifting* your *Attention* to the end of the stick. Continue walking, and notice all your *Sensations* that change.

After you have the sense of this, stop and *Shift* your *Attention* to way *beyond* the end of the stick (eyes still closed!), as if your *Attention* were a firehose streaming from the end of the stick. Continue walking for some distance.

Keeping your eyes closed, and continuing to walk, suddenly *Shift* your *Attention* all the way along and back up the stick, up your arm and onto the tip of your nose (eyes still closed!). You can request your partner to tell you to do this without warning, simply by uttering "tip of the nose," after you have walked some distance with your attention extremely extended. Notice what happens.

I recommend you repeat this activity a few times, with a particular focus on tracking the *Difference* between *Attention* extended all the way out beyond the end of the stick and when *Retracted* to the tip of your nose.

So what happened?

WARNING: Spoiler Alert

Look, I know this is a book and you are probably about to read what happens next. But I highly recommend stopping right here (or making sure you commit to testing this exercise out for yourself), because learning from experience is far more powerful than reading about it in a book.

If you would like a script for you and your partner to help you run this exercise together, then email me at help@robertscanlon.com and I will send you an activity worksheet with precise instructions, including tips for what your partner should say to help you facilitate the best learning outcome.

Back to the question from the exercise: what happened?

Probably the same thing that happens to almost every single person I've ever taught this to.

When your *Attention* is extended, you walk with a straighter, more upright posture, the stick raised high in front of you, with longer strides, and you appear confident (at this point, you can ask your partner what they observed). On the inside, it *Feels* more *Confident* and more in *Control*.

When your *Attention* is *Retracted*, your steps will be small and tentative, often your spine will be stooped or bent over, the stick feels out the path cautiously, and in the case of the sudden "tip of the nose," you may even feel as if there is a physical barrier in front of you and you must stop. Many people experience more fear and anxiety. If you haven't tried this exercise, I urge you to do so now, as just reading about it doesn't even come close to the actual experience you will gain.

What conclusions can we draw from this, and how will this translate to your *Public Speaking* and *Presenter Identity*?

If you think about it, the conclusion is stunning.

You have just learned to manipulate your *State*, and where you place your attention.

You have learned that, when your attention is extended, you can feel bold and confident. Your posture is upright and you are less aware of yourself and more aware of your surroundings.

You have also learned that this *State* can quickly be switched into a retracted state, where you feel cautious, tentative, nervous.

Same person, same equipment, same environment. Two different results.

So why is this "*State*" thing important? Because it is firmly at the root of everything you do, and the behavior it causes.

Let's look at the correlation of state to *behavior*. If someone is feeling happy, they might skip along the road and smile. If they are feeling sad? They may mope around all hunched up, complain about the world, or their lack of results. Our internal experiences are modeled by our physiology.

Put your objections to one side about causation. Experience tells us that *State* affects behavior, and since you now know you can influence your own *State* to model a state of *Extended Attention*, I'll demonstrate how to use this to make a massive difference to your public speaking.

Remember at the start of this book when we saw the *State* of the nervous presenter, and the possible similarities to your experience? Sweaty hands. Heart racing. Thinking about their first few words. Wondering if the audience will like them.

Where is your *Attention* when you are having that poor experience? *Retracted*, right? Deeply focused on you (your sweaty hands, your heart rate, and so on).

So with your *Attention* so far retracted, it is nigh on impossible for anyone, even the most experienced presenters, to be confident, polished or even appear that way.

Now we'll return to the stick exercise. We only experimented with extending your *Attention* in a straight line.

But what if you could do that in three dimensions? Extend your *Attention* in a sphere, all around you?

Yes you can. Try it now. Get up and walk around, and practice pulling your ***Attention-Bubble*** inside your head, then ***Expanding*** your ***Attention-Bubble*** way, way out until it fills the room or space you are in (if you can't walk around right now, try doing it statically, from where you are sitting or lying down. I promise you the effect is just the same!).

Notice how different you are when your ***Attention-Bubble*** is expanded?

This is the ***State of Flow***, even of *genius*, that Grinder and DeLozier were recreating. A state where peripheral vision is enhanced, and where one's awareness of one's *self* is significantly diminished, to the degree where we are unaware of ourselves and can even feel "at one" with our environment, or task.

Exactly as Professor Csikszentmihalyi describes the ***State of Flow***.

As a confident presenter, everything builds from you pushing your ***Presenter Bubble*** (which is what we will now call your ***Expanded Attention***) out as far as you can. Ideally, make your ***Presenter Bubble*** fill the entire space you are in.

Have you ever seen those people on stage—musicians, performers, speakers—who appear "larger than life"? Guess what they are doing—albeit unconsciously for most—with their ***Presenter Bubble***? Yes, that's right, their ***Presenter Bubble*** is itself larger than life.

Split Attention and Recovery

I wrote previously about ***Recovery Skills***. Now that you know the power of the ***Presenter Bubble,*** we can add a valuable ***Recovery Skill*** to your toolbox.

Currently, if something doesn't go quite right in your presentation or speech, where do you think your attention goes? That's right, it zips right back inside your head.

Here are some other common experiences. While presenting, have you ever become acutely aware of what you are saying and how you are speaking? Or something innocuous, such as the color of the slides, or somebody's tie, or what you're having for lunch?

Presenter Attention Bubble
too focused on self

We call this "split attention," a unique and often helpful human skill.

But not when you are presenting! All this means is that a part of you has retracted into "observer mode". The solution? Simple. Push your *Presenter Bubble* back out. And yes, this is something you will probably want to practice, over and over. See the *Drills* at the end of this Chapter.

Competing Attention

"But that's easy for you to say, Robert! Have you tried to push your bubble out when everyone is staring at you?"

Precisely. Where do you think their attention is? On you. Not on themselves (ignore those who are feverishly tweeting your show).

Your bubble must be *consciously* influenced, as to you it seems as if you are in competition with your audience, and the intuitive thing to do is to retract yours.

This could be even more tricky, especially if you are not naturally outward or gregarious, or you are simply an introvert.

While we're on the subject of introversion and extroversion, let me ask you a quick question: Which "type" do you think may make the better presenter? The extrovert or the introvert? The answer may surprise you. Here's a brief summary of the differences:

An introvert is simply someone who replenishes their energy by being by themselves, or with one of two close friends or family. Large, voluble groups cause the introvert to *expend* energy.

An extrovert, on the other hand, likes to recharge in social groups, or on the phone with friends. Spending time by *themselves*, or in isolated circumstances, causes the extrovert to expend energy.

When it comes to introvert presenters, they can be so anxious about the amount of energy it takes to make a speech that they will design and practice way more than some extroverts are inclined to.

However, *both introverts and extroverts must consciously expand their* **Presenter Bubble.** The difference is, for the introvert, it may feel counter-intuitive.

Much better extension
of attention

Expanding your bubble is not a war of attention. Despite the fact that the entire audience has their attention on you, it only makes it FEEL as if your "bubble" is competing with that of the audience. In practice, this is not true: for yours to expand and fill the space, theirs does not have to retract. They are not two competing forces. Yours can easily *encompass* theirs, something most audiences long for, and a key ingredient in any highly successful performance. So just understand the sensation of competing attention may feel strange at first. The solution? Smile and expand *your* bubble!

Presenter Attention Bubble
Ideal projection

The effects of an expanded Presenter Bubble

Having spent many years coaching people to "extend their attention," later reframing this concept to an easier "expand your Presenter Bubble," I can tell you some common—and significant—effects that are noticed by the audience, but not necessarily by the presenter. Remember, the presenter has his or her attention extended. So it makes sense that they track less about themselves. This is important: The butterflies might still be there, but they are learning some new flying formations behind the scenes!

Here's an experiment for you. Ask someone to read out loud a page of text to an audience (preferably text that comprises several paragraphs of prose—not bullets or lists). This will establish a baseline style. Notice how much their facial expressions change, how often they look up to make eye contact, how much they move around (or not), and very specifically, how easy are they to understand. If you are able, also notice how their sentence rhythms and natural pauses work.

Now ask them to *retract* their attention and put it on the tip of their nose.

- Typically they will raise the work they are reading from closer to their face;
- They will become quieter;
- They will stumble over words;
- Their cadence and rhythm will worsen dramatically;
- It will become harder to comprehend the meaning of the words being read;
- They may become glued to the spot and make no eye contact;
- You may notice a myriad of additional differences that compromise their speaking prowess in front of a group and the impression they leave upon it.

Remember: This is the same person, same text, same group, same task. The only thing that changed was *something they did in their head.*

Ask them to stop, straighten and take a deep breath. Breathe in again, and on the next breath, imagine they have extended their **Attention** and their **Presenter Bubble** to fill the room. It may take a couple of repetitions until they feel they've nailed it, but you—and more importantly, the audience—will notice a difference.

Ask them to read from the same text again (from the top).

You should notice a vast array of changes for the better.

- Sweeping eye contact;
- Smiling and use of varied facial expressions;
- Deliberate pauses;
- A more interesting variation in tone and vocal cadence;
- The text is easier for the audience to comprehend;
- They may move, and/or use expressive gestures;
- They will probably raise and lower the page of text, and will generally hold it low enough so they can make significant eye contact with the audience.

Time and again, I have witnessed this often dramatic change in the most timid of presenters.

But there is something to note —and to feed back to the person undergoing these changes: the changes that are incredibly obvious to you in the audience may not *feel* huge to them.

Generally however, they will sense less "nerves" and a feeling of better engagement with their audience.

I like to say that this is: *"The one thing that changes everything, and you only need to do it in your head."*

Your Presenter Bubble in your daily life, including "how to be charismatic"

Here's the extremely interesting thing about the **Presenter Bubble**. It works for areas of your life that have absolutely nothing to do with presenting.

Want to be noticed when you arrive at a party? Or be the "life of the party"? Simply extend your "bubble."

Want to feel more confident and positive? Try extending your bubble when out and about, or when walking down the street. You'll feel your body straighten, you'll breathe more deeply, and you'll feel more "in the flow."

Note: "Bubble" is only a word I use to make this a more convenient term for public speaking. What you are really doing is extending your *attention*. Anytime you extend your attention in this manner, you have much more likelihood of becoming more noticeable, more attractive, and even more charismatic.

But what about those times when you *don't* wish to attract attention?

Such as walking down a less than salubrious street?

Or entering a conference room while the conference is in progress?

Here's a tip for these occasions: *Retract* your "bubble," but remain in an assertive posture. Do not make eye contact. You'll find it much easier to appear invisible.

But ... at this point, we're more interested in making this work every time for you when you speak in public. Here's what you need to do:

Encourage your **Presenter Bubble** to extend out at every opportunity (and please use the practice drills at the end of this chapter over and over to further enhance it). Force yourself to expand your **Presenter Bubble** as large as you can imagine well before any presentation or speech. Please *please* don't wait until you are center-stage: you'll find it is far more effective when you begin the process off-stage.

And if you are interested in a way to totally *automate* your **Presenter Bubble** state, then the next section is just for you ...

1.5 How To Trigger Automatic Confidence

SO YOU'VE TOTALLY GOT THE *Presenter Bubble* nailed, and the difference is staggering, right? Bzzz.

I understand. Remember, for a long time now, you've been triggering yourself to have your attention unknowingly retracted. So just by practicing a new technique a couple of times to "get" the feel of it won't necessarily ring in permanent change (though for some it surely does. I can testify to that, since I was one of them).

A quick aside: I realize it's also possible that you have only read about it and not tried it for yourself. If you haven't yet completed the activity in the preceding section, then make a commitment to yourself. Do that now, because until you have actually experienced it for yourself it remains just an intellectual exercise, and since the *Presenter Bubble* is referred to a great deal throughout the book, you'll thank yourself for experiencing its power rather than just reading about it.

For now, I'm going to assume you *have* conducted the exercise in the previous section, and you are ready for me to teach you how to systematize using it. You'll learn how to consciously, deliberately and specifically trigger your very best *Presenter Bubble*, *without having to think about it*. (Yes, I know. A contradiction: "something conscious, that you don't have to think about"—what is that? Stick with me and you'll see ...)

Triggers and how to apply them

What we're going to do right now will be useful as a building block for everything else we will do together in this book, and we will begin it by cementing your *Presenter Bubble*.

Eventually you will want to call on an entire suite of techniques during your presentation or speech, and the last thing you need is to try to consciously recall anyone of them. All you will end up with is split attention, and we don't want that.

By using a very specific trigger—and stacking this trigger with every technique and method you successfully practice—you can employ the extensive network of out-of-awareness skills that can be directed unconsciously. Note: By "unconsciously" here, I am using the word to mean *anything outside of normal conscious awareness or access*. Not unconscious as in knocked unconscious. The term *subconscious* is generally used for anything *temporarily* out of awareness that may be consciously recalled, but for our purposes I prefer to refer to the *un*conscious mind, since it is where much of our involuntary or habitual behavior resides.

How many times this week have you had to stop to think how to make a coffee? Or how to drive a car? Or even walk/run/breathe?

These are all things over which you have some degree of conscious control, yet are now largely out of your awareness.

But I bet that you do not consciously trigger yourself into a "driver state" each time you get behind the wheel. If you don't drive, perhaps you ride a bicycle, or something similar. If you have a disability and are not able to walk, ride or drive, I'm certain there are similar routine activities that you no longer have to "think" about.

So what we will do now is to consciously create a new trigger specific to your *Public Speaking Identity*, which first we will use to call up your *Presenter Bubble*, so you don't even have to think about it.

Eventually, this trigger will work so fast, that before you know it, you will feel completely different about any presentation or speech.

A trigger is ... what, exactly?

A name; a word; an icon; a very specific physical touch, such as quickly pinching the skin between your left thumb and index finger using your right thumb and index finger.

Have you ever heard a song that suddenly transported you back to a very specific time or event; actually evoking your emotions of that day or time? Most people have. Or have you ever smelled a trace of perfume in the air, and it reminded you of someone from your past?

Possibly the most powerful example of a highly personal trigger is your own name. You've been hearing it from birth. Its power is such that you can pick out your own name uttered in a crowded noisy room.

All of these are triggers are unconsciously installed, and reinforced over time. Each time you heard that song, or your name; every time you remembered a certain event or person, the association was triggered until it became completely rote and baked into your physiological responses. You and I will now take full conscious advantage of this powerful human facility.

We will take your *Presenter Bubble*, and slowly add new elements to the trigger, until invoking your trigger not only expands your *Presenter Bubble*, but also has the rest of your mind-body producing its best toolbox, ready and on-hand for your every need. *Without you having to think about it.*

By the end of this book, you will be able to combine your trigger with another technique you can call on that will deepen your entire *Presenter Identity*. Something that will become a lifelong skill, and useful in more contexts than simply speaking in front of a group.

But I'm getting ahead of myself.

We will take baby steps together.

The simplest form of trigger is a specific word, or set of words. Ideally they are completely unique to the state you want to trigger. As an example: The word "Strong" would be too vague, and can be used in many other contexts (strong coffee anyone? Strong smell?). Ambiguous statements or words will confuse your unconscious mind: it wants to be told *exactly* what you're searching for. Be very clear about what you choose, and make it impossible for it to be mistaken for anything else.

But guess what? We already have something you can use right away.

Presenter Bubble. It might sound trite, but it works, and it's not something you will find yourself easily mixing up with anything else.

You can also use a phrase (or word) such as "*It's showtime.*" This is the one I use personally as I find it also triggers additional performance states. You will, of course, discover more and more ways to deepen your use of *states* and triggers as you progress through this book.

But for now, pick either one, and let's make your trigger.

Installing your trigger

"Installing"? What do you mean, Robert? Do I have to hire a tradesperson?

Fair point. By "installing", what we mean is to carefully craft the correct mind-body response to the trigger. All it takes is some time to yourself and a few minutes to practice.

Then I strongly recommend you integrate the installation with some practice, by calling on it in any situation. In the same way that you might install a new kitchen. Not much point doing that unless you *use* it, is there?

The good thing about your trigger is that you can use it whenever and wherever you wish, since it is totally portable and you take it with you everywhere you go.

Ready? Good.

Step One

Think of the words **Presenter Bubble** (or "**It's Showtime**") and immediately imagine your attention instantly expanding outward. If it helps, reenact the same physiology from the extended attention exercise: an expansive feeling; an upright, proud posture; a lifted chin, a big smile; expanded chest, and deep breathing.

Step Two

Now shake your whole body out, stand up and move around a bit to "scramble" your state, and come back to neutral.

Repeat

Repeat the exact process by thinking of those words again: "**Presenter Bubble**" → Instant Expanded Attention. Revel in it, and let it sit in your body for a few seconds, then shake it out.

Now rinse and repeat until it becomes second nature, *inevitable*. And as soon as you begin to say the words **Presenter Bubble**, your body takes over.

Excellent!

You can also have a lot of fun with this.

An extended attention makes a big contribution to how *charismatic* you are perceived by others. The next time you visit your local supermarket—or any crowded mall or public place—invoke your trigger and notice:

1. **How it feels**
2. **The reaction of others**

Even just before going into a party, or social event, if you'd like to feel more like "the life of the party" or the celebrity that everyone has just been waiting for, get busy with your trigger.

Practicing using your trigger-word in this way will help you engage the state of expanded attention and confident appearance, and you will stack the cards in your favor by repeating it in non-threatening situations. Your unconscious mind will find it much easier to employ when the stakes are higher, such as before or during a presentation or speech.

You'll be surprised by the magnitude of the difference this simple, yet fundamental, technique will make for you. It reliably sets off a new sequence of connections in your own brain and prevents the old anxieties from gaining any foothold.

As if you were choosing a fork in the road. Once you are a some way down the better path, there's no looking back.

Coming up next, I'll talk more about how your own "state" influences that of your audience. We'll look especially at the things that affect your state *that are under your direct control*: Eating, drinking, the time of day, caffeine ... you name it.

1.6 The First Rule Of Presenting

FOR THE MAJORITY OF SPEECHES or presentations, two things will be quite likely:

1. You will be standing; and
2. Your audience will be seated.

There are a couple of things that this immediately influences, such as presenter-audience rapport, and your establishment as an authority. We'll work on both of those at a later stage, because of greater significance is the audience's state and your state.

Have you ever fallen asleep while watching a movie? Or when reading in bed? I bet you were not standing up on either occasion.

So one thing we know straight away is that your audience has the propensity (while seated) to easily access a soporific or lethargic state. This means they will have to work harder to follow you, and their "mental tempo" may well be lowered as a result. Contrast that with *your* state: You are up on your feet and doing your best to be animated, expressive and interesting. The two states can be quite different, and to you, "on stage", it may even feel as if your audience is "slow."

However, there are techniques you can use to help your presentation work for you and your audience.

Exaggerate your gestures and emotional expression

Have you ever been to, or seen an example of on television of a rock/pop concert in a stadium setting? You go for the atmosphere, the huge wall of sound and your favorite artist's music. So why do they have big screens close to the stage? It's because the (often dramatic) showpersonship adds to the show—and if you can only see your favorite rock star at the size of an ant from a distance, it is way less engaging.

Engagement of your audience is critical in any presentation, regardless of the type of presentation: concert, speech, classroom environment or interactive meeting.

So the first rule is to always make what you say and do "larger than life," especially once your audience exceeds a dozen or so people. I don't mean cartwheeling across the stage and telling bawdy jokes, but rather turning up the volume, or what I like to call, "amping up" everything you do. For example:

- Gesture wider.
- Smile bigger.
- Move emphatically.
- Make hand and arm emphasis grander and easier to see.
- Exaggerate emotional moments more (and if you are able, reflect this in your facial expressions. Introverts, don't be concerned: it comes with practice!).

An easy way to incorporate this is to become more grandiose in your delivery when you are relating stories or examples: see the section on bringing your content to life for story and example techniques.

What you convey with your expressions and your body is one of the most powerful ways to enhance your delivery, and is a key part of your state. Of course, what you choose to "amp up" should be relevant to the content of your speech or presentation. A thoughtful and moving eulogy definitely doesn't call for clowning around on the stage.

But what if you don't feel like doing that? What if you're the after-dinner guest speaker at a conference and you took advantage of the scrumptious and bountiful buffet, and right now, you'd rather have a nap? What's that? You had a couple of glasses of wine too?

Let's be sensible here: Don't do that. Ever. Or at least if you do, make it only once and let that be a lesson to you.

A fundamental rule of presenting is controlling and influencing your own state.

That's why we spend so much time working on your ***Presenter Bubble***, and getting those pesky butterflies lining up.

It's time to add your ***Presenter State*** to your swag-bag, since it is something you can easily be aware of and influence. I'll start with some obvious pitfalls of not paying due attention to proper presenter state. For example:

- If you are giving a breakfast talk, and you've had half-a-dozen more coffees than the group: then beware your tempo.
- If it's five o'clock on a Friday afternoon in almost any 9-5 workplace, then your own state may be in rapport with your audience's: "I'm tired and I want to go home."
- If you didn't sleep well.
- If you have a cold.
- If you just heard some awful news. (I was once given news of a friend's suicide while I was in the middle of running a five day conference.)

The professional presenter, most of the time, will rely on their "show must go on" attitude to underpin their state. Sometimes you just have to grin and bear it.

However, there is a huge upside to what you *do* have under your control: there are actions you can take to deliberately keep yourself in the optimum state before a presentation or speech.

- **Keep hydrated** (but ensure your bladder is empty before presenting). Little sips work well. I personally like to add a small amount of juice to my water (about 10%) as it seems to prevent the dry mouth that happens when copious amounts of water wash through it. This is especially useful to keep your energy up through the day.
- **Eat minimally.** In fact, I would argue that presenting while slightly hungry is often advantageous. It's better not to have a significant portion of your energy diverted to digesting, and hunger might give you an 'edge.' Of course, if you have no choice—for example, you are unexpectedly called upon to speak after a conference dinner—then you know what to do: you must override that energy drain and pick up your Presenter State.
- **Give your body some energy prior to going "on stage."** For example, if you have been in the audience yourself listening to the previous speaker, then make sure you get up and get your blood circulating well before you are on (see next bullet point for ideas).
- **Speaking of getting the blood circulating** … If you have the opportunity to "get into state" well before your speech or presentation, for example, you are in the room before your audience and have it to yourself, or with only you and your assistants and sound person, then take full advantage. Warm up. Talk loudly. Do some breathing exercises. Stride around the room (an activity that has deeper benefits which I will address later). Put some rousing music on, or better

yet, your favorite song. Once again, think about the music analogy: A "sound check" doesn't just make sure everything works: It also sets up the performance. It's the same with full dress rehearsals in any stage show: you are cementing for yourself your *Presenter State*. Take advantage of every opportunity you get.

The Audience State

We've looked at the *Audience State* briefly at the start of this section, but now you understand the impact of your own *Presenter State*, it's time to take a deeper look at how to affect your audience's state—and what else is influencing them.

Your audience will be largely unconscious of their own state, but that doesn't mean you should be. Many things will affect them:

- The time of day;
- The subject matter;
- The previous presenter (if any);
- Your introduction (if any. I will show you how to control this);
- Session length and break times. Is your speech just before lunch? Then don't risk running over time, or you will fight the audience's irresistible and all-consuming thoughts of lunch (and perhaps your own), and much of what you say will be missed. Just when you might be making your most important point!
- Your speech is immediately post-lunch or dinner, where the tempo of your audience can be slow and people find it difficult to pay attention;
- You are following multiple presenters;
- You are following a comedian;
- You are following someone who made your audience angry, or stirred them up with controversy;
- It is very early—pre-breakfast;
- The environment is distracting. For example, three of the four sides of your conference room are picture-windows looking out onto a luxury yachting marina—and it is a Saturday morning. Be prepared to work hard to gain attention. And yes, I have had that exact experience. With a group of sixty lawyers *required* to attend, and the original room downstairs was flooded out due to a raging overnight storm and we all had to traipse through puddles of water in the room downstairs to access the "Plan B" venue. Fun stuff. Wait until I tell you about the major blunder I made in the first five minutes (recounted later in this book), and how I recovered.
- Some news the audience was just given (either prior to attending your speech and outside of your knowledge; or just before your speech and in front of you). Could have been good news (extra staff bonus!), startling news (the CEO was sacked), bad news (layoffs being announced that will affect 50% of your audience). Your audience may be more interested in discussing this news among themselves than paying attention to your presentation.

As you can see, it pays to find out everything possible that can affect your audience's state—and their receptivity to your speech.

Now what can you do about it?

When elements of your audience's state is predictable, you can take it into account when deciding:

- The content of your presentation (The next chapter specifically focuses on how to ascertain your audiences' state, and how to use it in your design);
- The style you will use (Interactive? Fast? Considered?); and
- Your own Presenter State.

You will have to work harder after lunch and after dinner (even breakfast will slow them down for a while).

If you have dry content, or spreadsheets to discuss, try not to do that after lunch. Just before morning tea is much more effective. But if you *have* to take the after lunch slot because it is outside your control, there are things you can do, knowing that your audience is sending blood to the stomach and not the brain. For example, you could design a quick quiz to run at the start of your show. You most certainly would not design busy and data-rich slides. You might include interactive elements—handing out worksheets, using props, starting with an impactful showreel or music piece, or even an audience activity. As I briefly indicated, we'll cover the design and structural aspects of your presentation elsewhere in this book, including more ways to assess your ***Audience State*** and what to do with it (See the section on What You Must Know About Your Audience and Index Computations. Right now we are simply discussing the importance of "state" and how to influence it).

Speaking of state ... what is one of the "must do" tasks before any speech that is the number one failing of many presenters, yet is one of the things that will transform your presentation from stumbling to stunning?

1.7 What Most Presenters Don't Do ... And Why They Fail

THE NUMBER ONE FAILURE FOR many budding public speakers and presenters is simply this:
The failure to practice out loud, multiple times.

Think about it. Would you attend a classical concert where the orchestra advertised *"First time playing this piece, ever!"*? Well maybe, for fun.

Yet many speakers unknowingly telegraph their failure to have practiced their speech to their audience—stumbling over slide titles, being surprised by what comes up on the screen, peering around behind them at the projected images to simply read the words on the slide (don't get me started on this. I'll show you far better methods as you move through the book).

"But wait. Are you saying I must memorize my speech or presentation word-for-word?"

No, far from it. What I want you to do is three-fold:

1. Avoid the mistake of writing out your speech long-hand, over and over.
2. Avoid the mistake of reducing your speech to mental rehearsal only.
3. Discipline yourself to rehearse your presentations *out loud wherever remotely possible.*

That last point (#3) is key.

One sure-fire truth about any very polished presenter is this: they all have plenty of "hours-on-stage" under their belt. For which *there is no substitute.* It is the fastest way to improve, and even faster when you know *what* to improve.

- You can't learn to drive a car better just by imagining it. Although, as research shows, it helps.
- You *will* make huge gains in the number of your "hours-on-stage" just by practicing.
- Yes, it's not *quite* the same as having a real live audience, but it's the next best thing.

And to do that, you *have* to practice out loud. Standing up. As if you had an audience. *And not reading from a longhand or typed piece of paper.*

Practicing as if you were in front of an audience establishes a "muscle-memory" connection between your brain and your mouth like nothing else will. No amount of running through it in your head is anywhere near as powerful. As I said, it still helps, but it comes with its own pitfalls.

Get into the habit of walking around your office, lounge room, hotel room, bedroom, meeting room, conference room, board room—anywhere you can. Preferably the very room in which you will be presenting, because that is the ultimate dress-rehearsal space.

Pay particular attention to the critical elements of your speech:

- The start (your first one to two minutes, and I cover this in depth later in the book in the section How To Make Your First Two Minutes Super-Strong);
- Key transitions and links you might be making for the audience (I'll show you plenty of options for doing this elegantly and deliberately);
- Your "take-away" message(s);
- Any dramatic moments.

And practice them until they are second-nature.

At this point, if you can rustle up a willing colleague or friend, it helps. You can give them the tracking and feedback sheet at the end of this chapter.

Having been down both paths of either writing out my entire speech longhand, and/or doing *only* mental rehearsal (with minimal and vague bullets for my notes), I can tell you from experience they are to be avoided. How you make your running notes varies from person to person, but once you have practiced out loud in full, at least three times, you'll have a good sense of how to structure your presenter notes, which is an art in and of itself. (I will be covering presenter notes later in the book, including how to best remember what you want to say.)

You also gain some wonderful things from doing this if you are serious about improving your public speaking game. And if you need more proof that simple, *purposeful* practice will make or break your skills, or if you still believe that some people are simply "naturals" when it comes to public speaking, then I highly recommend you read Matthew Syed's book, "Bounce: Mozart, Federer, Picasso, Beckham, and the Science of Success." Syed clearly illustrates why purposeful practice differentiates the mediocre from the extraordinary, going so far as to single out record holders in both sporting and intellectual pursuits. He demonstrates that these "experts" were not "born with the talent," but instead gained their prowess because circumstance and history conspired to drive them to purposeful practice.

You, however, do not need to wait for circumstance and history to converge. You can deliberately orchestrate it. As you go through this book, you will pick up a long list of skills, techniques and mindsets to adopt—all of which can be incorporated with *purposeful practice*.

But for now, as well as embedding your content into your brain and physiology by actively talking and walking out your speech, be content with purposefully practicing and incorporating your **Presenter Bubble** (which you *must* set up before every practice. *It's Showtime!*) and your **Presenter State**.

What you will quickly notice is how effortlessly you begin to learn where the "marks you need to hit" are in your presentation.

- Which memorable moments you can emphasize.
- Where to pause for effect.
- Where key points can be repeated, connected and reviewed.

Thrillingly, and to your great relief and joy, you'll feel far less reliant on your notes.

After all, if you were sitting in an airplane and happened to glance up and see the pilot reading the manual at the section *Taking Off For Beginners*, some apprehension would be natural, would it not?

So don't cut corners. This is one drill that can leap you ahead by years, and the lazy presenter will avoid doing at all costs.

Speaking of being lazy—did you know there is one thing that so many presenters do that *forces* them to be lazy?

Luckily, it's very easy to avoid. Let's see how.

1.8 The Most Dangerous Way To Be A Lazy Presenter

HAVE YOU EVER WATCHED A speaker or a presenter look at the next slide and read from it? (We'll assume they are using a computer-driven PowerPoint/Keynote presentation.)

I'm sure you have.

May I double-check something? You *can* read, yes? (Presumably, since you have this book. Of course, if you have a visual or reading impediment and are using a text-reader to read this aloud, please excuse my cheeky joke. I'm sure you still understand my point!)

An audience can read the slide to themselves faster than the presenter can read it out loud. There is *no* reason for any presenter to read verbatim from a slide. It's insulting to the audience's intelligence and a waste of their time. The audience is there for the presenter's expertise, not their reading skills. The effect on your audience of using just *one talking point* per slide as opposed to reading out reams of text from each slide is worlds apart.

If it's important to you to disseminate accurate information, there are specific ways to provide this in takeaway form, using pre- or post-presentation notes. There is a section of this book dedicated to the use of props, handouts and other support materials. For now, it's enough to say that *all* materials, including your delivery and what you physically give to your audience, have an effect on your presentation. Your job is to maximize this effect. I assure you, by the end of this book you will have a suite of tools at your fingertips to present something far more memorable than those colleagues of yours still reading from slides.

But we're still confusing what a presentation really is.

Underline or highlight this point: *Your presentation or speech is all about YOU, not your slides or the words on the screen.*

Think about the last speaker you saw who made a lasting impression on you. What did their slides say?

My point exactly—we remember the *person* and the points made by a *person*. A text-filled slide cannot convey expression, tonality or (much) emotion.

So why do some presenters merely read slides? (Or read them out loud first and then talk.)

Reading slides out to an audience is the work of a lazy presenter. Those who do it are simply relying on their slide-text as their notes. Possibly the result of rushed work or poor planning. In many corporate management scenarios, someone else may have constructed the presenter's slide deck for them and they may be seeing the slides for the very first time.

Presenters who insist on reading their slides are failing their audiences. At the very least, it is demonstrating a lack of respect for the audience's time and value. I don't care how "important" the speaker is, nor how highly paid they are. If they insist on wasting precious seconds of my life because they could not be bothered to rehearse or make sufficient notes to be able to speak outside of the content on your slides—

then expect me to walk out. I have better things to do with my life. Now let me adopt a more gentle tone for you, the reader: If you have been guilty of reading slides, please make a commitment right now to stop.

The presenter who uses slides wisely, will make certain their slides *enhance* the person presenting them. I'm a proponent of no slides at all, or simplification to as few as you can, but I recognize this is not always possible. But remember: YOU are the presentation.

I recommend you study the variety of ways in which speakers showcase their talks. There is probably no better current example than the ubiquitous TED talks, and Garr Reynolds of Presentation Zen has a great run-down on the many different ways TED presenters do and don't use slides:

http://www.presentationzen.com/presentationzen/2009/05/making-presentations-in-the-ted-style.html

If you don't know of Garr Reynold's book, Presentation Zen, I strongly recommend you get yourself a copy, especially if you have to present material visually on a regular basis. I'll reference this again for the sake of a pertinent reminder in the section specific to props.

Remember that slides are a tool and not your presentation. With that in mind, I'd like to end this section with a checklist. Ask yourself:

- How are your slides supporting and/or enhancing your presentation?
- How do your visual aids help showcase *you*?
- And double check this: Are your slides driving your presentation, or worse, are the slides *equal* to your presentation?

If you suspect that your visual aids have been the main focus of your talk, then you have some work to do. First, finish reading this book. Then review your presentation outcomes; rework your slides; review the rules, checklists and use the practice drills.

I promise you, your audiences will thank you for it.

<High speed whirring noise>

What's that you hear?

Oh yes ... a drill. Coming up next.

1.9 Drills

Before you present:

Continue to reinforce your *Presenter Identity*: take your statement or statements and turn them into affirmations. I recommend you place them where they will attract your attention. For example: Pin them up on your desk, attach them to your keyring, write them out a few times every day: do whatever *you* need to do to keep this front of mind until it sinks into your psyche.

Each time, before you present: Take a deep breath, and as you let it out, expand your *Presenter Bubble* to fill the entire speaking space. This is not a time to be shy: think big.

Practice extending and then retracting your bubble in contexts other than public speaking—while out walking, at the shops, or in a restaurant, in a busy public space—and notice the effect on your inner state. Take note of what you do and don't notice in your environment as a result.

Redesign any slide that requires you to recite the words on it. Free yourself from repeating information on slides and instead use visuals as prompts for you to speak to. This will become even easier once you've studied a superior method of designing and structuring your presentation that I will teach you later in this book.

Practice your speech, talk or presentation at least three times out loud. Make sure you are standing up when you do this. If you can enlist a willing partner for feedback, then do a fourth run-through with them. You'll be surprised at how having even just one person in front of you can change the dynamic, and reveal gaps in your speech, including sections where you feel obliged to clarify something you said.

Before standing up to speak:

Employ your trigger!

Envisage yourself being in your ultimate "showtime" state.

Take a deep breath, and allow your bubble to fill the space before you reach your "stage area."

During your presentation:

You might not have the wherewithal to track this initially, but at some point, you'll be able to feel how extended your *Presenter Bubble* is (or isn't) during a presentation. Practice extending it during your presentation, at any opportunity.

Post-speech:

Run a post-speech scan on your "state." Did you collapse it inadvertently? Where is your *Presenter Bubble* now? Assimilate the good stuff and notice what you did well in order to build on it.

Focus on keeping your post-speech *Presenter Identity* and *Presenter State* as strong as you can, to allow better integration of your new *Identity*.

Important: Stack everything!

Your *Presenter State* trigger will become more powerful as you grow. I strongly recommend that from now on, you deliberately add new positive experiences from your presentations and speeches to your trigger.

How do you do this?

It's simple, but the order is key. First you must trigger your *Presenter State.* *Now* you recall those moments of success. Stir them in to your *Presenter Identity* and immerse yourself in your strength. Immediately after doing this, practice using your trigger a few times so you can experience the additional confidence, and anchor it in by repetition.

Tracking Sheet

As promised, here is the tracking sheet. Feel free to download, print and use with your peers, friends or family for support.

http://robertscanlon.com/tracking-sheet

CHAPTER 2: HOW TO USE YOUR VOICE, YOUR BODY AND YOUR WORDS FOR MAXIMUM IMPACT

2.1 Nothing More Powerful Than An Audience Who _____ You

I'D LIKE TO BEGIN THIS chapter with a quick nod to a line from Chapter 1.

"Your presentation or speech is all about YOU, not your slides or the words on the screen."

The success of your presentation relies on *you*, literally. I believe you can be a better presenter simply by being *more of who you are* at the front of the room (or on stage, or in a group setting).

In Chapter 1, I introduced the notion of making grander gestures and emphasizing expression and emotion, especially with larger audiences. This chapter we dive into the details and drill further into how you can use your voice, your body and your words to reach your audience in ways you may never have dreamed. Are you ready?

Making an impression

The hackneyed phrase, *"You never get a second chance to make a first impression,"* still holds true for anyone speaking in front of a group of people.

In the first few seconds of your speech, audience members will make up their mind about you and jump to whatever conclusion they will.

How well you project (your ***Presenter Bubble***), your perceived charisma (***Presenter Bubble*** and ***Presenter State*** combined), your supporting materials and confidence with your content (did you practice out loud?), all conspire to determine the impression your audience receives in the first minute or two.

But you can take a great deal more control over this process—and build on the foundational ***Presenter Identity*** you are already deliberately creating—by drilling down into the practical techniques that will steer your audience into your presentation and have them eating out of your hand.

If you are presenting because you need to:

- Persuade;
- Educate;
- Sell;
- Inform;
- Entertain;

then you will want to first ensure you have rapport with your audience. Nothing is more powerful than having an audience who *likes* you.

But can you *make* an audience like you? And if so, is it ethical to do so?

Let's work our way through these techniques before we address—and hopefully answer—that question.

And there is no better place to begin than well, the beginning, of course.

2.2 How To Make Any Speech Memorable

THE START OF ANY SPEECH or presentation is your chance to win your audience over ... by making your first impressions count.

And yes, of course, if you fluff the start, then it is always possible to recover at any point in a presentation, but by crafting your starts (and finishes, which we'll get to later), you give yourself the best chance to begin a success-spiral with your audience. They warm to you quickly; you react both consciously and unconsciously to their positive feedback and it shines through; they warm to you even more ... and so on.

It makes everything easier.

So, especially if you are just beginning to speak in front of groups, I recommend you spend more effort on really nailing your first two-to-three minutes. You'll be surprised at how much further this reaches than just "first impressions." (There are some specific techniques for this in the section on "How To Make Your First Two Minutes Super-Strong.")

If it is simpler, think of your speech as a great novel or movie, compared to one that leaves you cold. Most of us enjoy a book or movie that grabs us instantly, and not necessarily just because it is fast-paced. Perhaps the writer or director was able to quickly make an authentic connection. Hooking your audience, holding their attention, and making an authentic connection is exactly what you need to plan on doing with your audience.

Detailed rehearsals for your first three minutes will also make you feel supremely confident and help remove the "fear of the blank mind". Most experienced presenters will tell you that once they get into their stride, any apprehension fades into the background. Yes, you are correct: By admitting that their apprehension has faded, they're telling us *they have successfully removed attention off themselves, out onto their audience, and pushed their bubble out.*

A second key impression point—and one also well worth rehearsing over and over—is the *end* of your talk. But before I delve into this, we'll take a quick aside to understand the social psychology behind beginnings and endings—just enough to give you an insight into how and why these skills are key.

Why do starts, finishes, and interruptions need careful crafting in your presentation or speech?

There is an effect known as Serial Positioning, where we tend to remember more easily certain elements in the content of lists, movies, and books, depending on where the item was placed. Specifically, research shows that the Primacy and Recency effect makes a significant contribution to making anything memorable.

Primacy = what came first.

Recency = what came last.

Or in layperson's language: beginnings and endings.

So if you want your presentation to be more memorable, and to leave a lasting impression, casting a critical eye over your starts and finishes is more important that just making sure you don't fluff your lines.

"*Wait,*" I hear you say, "*didn't you say something about 'interruptions'? What's that got to do with my speech? Surely I need to avoid any interruptions?*"

Well yes and no. Yes, in the sense of managing audience interruptions, which I will cover in due course.

But no, in the sense that a deliberate interruption is another technique for improving how *memorable* your presentation will be.

We can take advantage of a human tendency known as the *Zeigarnik Effect*: Essentially we are inclined to remember interrupted tasks or anything incomplete. Rather than taking your time up here to explain the research, I've included a link with a good overview here:

http://www.managetrainlearn.com/page/the-zeigarnik-effect

From a presenter or speaker's point of view, this gives us yet another tool to use, and one that can end up transforming your presentation when used properly. Even more exciting is that this technique can be used in an advanced fashion to create what we call *nested loops*. The easiest example to give you here would be a top-level comedian, who begins one story, but doesn't finish it, and you think they've just distracted him or her self ... but the story returns later in the show. Billy Connolly is a great example of someone who uses this technique and makes it look seamless. (Here's an example. Warning: not safe for work! https://www.youtube.com/watch?v=Vg3hbbms-48). Similarly in movies, Quentin Tarantino uses multiple "unfinished loops" to enhance curiosity.

Now where was I?

Ah yes. So whenever you take a detour (a planned detour!) in your speech, you leave your audience with an unfinished task, or incomplete loop. Done well, this is beautiful to be a part of, and allows the presenter to weave wonderful stories around their content.

Overdone, or clumsily executed, it will drive your audience nuts, and possibly make you memorable for all the wrong reasons, especially if you neglect to finish a story, or deliver a promised point.

Which is why it is an advanced technique, and one I will be addressing in more detail much later in the book, in the section called, "How To Use Props, Visual Aids ... And Even Slides"

So, a quick recap:

The Primacy Effect: We remember what came first.

The Recency Effect: We remember what came last.

http://en.wikipedia.org/wiki/Impression_formation#Primacy-recency_effect

http://www.simplypsychology.org/primacy-recency.html

The Zeigarnik Effect: We more easily remember anything interrupted or incomplete.

But wait ... there's more.

Another handy tool, which again can be used as an advanced technique, but worth knowing about now, since you can also use it to jazz up your first few minutes and stir up your audience, is something called by a dastardly sounding psychological name ...

The Von Restorff Effect: We remember things that stand out (as different: For example in lists).

Look at the list below:

Red

Violet

Blue

Green

Yellow

Black

A herd of elephants

Indigo

Orange

If you were shown that list for only a few seconds, I guarantee you, there is one item almost everyone will remember without any issue at all, along with a couple of the others.

That's right: Yellow. So out of place isn't it?

Bzzz. The *elephants*, of course!

So how do you use the **Von Restorff Effect**, other than designing those cute "spot the difference" cartoons or "tell me the odd one out" lists?

Perhaps you wish to shock your audience with a particular statistic; or to use a controversial question, and these will be in your opening minutes.

This gives you an opportunity to craft this element—remember it is what stands out that becomes memorable. So even though your statistic or question may stand out just by its very nature, you also have the means to make it more dramatic.

For example:

- Make the slide for that part radically different to the rest.
- Use a completely different tone of voice.
- Move to a different part of the "stage."
- Bring out a prop to illustrate only *this* point (there is a complete section in this book dedicated to props).
- Use a sound effect (sparingly please!).
- Stage something unusual (for example: ask for a volunteer to help you demonstrate something; have someone come onto stage and hand you something eg "late breaking news").

The list is as endless as your imagination.

Warning: humor does make things memorable. But that means you have to make it funny in the first place! If you know you have a dry sense of humor—if you often tell jokes that take a while to sink in—then I recommend you practice this particular part of your speech with a friend. Delivery is everything!

I'm sure you're starting to get a sense of why the beginnings, endings, and well-differentiated elements of your talk are critical to making it more memorable.

Your start will stand out, purely because it is the start. By working on it, crafting it, rehearsing it, you kill many birds with one stone: You will make a better first impression, you will feel more confident, you will get into "flow" more easily and generate positive audience feedback for you to feed off, you will find it easier to extend your attention ... and your content will come alive.

Now I must read you the riot act about endings.

I've seen a lot of presenters start well, then end badly. Endings are worth designing with as much deliberation as your openings.

The last thing you want to accidentally deliver is what I call a "dribble" ending, where the speaker appears to thank the audience and doesn't really understand how to use body language to signify that this is the end then they feel uncomfortable because some people are raising their hands as if to clap, so they try to make one more point and attempt a smile and then someone claps anyway in the middle of what they are trying to say so it ends up dribbling away because some people at the back are already talking and some are getting up at the side and leaving through the door where the organizer has poked their head through to see if ...

I'm sure you get the idea.

Movies without a definitive ending leave us uncomfortable, so don't do this to your audience.

Make your ending short, sharp and definitive.

Job done.

2.3 How To Perfectly Position Your Presentation ... Without Your Audience Realizing

WOULDN'T IT BE GREAT IF you had a reliable method for helping your audience feel totally comfortable, both with your talk and with you as an authority? A method which boosts your own confidence in where you are taking them?

Of course, the answer is yes.

But how do we do that?

Let me ask you this question: Why do we put paintings in frames before we display them? Answer: Because it sets them off and makes them look even more spectacular. To the human eye, anything "framed" has an already implied sense of proportion.

And so it should be with any speech, talk or presentation.

So what is "framing," and why will it help with public speaking?

In exactly the same way that a picture or photo frame defines a piece of visual art, **Verbal Framing** works to define what is inside and outside of your content. It's the art of setting up both the process *and* content in your speech in a way that the audience doesn't have to put any extra work in ... they just sit back and enjoy the show.

Just like real picture frames, **Verbal Frames** come in various types, sizes and styles—and there are elegant ones, and ones that are just ... ugly.

But I hear you say: *"I still don't understand what they are?"* You may already be aware of some **Verbal Frames**, but haven't yet labeled them as a frame. Here are some common examples:

Time [frame]: *"My talk runs for about 30 minutes."*

No questions 'til the end [process frame]: *"I'll take about 10 minutes to share my story with you, after which I'd be happy to take questions."*

Content frame: *"I will give you an overview of Topic A first, then we'll get to the nitty-gritty details."*

There are a plethora of ways to frame up your talk or your presentation—and as I hinted, not all meet with what I believe is an "elegant" approach.

Here is a commonly advised approach that I recommend avoiding: *"Tell 'em what you're gonna tell 'em, then tell 'em, then tell 'em what you told 'em."*

While this might *seem* okay (in that the audience will get some kind of up front framing and summary), it lowers the common denominator for how we appreciate our audience's ability to connect the dots for themselves ... assuming a decent presentation design. Your audience will not appreciate being treated like a kindergarten group. (Unless they *are* a kindergarten group. Even then, I'd argue this is a tired and inflexible concept.)

Another frame that has its uses, but can also kill the energy of the audience, is the "Agenda Frame." The presenter might run through the entire agenda outline (possibly including housekeeping). If you are required to do this, you could find yourself having to draw on all your audience rapport techniques just to get through this dry part of the proceedings. Good design skills will also help to break it up; inventive delivery will help it come to life. (See sections in Chapter 3: The Smart Way To Divide Up Your Presentation; The 7 +/-2 Method and Chapter 4: How To Take Your Audience On A Journey.)

When framing is elegant, it bypasses your audience's conscious attention. They'll simply be left with the feeling they are on the same page as you. Note that this is possible even with controversial content, as you will see in Chapter 4, "How To Deal With Difficult Audiences."

Framing is especially critical at the beginning of any presentation or speech, as your audience is unconsciously categorizing who you are and what your talk will mean to them. By putting frames around your opening statements, you give them a clear idea of what to expect. Tip: You can still surprise them later by not showing your entire hand. There's more on this in the Chapter 5 of the book, "How To Be Engaging, Enthralling And Entertaining."

Let's take a look at a fairly standard opening and the frames contained within:

"Good morning! Thanks to Sarah for the wonderful introduction—and as she said, this morning I'm hoping, in exchange for the next fifteen minutes of your life, to share with you three of the most dramatic improvements in your personal energy I believe anyone can easily incorporate into every waking day. I'll give you some concrete examples and actually have you practice that with a partner (don't worry, no embarrassing tricks here!), so that by the end, you'll know exactly how to do each of them, beginning right after my talk.

I will take questions at the end, but we'll get going right away, because you might be wondering, 'Who on earth is Brenda Weston, and what qualifies her to be an expert on personal vitality?' And that's a great question, because three years ago. I was on my last legs, barely able to scrape up enough energy each day to get out of bed. [shows funny slide of herself looking very sick and ill] ..."

And so on.

So, for this fictitious opening, what do we already know from deconstructing the frames that Brenda used?

- Brenda will talk for fifteen minutes.
- She will share three techniques.
- The techniques have something to do with improving our energy levels.
- They should be easy to learn and use on a daily basis.
- She will take questions after her talk.
- She is prepared to be humorous and self-deprecating (the first slide/photo).
- She has framed up a possible "objection" (who are you to tell me this?).
- She will give examples.
- The audience will be able to apply the techniques immediately after her talk.

There are also some elegant presuppositions used in her frames:

"... actually have you practice that with a partner ..."

The frame introduced here is that at some point in her talk (we don't know when, or how), the focus will move to the audience, who will be expected to practice something. More subtle is the fact that there is some tension and an element of surprise, since we are still "blind" to the content. This is one example of a Blind Bullet Frame—see Setting Up Response Potential for more info).

"... (don't worry, no embarrassing tricks here!) ..." The frame cleverly introduced here as an "aside", helps settle the audience, some of whom may have had their tension raised *too* high by the previous phrase (*"have you practice that with a partner"*), possibly unwittingly interjecting performance anxiety, so Brenda has simply tacked on a "***Pacing Out Objections Frame.***" (For more on Pacing Out Objections, see the section on dealing

with controversial topics or hostile audiences.) Most of the audience would be reassured at this point—probably reinforced by Brenda's breezy style—that this is nothing to be concerned about. No doubt she would re-use and possibly deepen this frame at the point before which she introduces the activity itself.

Do you always need frames?

If you are just beginning your journey as a public speaker or presenter, I recommend you practice using them, incorporating them whenever you present. What you will begin to notice is that the odd time you leave one or two out, you will notice the unease in your audience. Tune into that, and ask yourself what you could have "framed up" more effectively.

Once you have those fundamentals in play, then yes, it is permissible to play around. But remember, acrobatics are not performed by novice pilots. Always start with—and practice—the basics.

And you most certainly need to be fully aware of how to make, break and recreate *Audience Rapport*. Speaking of which, shall we? ...

2.4 The Skill Of Influencing Elegantly

WOULD YOU LIKE YOUR AUDIENCE to like you? To feel "in tune" with you?

What about developing deep rapport with your audience?

Many inexperienced presenters (and some experienced ones) imagine a hostile environment where the audience will judge them harshly and give them a hard time. But in my experience, given the chance, audiences do not want you to fail. After all, they have a vested interest in having a good, enjoyable and or informative time.

So we'll start with the premise that most audiences *want* the presenter or speaker to succeed. Your job is to give them reasons to develop that empathy and rapport, and do it from the moment you walk on stage.

As well as a measure of how well we are liked, rapport is a key influence skill. We "buy" from people we like. I strongly recommend you read Robert Cialdini's masterpiece, *Influence—The Psychology of Persuasion*. Here's a link to it:

http://robertscanlon.com/cialdini

Cialdini shows how easily we are persuaded—and how to resist it when you don't wish to be manipulated. In his six broad categories of influence patterns, you will find one entirely devoted to "Liking and likability."

Making yourself "like-able" to your audience is a key skill, and it might surprise you to know that there are techniques you can add to your toolbox that will make this easier. Despite what you might think, likability is not due solely to personality.

Caveat: At first glance, what follows can be perceived as highly manipulative. Some of these techniques may be used as strong influence patterns in any situation, and you may recognize certain elements encountered in less salubrious sales professions, particularly when high pressure is exerted. I urge you to first learn these techniques and apply with integrity, before dismissing them simply because they are also used (badly) by dodgy salespeople.

In my opinion, when used well, and with skill, these techniques are not received by audiences as manipulative. But like any tools, if overused, they quickly lose their effectiveness. As a pleasant side-effect, understanding how these rapport-building techniques work to influence likability will also help you avoid being unwittingly manipulated. When they are overused, used badly or purely for personal gain, you'll see right through them. As they say, "*A ploy perceived is a ploy undone.*" So keep an open mind, and we will continue our journey.

Here's a key principle of rapport: Rapport increases when the degree of sameness increases; we tend to like and agree with people we are similar to, and in rapport with. (Or stated a little more cheekily: "*You must be very smart: You agree with me!*")

Now look at this from the opposite point of view to better understand the effect of sameness and difference on rapport with others: *We are least likely to influenced by those most different to us.*

For example: If you are a non-smoking teetotal vegan body builder, you are not likely to be influenced by restaurant reviews from a beer-drinking steak-fan. Before you laugh, yes non-smoking teetotal vegan body builders *do* exist: http://www.veganbodybuilding.com/. Please note, I have no connection with this website, nor do I specifically endorse the claims being made. I merely present it as an example. Here's another, more common example: a high degree of *sameness* is behind our desire to belong to clubs and associations, playing or watching a sport we love, attending concerts and so on.

So you can see that in general, rapport is deepened when differences are removed and sameness is increased, and as Cialdini points out, "likability" improves.

Now we'll look at how this works for Public Speaking.

You and your audience

One clear difference that is hard to minimize is that you are the presenter, and the audience is, well ... the audience. There's a strong argument that suggests the speaker or presenter should always be perceived as an authority to the audience. Assuming this is the case, then there are some differences you may want to *emphasize*, rather than remove, such as the way you dress and position yourself to enhance your authority status. To some degree, this will depend on the outcome of your presentation. We'll be covering outcomes in great detail in Chapter 3.

However, positioning yourself in this way doesn't mean to have to send out signals of *"I'm different to/ better than you."* It simply means you choose to use some points of difference to establish your authority.

At the same time those circumstantial differences have to be taken into account so that you do not overly dis-create rapport.

The fact that:

- You may be on a stage (and probably raised above your audience),
- You are dressed to present,
- You may be behind a lectern,
- You are in all likelihood standing up and your audience is sitting down,
- You are speaking and they are not;

emphasizes *differences* that may conspire to *lower* rapport levels, and so in order to maintain and develop rapport with your audience you must work harder.

So what will create sameness in this situation?

I want you to think about this carefully. Take a look at humor. Why is humor so successful in creating likability? It's because this is a common shared experience. When we all laugh together, we momentarily "become one." The reason a movie can be more enjoyable and satisfying in a packed movie-theater is in no small part due to the unconscious rapport created by the fact that "we've all been on the same journey of oohs, aaahs and laughs together."

If you've ever been on a flight where there has been a very bumpy ride from turbulence, the sense of relief on landing can often provoke spontaneous applause—but why should this be different to any other flight? Why don't we clap them all?

It's because that shared experience inexplicably bonds the "audience."

Making your audience laugh (while in no way an easy thing to do) is one of the most effective rapport-building activities any speaker can do, as it enhances sameness: we are all laughing, often together with the speaker.

Before you rush out and purchase a library of joke books, I'd like to point out that humor comes from a variety of situations, and about the worst way to generate it is from joke-telling. Far from it. We'll leave telling jokes to the pros. However, it's important to understand that being humorous works to build underlying rapport simply by creating a common experience (or what I call "sameness"), and now that you understand how this works, we can take it further. (And if you specifically want to discover how be funnier, you'll be excited to know I'll show you in Chapter 4: "How To Be Fantastically Funny" and again in Chapter 5: "How To Flex The Funny Muscle Some More")

Now to the nitty-gritty. In order for you to successfully deliver your content to a willing audience, you need to build that rapport bridge. But apart from humor, how *do* you create sameness and build rapport?

Fortunately there are plenty of easy rapport-building techniques that you can use anywhere and at any time. Let's take a detailed look at them.

Unconscious agreement

Any time your audience is in agreement with you, you rack up more rapport points. This will often be out of their awareness, but if we were to define it, it's a simple unconscious check—a, *"yes, that's true"* moment that occurs in the back of their mind.

Therefore, in the moments where you most need to develop rapport, you want to have the audience *agreeing unconsciously* with what you say. This is known as "pacing." Think of it the same as you would "keeping pace" with someone out for a walk, where in order to continue a conversation, you must match their speed. In the same way, you are *pacing* your audience's thoughts and feelings by matching them.

To do this successfully, you must develop the ability to speak generally, *but still sound as if you are only ever talking to one person.*

Asking rhetorical (or real) questions is a great way to start practicing this.

Notice the difference between these two questions:

"Have you ever had your hair cut to almost a shaved head?"

"Have you ever had a bad haircut? Or just a bad hair day?"

The former is much harder to agree to. In all likelihood, most of your audience will be saying no (in the back of their mind), thus dis-creating rapport. The question is too specific.

The latter has a much greater chance of almost everyone in the audience nodding—or at least granting you permission to be right, even if it has not happened directly to them. This is a key point: They are giving you *permission* (unconsciously) to continue.

So your first step is to devise questions that almost everyone, on almost any day, could answer "yes" to.

"Have you ever been busy at work?"

"Have you ever seen a bad movie?"

"Have you ever read a great book?"

"Have you ever experienced a bad driver?"

Notice the examples so far all start with the "have you ever." That's okay for now. Later, as you become more skilled, you'll pick up a variety of ways to make general statements that has your audience nodding in agreement. For example:

"You know that moment when you've just said something and then you immediately realize it was the wrong thing to say?"

If you've done a good job in your intro, most audiences will agree that this could be a true statement for them—if not recently.

But what if it isn't quite general enough?

Then we must catch a C.A.B. (or Cover All Bases)

How? By using a catch-all, that will restore the nods of agreement. So when I gave the example:

"Have you ever had a bad haircut? Or just a bad hair day?"

The second of those two questions was designed to catch those who have never had a bad haircut. And even this question may leave out a third group: those who have no hair. A further C.A.B. might be to sweep in those last remaining follically-challenged folks: *"And even if your last haircut was many moons ago, I'm sure you can recall what those bad hair days are like!"*

Or if you're feeling very cheeky and already have your audience in the palm of your hand: "*Have you ever had a bad haircut? Or just a bad hair day? Hmmm. Looking at you, it might have been quite some time ago.*" (Be careful! If you try this type of playful comic banter without first building sufficient audience rapport you'll be in big trouble.)

The idea of covering all bases is that you can quickly add more parameters to your "general rapport-building question" if you realize in the moment that you may have inadvertently excluded a group of some people. Don't be like one lovely man, Greg, who I had in a training session. Greg became very embarrassed when we discussed this technique. Only the week before he'd had the experience of explaining something technical to a quite large non-technical group, and in frustration had chosen to use an analogy: "*Look, you can all walk, can't you?*" he said. As he saw some audience members glance off to the side, he realized in horror that there was a small group of wheelchair-bound people in the audience. Being the extremely warm man that he is, he recovered gracefully. Using the C.A.B. method meant a lot to Greg after that experience.

Principles of generalized statements that create rapport

Use of *Universals*

Universals are statements that an audience will hold to be generally true for them (as individuals), or at the very least, will allow that they could be generally true at some point. More often than not, these are in the form of generalized statements as described above. To make it easier for those in the audience who may filter their world more pedantically, or continually track for exceptions (to anything you say), you may find it helpful to use modifiers such as:

- *Most* people ...
- *Many* people ...
- You may have ...
- You've *probably* ...

Here are some examples. Test them in your own head—could you reasonably agree that this would be (or could be) true for you? Do you feel that internal "yes" happening in your head?

- *You've probably felt the pressure of an impending deadline ...*
- *Most of us experience emotional ups and downs on a regular basis ...*
- *You may have had the strange feeling that you've forgotten something ...*
- *Many people feel anxious about public speaking ...*

Think about your own talk. What **Universal Statements** could you develop in your repertoire?

Once you have a suite of them, you'll be able to use them—and more importantly, use them to *connect your content to your audience.*

Now I'll add in some **Cover All Bases** [C.A.B.] statements, so you can see how they can work together:

- *You've probably felt the pressure of an impending deadline—and even if you haven't experienced this recently ...*
- *Most of us experience emotional ups and downs on a regular basis—and even if you don't, perhaps you know someone who does ...*
- *You may have had the strange feeling that you've forgotten something, and if you haven't, perhaps you've just forgotten that you did ... [:-)]*
- *Many people feel anxious about public speaking, and even if you are never anxious, you've probably seen people who are. Whether you get anxious before a talk or not, we're going to look at some methods for really connecting with your audience ...*

The use of *Truisms*

Truisms are powerful because they are undeniable. The person hearing them has no choice but to acknowledge that the statement is true for them, *at that moment in time*. It sets up an immediate and often unconscious influence pattern that lets the person on the receiving end of the statement know that the persona making it is being truthful.

Used well, *Truisms* become a part of your rapport-building repertoire. Overdone, they sound odd.

And once you know what they are, you'll see how chaining them together assists in creating rapport-building statements.

Here are some sample truisms related to your experience right now:

- *You are reading this book.*
- *There are words on the page.*
- *You are breathing.*
- *You are alive.*
- *You are reading about public speaking.*
- *You are part of the way through this book.*

These are statements of truth, which by themselves don't mean very much, but they create that tiny bridge of agreement between the speaker and their audience, and help *enhance* the rapport-building process by creating trust.

Caveat: Simply uttering a string of truisms doesn't make anyone become instantly trustworthy. Trust is earned and built over time. But in the case of public speaking, where you have very little time to create those all-important first impressions, any "micro-technique" you can employ to strengthen audience trust in your presentation is helpful, and in this case, truisms are not only helpful, they are extraordinarily powerful.

Here are some examples related to public speaking (after which I will show you what happens when you string several *Truisms* together along with a sprinkling of *Universals*):

- *It's the morning session ...*
- *We're here to discuss ...*
- *In Michael's introduction, he said [...] ...*
- *I'm rather tall ...*
- *I have an accent ...*
- *I'm here to explain ...*
- *It's Tuesday ...*
- *It's Friday afternoon ...*
- *On this slide you can see ...*
- *The flipchart on the stage ...*
- *It's 9.30am ...*

As you can see, there is a myriad of possibility for creating truisms: in fact they are everywhere in our daily lives. Think about the news announcers: *"Good evening, this is the news at nine. I'm Brian Smith and on this Wednesday the fifth of March, we lead with the breaking news ..."*

There's an entire string of truisms beginning that news announcer's introduction—all designed to give the perception of trustworthiness. Here is the unconscious process:

"Good evening [check: Is it evening? Yes. He is correct], *this is the news at nine* [check: Is it nine pm? Yes. He is correct again]. *I'm Brian Smith* [check: Is he? Look at convenient logo and name. Yes. He is correct] *and on this Wednesday* [check: Is it Wednesday? Yes. He is correct, yet again. Amazingly.] *the fifth of March* [check: Is it the fifth of March? Yes. He is correct! Incredible. Does this guy know everything?], *we lead with the breaking*

news ..." [check: Is this breaking news? ... well he was right about everything else, so I suppose it must be? Do go on and tell me what is breaking ...]

This may be a simplistic example, but it illustrates the continuous and instant evaluations we make in our heads: *Is what they are saying true for me, or not? And if it is true, I must agree with them. I can be in rapport with them. I can trust them.* Remember rapport is simply minimization of difference, and it's hard for differences to persist with someone we agree with and find trustworthy.

Once again, I'll give you a typical public speaking example, and this time I want you to experience what happens when I roll a few universals in (and a couple of CABs too), so you can understand how it all comes together.

"Good morning! Thanks Alison for that wonderful introduction. I thought I'd begin this morning's session about personal security with a couple of questions to ponder: Have you ever suddenly been aware of someone watching you? Ever had the hair stand up on the back of your neck for what seemed to be no reason? Most of us have had a similar experience—and even if you haven't, I'm sure you've heard friends and family mention it. Now take a look at my first slide. [Switches to first slide and pauses. Slide shows blissfully unaware woman in a railway station surrounded by cartoon devilish-faced characters, reaching to pick her pocket, rummage in her handbag, and about to steal her luggage. The caption says '99.9% of personal security is all about being aware'.] *When you've had that sense that you might be being followed, or that someone is watching you—or for whatever reason, you're feeling uneasy, it is almost certainly because your senses have noticed something that your unconscious mind has not been able to decode and bring into your conscious awareness. As you look around the room now, I'd like you to sense how much information is already available to us, and notice what you had not seen before. Now as you do that, please tune into the sounds you can hear in this room—and outside it if you can—and again, notice things you hadn't heard before. Finally, as you twist around and listen, I'd like you to use your sense of your body—touch and movement—to discover what it is telling you. How does the chair you are sitting on feel? Can you sense the person next to you? The heat from their body?* [Pauses and looks around to be in rapport with the audience] *Okay, that's enough for the purposes of this introduction. Let me take a few responses from anyone willing to share ... first let's look at what you noticed visually ..."*

And so on.

As you read the sentences above, I expect those **Universals**, **Truisms** and **CABs** stood out—*now that you know them.*

But test it out. Read the presenter's introduction out loud, to a friend if you wish. Do they pick out the rapport-building phrases? No. Because these are a normal part of everyday language. However ... without them, you risk *dis*-creating rapport.

I'll give you the opposite example, just for the sake of contrast (and in the hope that you never do this!):

[Nods stiffly at audience] *"Personal security is all about becoming aware of things you were previously not.* [Skips through first slide and straight to next slide entitled 'Decoding important information from your senses'] *I'll teach you how to get critical information from your senses."*

Yes I know, it sounds silly, doesn't it. But it's not so far removed from how a speaker who lacks the understanding about the need to create rapport in the first few minutes might behave.

Design it in

Don't leave rapport-building to chance. I recommend you deliberately* design it into at least the first few minutes of every presentation, *even if you think you already have rapport with your audience, or that they know you well.* Then rehearse it thoroughly.

Both you and your audience will feel so much better for it.

* In Chapters 3 and 4 we will continue to build on these skills. You will learn practical techniques with solid examples to help you divine what content will be needed in your rapport-building statements. Statements that will be much more convincing, and less general. Why? **Because you will be joining the conversation that is already happening in your audience's heads.**

Stories are powerful

"But Robert," you exclaim, *"I find these types of statements a little unwieldy and they feel cumbersome."*
So? Your point is?

Just teasing! I can understand that you could feel at first that any new technique feels a little clumsy or even contrived. You must also expect techniques that you haven't used before to *feel* unfamiliar and even *uncomfortable*, as you first begin to use them. If you learned a new language, would you be speaking it fluently the day after beginning your education?

You must immerse yourself and be prepared to make this a learning journey. Almost all of the techniques in this book are straightforward to learn and to apply, but to become second nature and more comfortable will take some degree of practice and rehearsal, and some hours under your belt.

But knowing them to begin with will give you a huge boost in confidence.

When I first forced myself to confront the fact that if I wanted to be more successful (than I had previously been), then I would need to present more effectively in group situations, I was petrified. I am, after all, very comfortably introverted. Why would I put myself through this? On more than one occasion, as I've been walking up to the stage, I have felt like turning around. Then I look at the audience, expectant, bright-eyed, and I take a deep breath, realize I have my suite of well-practiced tools, and know that "it's showtime" and I can truly do this well. And the butterflies line up again, obediently.

These techniques for rapport-building work, and work well. There are many ways to slice this up though, including the use of storytelling as a rapport-building tool. We'll cover this in more depth in Chapter 4 when we talk about the art of storytelling, but while we are here, let's take a quick look:

- Stories are as old as mankind.
- They are used to teach and impart knowledge. (Religious texts, parables, Greek mythology)
- In some cultures, stories *are* the culture. (Aboriginal dreaming)
- They are on the news and in the movies on a daily basis.
- We easily identify with (or create separation from) people in stories.

So if you know you have some great stories and examples—they don't all have to be funny, sad or monumentally life-changing—start noting them down and keeping a journal. You'll be using them later.

The fact is, good stories can be extremely rapport-building, because they give the audience a place to share their experience, either with you, or with the person in the story, or by laughing.

Stories, examples and case-studies are extraordinarily powerful methods of not only building rapport, but in influencing in general. The next time you go to see a "motivational style" speaker, make a note of how many stories and examples they use.

Words. They are important. Words have started wars, and ended wars.

But here's a secret: We haven't even begun to plumb the depths of how you influence an audience. Words might be mighty, but they pale into insignificance against the might of ...

2.5 How To Speak With More Than Words

AS A PUBLIC SPEAKER, YOUR words are important, right?

No question about that. As we've just seen in the previous section, the words you choose can make a huge contribution to the connections you make in the minds of your audience.

We might say that your words are your content—but what about the meaning?

Here's the problem: so much of our communication is received non-verbally. There is a field of study known as Kinesics, or the interpretation of body motion in communication, commonly referred to (and misnamed) as "body language." (See http://en.wikipedia.org/wiki/Kinesics.) *Ray Birdwhistell* pioneered this concept, but resisted equating any one specific "body movement" to a particular message (eg "arms folded" = "closed or resistant"), as he felt there were insufficient universal gestures or movements to code so-called body language in this way.

Professor of Psychology, *Albert Mehrabian* (see http://en.wikipedia.org/wiki/Albert_Mehrabian) conducted another study (also widely misinterpreted as we shall see), implying that our communication is delivered in the following fashion:

7% via *Words*

38% via our Tone of voice

55% via *Nonverbal behavior* (for example: facial expressions, gestures—as in the kinesics described above)

The misinterpretation results from the fact that Mehrabian's work was only designed to examine how the *meaning* was conveyed in a simple "like/dislike" response, but has been unfortunately generalized into popular culture as being a constant across all situations.

Nonetheless, the pioneering research by both Birdwhistell and Mehrabian provides us with great insight into how we are able to align our communication for maximum impact and influence. Just so you're clear on the limitations, and we don't all fall prey to a continuance of the misinterpretations, let me first give you an example of where it falls down. Then we will take both concepts and see how we *can* use this to improve your public speaking.

If I said to you, "*Please cross the road now,*" even if my tone conveyed a sense of warning or danger, you might still take this to understand that you should cross the road.

But if I said "*Please do not cross the road now,*" using exactly the same tonality, then clearly I mean something different.

In my view, words are important—even critical.

But for your meaning to be *unambiguous*, this is where Kinesics and the "7%-38%-55% Rule" can lend a huge insight.

As a presenter, you need our audience to hear your words and unconsciously interpret them to match your non-verbal communication.

If they match = audience trusts your communication.

If they do not = audience may at the very least, feel uneasy, or at worst, negate your words.

In many cases, they may not understand consciously why this is the case. If you've ever met someone, spoken with them for a while, and had the feeling or intuition that somehow they are not quite what they seem, or you are not hearing the full story, the likelihood is that you are "reading" their non-verbal communication and interpreting it in a certain way. NOTE: As Birdwhistell points out, this is not necessarily factually true (there may be nothing inconsistent about their communication), but it is certainly *true for you in the way you are receiving it*.

And this perception is the key.

As a public speaker you must become skilled in the use of your vocal tonality and your gestures and movement to help enhance your presentations and talks.

Or at the very least, understand their impact.

This is why it is extremely helpful to video your presentations, or get post-presentation feedback from someone who knows how to track your communication. Without the camera's eye or reliable third-party feedback, it is tricky to self-assess your tone, your "body-language," or more correctly, *kinesics*. http://en.wikipedia.org/wiki/Kinesics.

Here are some examples:

The boring speaker. How to they speak? In a monotone. How to do they move? Not much. Could their words be important and interesting? Of course, but as an audience, we have to work hard to receive them.

The mis-matched speaker. They tell you how exciting the new initiative is. In a monotone. They tell you they are confident about the positive impact of the changes, but they look worried. Or they may tell us what a terrible choice we face—with a smile. All of which challenges their "believability" in our eyes.

The congruent speaker. They tell you a story. It's animated and conveyed very well in facial expressions. They express excitement (and other emotions) naturally in their vocal inflections. Their stance is strong. Or confident. Or interesting. Or whatever seems to be supporting their message at the time. We like them.

Now I hear the objections. *"But Robert, before you said you wanted us to be 'more of who we are' on stage? How do I do that when I'm a quiet introvert? Do you now want me to jump around telling the world how excited I am?"*

Far from it. What I am encouraging you to do is to understand how and where to guarantee your entire message is in alignment. Where your *words*, your *tonality* and your *gestures* all conspire to deliver the same message.

There is nothing wrong with a quiet and assured speech—if the message is clear. In fact, there can be much gravitas conveyed in this manner, and something that extroverts would do well to learn and become more flexible with.

Because flexibility is the key.

You need your skills to improve so that you can be more *adaptable*. You need to know that if your public speaking lacks confidence, there are *things you can do to bolster the audience's perception of confidence*, on top of getting your own **Presenter Bubble** under control.

We want precision and congruence.

Imagine attending a magician's show. This particular magician is imprecise. You see the card flick back into their sleeve. You catch a glimpse of the assistant climbing down a hidden escape hatch behind a loose curtain. It's not impressive—and you would most likely leave the show disappointed.

Think of your public speaking the same way. The more precise you are, the easier it is to wow your audience.

Precision in non-verbal communication is not about uncomfortably over-exaggerating your tonality and body language. It's about getting it right. And avoiding common mistakes. Here's what to watch out for:

Insufficient tonal variation

Minimal changes in volume, or inflection, or in conveying emotions; use of monotones.

This is common with nervous speakers. Flat tonality, verging on the monotone, and perhaps too quiet. All caused by excessive tension in the chest and throat, and insufficient movement of air through the lungs. Solution: Extend your bubble, breathe deeply into your diaphragm; possibly use some vocal warm-up exercises (singing is good); learn to verbally project perhaps by taking some dramatic classes. Ask someone to coach you in a large room: have them stand at the back while you try to vary your voice to extremes. On many occasions, I've asked presenters (in a coaching environment) to raise their volume, which they do (on the inside!), *but no-one can hear any difference.* Sometimes with tonality, because we are so used to the narrow range of our own speech patterns, it can be hard to move the boundaries. Practice, practice, practice.

You may also find it helps to practice in front of a mirror and influencing your tonality by varying your facial expressions.

Distracting body language

The most common one? Fiddling. Fiddling with money or keys in a pocket. Fiddling with a remote, or a marker pen. Fiddling with clothing, or hair. Learn to avoid fidgeting. Some fiddling happens because we are uncomfortable with the audience's eyes on us. I have had presenters who habitually fiddle come to the front of the room and simply stand in front of the audience in silence. It helps them anchor what it feels like to be still and quiet in front of others. It can be tough, but worth the re-training.

Here is a (non-exhaustive) list of typical—and common—physical movements and habits that can be distracting to audiences:

- Wringing hands.
- Imprecise gesturing: *"Look at the second line on the slide"* (while they throw an arm vaguely in that direction)
- Over-gesturing.
- Too many Umms. Ahhs, and other over-used fillers. (Yes I know, these are words and not movements, but they are incidental to your content and should be minimized.)
- Too much movement side-to-side on stage—for example, pacing the stage. Imagine an audience watching a rapid table-tennis match. Make sure your audiences' heads don't need to swivel rapidly to follow your presentation, or that your rhythmic movements are not causing them to fall into a trance.
- Too much time spent moving to a needed resource. For example, presenting from one side of a stage, but having to walk to the other side just to click to the next slide. Arrange your equipment suitably, and rehearse to avoid unnecessary pregnant pauses, unless you want them by design or for effect.

Incongruent body language

- Folding arms and asking for feedback. Yes, the presenter may not *mean* to be perceived as closed; as I said before, "body language" is not universal, but that doesn't mean it doesn't create certain perceptions in some minds.
- Similarly, saying *"Any questions?"* and then clasping hands together indicating closure. This question, in and of itself is a closed question. Learning how to ask –and answer—questions is a crucial skill, and is covered in Chapter 5, beginning with: *"Can You Ask Your Audience A Rhetorical Question?"*
- Appearing apologetic, or appearing to beg. Behaviors such as rubbing/clasping/wringing hands; bending forward the audience (as if praying) should be avoided. I call this "the Preacher." This body position tends to project a lack of confidence or fear. Solution? Stand up straight, leave

your hands by your side, or use one only to gesture. Men can get away with one hand partially in a pocket. Alternatively, you can stand up straight and hold your hands loosely together in front of your body (they will usually fall comfortably to your upper thigh area). This is non-threatening and is one stance helpful for listening to an audience member.

- Anything over-used. Not strictly incongruent, but after a while this grates. For example:
    - Using an accusative pointing finger all the time ("stabbing" at the air or at the audience). Same with the toned down politician's version—the flat hand held vertically, pointing to the audience. Occasional use? No problem at all.
    - Wide open arms and palms of the hands facing the audience (another version of "the apology"). Useful on occasions to demonstrate inclusion, or to invite responses.
    - The "Thinker." Usually one hand under the chin, the other folded across the chest. If a speaker always assumes this position, eventually they may appear aloof, overly logical, rational or unemotional. Again, occasional use is great to portray reflection and encourage thoughtful assimilation of your content.
    - Erratic, self-interruptive, impulsive movement on the ... wait, is that a squirrel? Any unfinished movements, or being "all over the place." After a while, the audience is exhausted. However, if your goal is to wake the audience up, or introduce a "pattern interrupt," or to bring a story to life, then erratic and impromptu movement can be stimulating ... if used wisely.
- Any aspect of the presenter's dress or movement that conflicts with their content: For example, the person speaking about grooming who clearly needs a haircut.

It sounds as if I'm implying that the audience will be casting a critical eye over your tone, movement, and appearance, but in reality, the audience simply wants you to succeed. Any critical response is largely an unconscious one which you can easily overcome using the tools in this book.

Demonstrating direction, miming actions or timelines "the wrong way around" for the audience

Almost all new and inexperienced presenters fall prey to this, as do a good many presenters who should know better.

Imagine you are in the audience and looking at the stage area. If the presenter shows you a slide of a graph with a rising line on it, you'll tend to expect that the low end of the graph will begin at the lower left of the chart, and that the higher end will be placed to the top-right. See my example below.

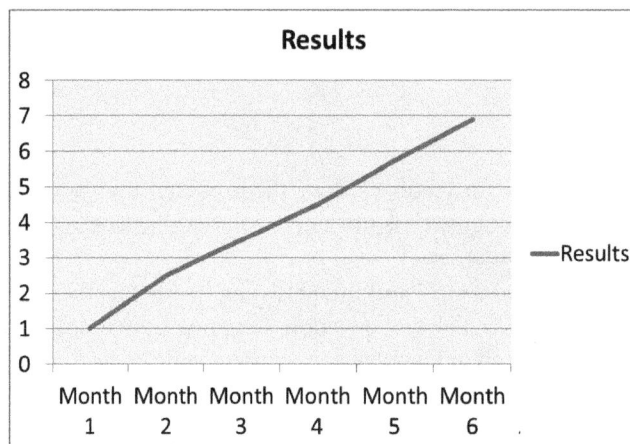

A Typical Rising Chart

Now imagine you are the presenter, and facing your audience. There is no graph behind you, and you must demonstrate an increase in something to them by using your hands (it could be sales; complaints; defects; phone calls, it doesn't matter what).

Your natural tendency will be to use your hands to illustrate this *the way you see it in your own head.*

The issue is that this mime will reversed from your audience's point-of-view, and it will be neurologically confusing to them—your words will not match your actions.

Consequently, everything we do on stage with our gestures must be designed to work for our audiences' unconscious expectations. If you are describing with your hands a mock "graph," it must match your audience's idea of what such a graph's visual appearance would be.

If you are gesturing to something that "happened in the past," most of your audience will expect (but not consciously) that this will have occurred on the left-hand side of the stage. We hypothesize that this is because we read left-to-right; that graphs showing a timeline will always show past on the left; that the rewind and fast-forward buttons on any device, even online, will be placed correspondingly on the left and right side of the play button.

Stage placement is counter-intuitive; meaning that you have to reverse what you might imagine in your head and represent it for your audience *in the way they might see these "images" in their heads.*

For example, if you suggest that *"in the future, reporting this way will be the norm,"* and you gesticulate to your right (or with some vague wave of the hand), the your audience will not perceive this as clearly as if you had pointed to your left.

In this example, pointing to the right is most likely your natural reaction. This direction is known as *"stage right,"* which is the *left* side of the stage from the audience's point-of-view, and the audience will "see," or code this as something occurring in the past. Pointing to your left is pointing *stage left;* which is the *right* side of the stage from the audience's point-of-view, and they will experience this as representing their *future.*

I will say now that this takes some conscious effort to retrain your own natural inclinations, and should wait until you have some experience and confidence before you try to incorporate it.

In summary

With any body language, acting-out or miming, your outcome should be to minimize any friction that is preventing you:

a. Building rapport, and

b. Creating unintentional discomfort or distrust in your audience.

Simple.

2.6 The Secret To Never Being Stuck For What To Say Next

PREVIOUSLY I SPOKE ABOUT MOVING around the stage: how to do it, what to avoid. How about we delve a bit deeper into this now? What's that? You can't move? You're stuck to the spot?

We need to talk.

I'd like you to (as you read this), become completely frozen and immobile. As if you were playing one of those "freeze when the music stops" games. Totally motionless, not a hair moves.

I'm willing to bet that you also feel your brain start to "freeze" its thoughts too and only focus on this one activity. (Not a bad thing when reading.)

Okay you can loosen up now. Most of us are constantly moving, fidgeting to some degree, shifting our bodies—even if reading. Our eyes move, we occasionally look around, reach for a drink, get up to visit the facilities, you name it.

Yet many people have had the sensation on stage of "being frozen and/or stuck to the spot."

At the very start of this book, I talked about the fight/flight/freeze response to fear. Being stuck to one spot is one way we manifest fear. So of course, if public speaking is a nerve-wracking experience, you are more likely to be predisposed to freezing up mentally.

And how do you think that plays out in your body?

That's right. If your mind freezes, your body will tend to follow.

And then we have the converse: If your body is moving very little, or stuck to the spot, guess what happens to your thoughts? They become more static (in the context of being on stage). This is why, despite having the apparently easiest question in the world fired at them, contestants on TV quiz shows seemingly freeze up and cannot think. It's a shame they don't know the trick.

What trick? A trick that you can learn, practice and rehearse as the ultimate get-out-of-jail-card for any "my mind has gone blank" situation. And one that will persuade you to practice moving around on stage, and to abandon relying on lecterns. Or learn to rely on them less.

I'll also show you a fantastic technique to allow you to recall automatically what you should be saying at any one time, which, for example, is fabulous for successful memorization of your introduction. Later in Chapter 7, we'll link this to making good speakers' notes.

Meanwhile, let's talk about moving around.

If you are stuck in one place on the stage, you are more likely to have difficulty recovering from a blank moment.

The solution is as simple as they come: move.

Time and again, I've had trainee public speakers and presenters get up in front of a group to present without notes. Some will hit that frozen spot, and time and again, our supportive group of co-learners will laugh, because guess what? That's right, they've assumed a "statue position," as if frozen in time chasing that elusive thought around inside their heads.

All we do is ask them to move around; to take their time, and to find their place again.

It's remarkable, on every single occasion, just like magic the train of thought returns and the presentation continues. Why is this?

I put it down to the movement. Perhaps the movement has a calming or relaxing effect, perhaps it allows a held breath to shift and flow to the next one, or it tells the brain to resume from pause-mode, or allows neural pathways to reconnect in alternative routes—it really doesn't matter. All that matters is that it works, and it works reliably.

Which is one very good reason why you should not habitually present from one specific place on the stage. This will tend to make you much more susceptible to the "stuck state," since your body is already not moving from its habitual position. If you do become stuck, you might find it doubly difficult to move away from your physical comfort zone, making it harder for you to get back into flow.

Therefore I encourage you to liberate yourself from presenting from one static spot, if only so that you understand that when you move, so does your presentation. There are other very good reasons you should learn to present from anywhere on stage, as we shall see in Chapter 6: "A Critical Technique: But Don't Let Your Audience Catch You Doing It!" All the more reason to start practicing it now.

How do you move around?

Purposefully.

To begin with, I recommend that you move in between sentences. Anywhere there is a natural pause.

But of course, you *can* move while speaking. Just remember, this is an art, and if you are looking at your audience, or at your slide (why???? Don't do that!), you might miss something important. Like your chair, or worse, the edge of the stage. Don't laugh. I've seen it happen.

You should also know that if you are moving across the stage while talking, it's much more distracting for the audience. It can also cause issues for those hard of hearing.

A great way to get a sense of how this is done well is to watch good stand-up comedians work the stage (watch live performances filmed and screened on TV). Yes, they can definitely talk while moving, but I bet you'll rarely witness them deliver a punchline on the move. Because they know it has less impact.

Equally, as described in the previous section, too much movement is distracting and possibly incongruent to your topic.

Overuse of one side of the stage compared to another should also be avoided. Almost all of us are "handed" in one way or another: right-, or left-handed. For some people this spills over into how they use the stage area, and which side of the audience they pay attention to. You may be unaware of it, thinking that you are attending to both sides of your audience equally.

I recommend you watch video footage, or get feedback from an observer to make sure you are reasonably balanced. This is even more critical if your presentation is already unbalanced from the audience's perspective, for example if you are using a laptop to drive your slides and sitting off to one side. You can still move out from your position from time-to-time, or throw your attention, and gaze, to the farthest reach of your audience. And extend your **Presenter Bubble**, of course.

Movement in your presentation should be both as deliberate and as natural as possible, and I promise you it will feel that way, once you have some decent practice under your belt.

Remembering to pause, and have space when *not* moving, in order to address your audience, also gives you an opportunity to make one of the strongest human connections anyone can make with their audience.

Read on to find out what.

(You know you want to.)

2.7 Do This Well ... Or Risk Looking Shifty

SHOULD YOU MAKE EYE CONTACT with your audience?

Think of it as "I" contact. You to me. An audience is not an amorphous group of eyes, it is a collection of individuals. (They may exhibit crowd behaviors, which is covered in Chapter 6, "How Not To Address An Audience")

Research seems to suggest that 85% or more of all human-to-human communication is conveyed via the eye. (See http://velvetchainsaw.com/2012/05/23/your-senses-your-raw-information-learning-portals/)

That's an extraordinary claim, yet it tells us much. It explains just why we might feel uncomfortable with people who make no eye contact; cannot sustain eye contact; do weird things with eye contact (stare, or appear shifty); and even those who have an eye disability (one eye that roams, "lazy eye", squints etc).

Which is why I like to think of eye contact as "I-contact."

"*But Robert,*" you say, "*there are over 80 people in my talks. How can I make eye contact with all of them?*"

Answer? You can't, of course. But you can make it *seem* as if you are, and you can roam your gaze around the room, to avoid overdoing eye contact with the front row (a trap for young players).

Learning to make frequent eye contact with your audience is a learned skill, and one that requires your attention to be well extended. I'll show you how to do it, then we'll look at some common errors. But first—why is this so important?

When you consider how much communication could be transmitted via your eyes, connecting to your audience with real eye contact becomes a key method for conveying rapport, trust and authenticity. For this reason, I recommend you make it your mission to make "I-contact" as much as possible.

If it helps, try taking the opposite view: imagine you avoided making any eye contact whatsoever. A presenter that makes no eye contact can seem removed, cold or indifferent.

Your audience will perceive you as someone who is willing to engage and connect. The fact that there is more than one human to make eye contact with makes no difference to them. Almost all of us have an innate need to feel valued, and one way to experience this is to feel connected with another human being. When we are noticed, and eye contact is held, we feel more present with the other person.

Think about a group of friends gathered at some social occasion, perhaps a barbecue, picnic, party, and each take turns telling stories, as we are fond of doing on such occasions. Observe carefully: Any time one person is holding the fort with their story, they will be seeking eye contact validation—and non-verbal eye-cues—from the others. It's something we are programmed to do (assuming no visual impairment).

I like to remind myself of this in any presentation or speech context —and to imagine that this situation is nothing different to a group of friends I am recounting stories to. It helps me to approach audiences in a way that makes it much easier to seek out eye contact, rather than be afraid of it.

To use eye contact effectively as a presenter, there are a some techniques I would recommend you take the time to practice:

Techniques to help you make good eye contact

- Linger an appropriate amount on any one person. (Too much is creepy!)
- Move from person to person, linger briefly, then move on. (See the drill at the end for suggestions for practicing this.)
- Look directly into their eyes, even if: You are a long way away; the lighting is bright; they are on the farthest side away from you.
- Cover the whole room and avoid any dependence or "handedness" (see "Things to avoid" below).
- Move naturally, even pause if you want to.
- Smiling helps tremendously (we all love a smiling eye!), as the person you have made eye contact with may smile back. Or they may have the most impassive face you've ever seen. Makes no difference. Just move on.
- Try to land in a different spot each time, especially for larger groups (over 20).
- For very small groups (under 12), make sure your eye contact is distributed evenly. No favorites. It's easy to get caught in the trap of making more eye contact with the most engaging person or biggest extrovert.

Here are some common mistakes.

Eye-contact "no-no's": Things to avoid

- Moving too fast—don't do it, it will make you look "shifty." Not good for audience rapport.

Don't look just above their eyes, or the audience will experience an odd sense of disconnection from you. Even if you are uncomfortable with eye contact, you're just going to have to learn to do it. Once you can, I promise you, from then on it's all easy.

- Lingering on one person too long. Unless you really want them to feel uncomfortable for some reason (it has been known!).
- Avoid having favorite places to look to. Some presenters tend to direct their attention only to the front row (easier to see). Others teach to a particular side (many of us have a particular visual preference to look either to the left or right side). Your presentation habits can be affected by the position of the podium, stage or lectern. Perhaps the hardest situation is when you have participants who laugh the most or you have someone who is always nodding in agreement with you. Avoid letting yourself be drawn to any one person or place.
- Avoid hard staring. Try to keep your eye contact light at all times—that's where your smile works wonders.
- Avoid squinting or peering into the audience (perhaps they are hard to see; perhaps the spotlight is preventing you, or making you squint). Practice a relaxed gaze when you are looking into bright light, or an audience in darkness, and looking where you imagine them to be sitting or standing, will work just as effectively. Being able to spend time in the room or on stage before your audience is present is a golden opportunity, so take it every time you are able. For me, it's mandatory to request room access prior to the audience being there: At the very least to survey the scene, and at the best to have a full-dress rehearsal type experience.

Your physical position

Where you are, in terms of relative height to your audience, will also determine how well this works. For example, if you are in a room of 100 people, all seated "banquet style," and you are not on a raised stage, then you will have to make more physical effort to make eye contact with your entire audience, but the payoff is well worth it. They will each feel as if you are speaking directly to them.

If you are high up on a stage, it can be disconcerting, as most of us are used to making eye contact at relative heights similar to our own. To be suddenly looking down at everyone, looking back up at you, can feel challenging (especially if the lighting is also strong). Once again, relax the muscles around your eyes, smile, and make any effort to look back naturally. If it helps, watch how some top music performers handle this on stage in stadium type environments and notice how they still manage to look around the "room." Some will even give the appearance of having noticed someone in the crowd, nod and wave, all to be more personable.

Note: I'm not suggesting that you *act* or try to be something you are not. Just "release the inner human connection" inside you, and you will be fine. Audiences are not to be feared, despite what that lizard brain of yours seems to be suggesting.

The one thing that will help your eye contact each and every time is the fullest extension and projection of your *Presenter Bubble* that you can manage.

Speaking of "projection," are you a mumbler? Can people hear the beginnings and ends of your words? Do you know how to project like a Shakespearean orator?

Let's look at how ...

2.8 The Art Of Presenter Ventriloquism

PROJECTION. WOULD YOU PROJECT YOUR slides so they appear out of focus or fuzzy?

Of course not. So why do some presenters use their voices so poorly? Probably because they have never been trained to do anything else.

You, however, will have an edge. In fact you already have a very significant edge over most.

Your *Presenter Bubble*. Believe it or not, if you didn't already experience it before, when you really focus on placing your attention on your audience and not on you, your voice immediately becomes more comprehensible. Your projection is enhanced, even if you have a soft voice, and you'll sound more natural ... all without having to think about it.

One more reason why the *Presenter Bubble* is a compelling skill to develop.

But now that you know that, it's time to examine some very specific ways to improve your vocal delivery, so that your talks, speeches and presentations, no matter what size the crowd, are always beautifully delivered.

Clarity of speech

A great training ground for speaking with vocal clarity is to watch the evening news announcers. First just look, and especially notice their mouths, how they breathe, their "stance." Almost everything they do is designed to open up their chest, shoulders and avoid constriction of the throat and neck.

So the first step is to make sure your breathing patterns are relaxed and deep. Place one hand on your abdomen and breathe "into" it. Feel your belly move out and in with each breath. Now on the out breath, keep your hand on your belly and say "My name is _____ _____." Feel how you can make this far more resonant by using more of your lung capacity and volume because you have used your diaphragm to pump your lungs (as opposed to relying on just your intercostal muscles—those attached to your ribs).

Singing helps too. More than one Presentation Skills Trainer I have met teach the use of singing warm up exercises to help public speakers work their voices more effectively.

You want to avoid straining your vocal chords. I'm sure you're aware of numerous tales of rock and pop stars who have had to cancel tours due to a strained "voice." Or worse, have undergone surgery.

So that's why you want to learn to relax, and why working on your *Presenter Bubble*—which in and of itself is a relaxation technique—will help.

If you think about nerves and stress for a moment, you'll realize why some voices sound weak. If someone is nervous and tense:

- Their breath will be in their upper chest (paradoxical breathing) and shallow. Hard to pump up the volume here!

- Their neck muscles and jaw muscles may be tight, resulting in tightened vocal chords. This is a recipe for strain. Ever felt like you're losing your voice after a speech? That's your nervous tension locking everything down.
- The pitch of their voice (high or low notes) will tend towards the higher registers, or even sound "squeaky." Why? Shortened vocal chords due to ... yes that's right: Tension, contracting the muscles (or not allowing lengthening).

Add all these factors together and it's already a problem—but what if you are the high achieving kind? Or someone who hates to be seen as "weak"? Chances are you will *force* your voice, which makes things worse, and significantly increases the chance of injury. It's also likely to lead to a shouting style of projection, which perversely makes you harder to understand.

Back to the news announcer. Steady breathing, open chest, shoulders and relaxed throat and jaw.

Take the time to really listen to them, especially to the envelope of their words. Can you hear the beginnings and endings of words? No laziness there, is there?

This is called enunciation and is related to the way we articulate each word. By focusing on speaking more slowly and taking great care that the beginning and ending of each word is clean and clear, your level of comprehension in the audience will improve dramatically.

How to do this?

Simple. If you've seen or heard of the movie "*My Fair Lady*" (here's a clip with the famous pronunciation scene: https://www.youtube.com/watch?v=MJr9SSJKkII), then you may already know this technique—but those news anchormen and women give it away when you watch their mouths.

- Open your mouth more deliberately.
- Use your lips to open and close consonants in an exaggerated fashion.
- Use your tongue to make more clicks when needed. Remember, "The rain in Spain, falls mainly on the plain."
- Practice speaking in front of a mirror and *learn to show your teeth when you speak*!

A word on accents: I'm not insisting you learn to speak BBC-accented English. And perhaps English is not your first language, perhaps you already have an accent (which can be attractive to audiences). No. I want you to practice a deliberate and exaggerated e-nun-see-ay-shun of each and every word.

Both breathing and a more deliberate focus on enunciation (especially when you work on distinguishing each word) will already help—assuming your **Presenter Bubble** is extended.

But we can also play with your speed, vocal variety and the introduction of deliberate ...
pauses.

Why? Because we need to be the opposite of the *boring* presenter, who speaks in a monotone, mumbles and slurs words together, and does not project.

We need to talk about your **AUDIO Presenter Bubble**.

Oh yes, it exists.

Remember how we talked about where you place your mental attention? And how extending this mental attention translates into using a **Presenter Bubble**?

For most people, your audio projection (how far your voice appears to travel) will ratchet up and down along with your mental attention.

But just like all the techniques in this book, once we put conscious attention on projecting and extending your **AUDIO Presenter Bubble**, you will be amazed at how well this works.

I bet you have never thought about where your voice "is" when you speak. This is exactly why many speakers' voices never seem to reach us effectively: they are still stuck in their mouth—or worse, down their throats. Think about it. We're all used to hearing the sound of our own voices, and very close to our own ears at that, so we've really trained our "bubble" to stay close.

But you can *extend* your voice. There's plenty of proof too: ventriloquism wouldn't work unless it were possible.

The next time you speak to someone—one-on-one—try placing your attention on where the sound of your voice is landing. Enunciate and expand your **Presenter Bubble** at the same time, and keep your breathing deep and long.

My bet is that you'll feel a notable difference in the *quality* of the communication between you both.

If you have a willing partner, try this:

One person chooses to be the "presenter," the other the "audience." Stand facing each other about one meter/yard apart.

Part 1: The presenter starts speaking (using a topic they know well or ad-libbed). The audience member moves backwards while facing the presenter until they feel that they have lost clarity. This may be while you are both still quite close, or it could be ten meters/yards.

The job of the presenter now is to "move" the audience further away, without actually raising their voice. This is a projection and **Presenter Bubble** exercise that gives you immediate feedback. At first you are likely to think you're shouting but it doesn't take long to work out how to project well. In this part of the exercise, the audience member keeps moving backwards until they lose clarity and comprehension, at which point they stop.

Part 2: Start again close together, but this time the presenter is to try speaking as softly as possible, while maintaining maximum distance where the words are completely understandable and audible. The audience member again moves backwards to demonstrate that the presenter can be heard at this new, longer distance. If the presenter becomes less audible or their words create less clarity for the listener, then the audience member will move *closer* until they re-establish comprehension.

I assure you, you will be amazed at how effectively you can make yourself understood over a large distance, simply by putting your attention on your **AUDIO Bubble**.

This exercise may appear inconsequential if you're just reading it, but when you do jump in and have a go, you'll have tangible proof that you can expend *less* energy and save your vocal chords from injury, while delivering a message that easily reaches everyone in your audience.

And yes, in case you're wondering, this works even when using microphones.

So to recap: You are demonstrating clean and clear "body language," you are using clear and rapport-building words, and now you have the means to make yourself sound clear and polished.

Now we'll turn our attention to using your voice more *expressively*.

2.9 What Is The Most Authoritative Tone Of Voice?

IT'S FINESSING TIME.

Think of your voice as a tool—a tool to support your message.

If you want to create a sensation of suspense in your audience, then how would you speak? Quietly, right? A "conspiratorial whisper" perhaps?

If you were describing a particularly poignant moment, would you shout? Probably not.

Imagine a movie where an intimate love scene is being depicted, and it takes place in the front two seats of a stationary car. Do you think the director would instruct the actors to yell at each other? No, that's reserved for arguments.

So in everyday-normal-world, we all *get* the idea that our vocal intonations, inflections and volume contribute to the meaning of the communication.

And that should be our guiding light: The *meaning* of the communication.

I can say the word "*No*" over and over, each time using a different tonality, and each time conveying a different meaning (strong, weak, unsure, danger-warning, OMG-a-truck-is-about-to-hit-me, or when my favorite sports hero loses).

In each case, the word is the same, but my tone is different each time. Most likely my body language also changes depending on the circumstance. We covered the effects of words, tone and body language earlier in this chapter (see How To Speak With More Than Words) and Professor Albert Mehrabian's research (http://en.wikipedia.org/wiki/Albert_Mehrabian). In this section we're referencing the same research, only now from the point of view of our auditory expression, or *tone*. I should point out again that the percentage of our "communication" commonly attributed to tone (38%) can be highly contextual.

Nonetheless, it's a great guideline as to just how *much* meaning is conveyed by our tone of voice, and therefore how crucial your tone of voice is when it comes to influencing your audience.

So if you don't want to be that monotonous public speaker, you will have to put some attention on how you speak.

As I pointed out in the previous section on improving enunciation, and as you'll discover throughout this book, putting effort into extending your **Presenter Bubble** will do a lot of the heavy lifting for you when it comes to making yourself heard. Indeed for many people, this is one of the keys to unlocking audience engagement.

But if you struggle to feel you are "interesting" enough, then finessing your vocal delivery may be the difference that makes the difference.

(Before moving on, if you have navigated directly here but haven't read the preceding section in a while, or at all, please make sure you are familiar with: "The Art Of Presenter Ventriloquism")

Here's the most important reason you want to find more variety in your vocal patterns: It's one way to significantly influence your audience's *state* that does not *require* any body language, though using your body effectively will certainly help with congruence. Note: We'll be taking an in-depth look at the notion of "state," and why it is so important to know what it is and how to influence it, in Chapter 3.

In the previous section we learned from TV News Announcers by watching their mouths and their physiology.

Now let's tune in to Radio Announcers and the more successful on-air DJs and Anchors. Staying clear of the overblown "advertising style" and closer to the classic 50's style of speech patterns, what can we deduce?

Listen to this quick segment from a well-known BBC Announcer:

https://www.youtube.com/watch?v=hIA-pdqoRSU

What we can deduce is that an interesting voice makes an interesting presentation.

But what makes the voice interesting—and how do you do it? Take a look at this list:

- A lower pitch tends to convey authority (it's hard to sound terribly convincing with a Mickey Mouse style of voice). Don't be concerned if you do have a higher voice though. Mine doesn't have bass tones like Morgan Freeman's either. No matter how high your voice is normally, there are things you can do to make it sound more commanding, beyond just deliberately choosing to use the lower registers of your vocal range. As touched on in Chapter 2, learning to use diaphragmatic breath is key, as is not rushing your words.
- Variety of intonation is crucial.
- Authority perception increases when the sentences end on a lower pitch. (Think of the "movie trailer guy," and note the speech patterns)
- Knowing when to make your voice inflection sound like a question, and when not. A sentence should only sound like a question when it is one (see "What to avoid?" below).
- Variety in speed and rhythm is perhaps even more important than variety in pitch. Good news for us squeaky-voicers.
- Pauses. Work. Especially for dramatic delivery, or to Make. A. Point.
- Naturally delivered phrasing is key for comprehension. Having breaks in the right places is vital, for example: Speaking as if you were reading and observing correct breathing breaks at commas, full stops, new paragraphs.

What to avoid?

- Avoid speaking within the same narrow pitch range the whole time.
- Avoid speaking within the same volume range the whole time.
- Avoid making everything you say sound like a question. Compare the speech patterns of the typical 'Valley girl" (where sentences go "up" at the end) with that of the "movie trailer guy." Finishing sentences with an upward inflection? It sounds like everything you say is a question? And will end up convincing your audience that you are unsure of yourself?

2.10 Drills

Before you present:

Pay particular attention to your beginnings and endings. Deliberately craft them for maximum impact. Practice them.

Practice making eye contact with an imaginary audience. If you can do this in a conference room or meeting room, all the better, but any room will do. Get your brain used to that lingering scan around the room (even if all you are doing is talking to empty chairs).

Design "frames" into your presentation that allow your audience to be taken by the hand and set their expectations. At first you might find yourself doing this very obviously, but as you become familiar with framing, you'll notice you're doing it in flow with your content. You might think some frames are simply obvious, but in my experience, when you really pay attention to designing frames into your talk it will help you gain the skill faster. Most importantly you'll see the results from the increased level of your audiences' engagement.

When you are practicing out loud (also see Chapter 1: "What Most Presenters Don't Do ... And Why They Fail"), try varying your tone to extremes. Not that you will actually speak this way when you are "live", you're only doing this to explore all the limits.

Deliberately practice using more authoritative tone and pitch. Imagine projecting your voice from your abdominal area to help focus on diaphragmatic breathing. Placing one hand on your stomach may help trigger this movement of breathing away from your upper chest, and further down into your lungs. As someone who practices yoga I can assure you that developing a larger and more effective breath capacity can take some time, however, placing your hand on your abdomen will help focus your intentions.

When you practice out loud, also practice *deliberately* moving around. Then try presenting just from one spot. Practice with your hands clamped down by your side. Notice what happens in all these instances, and practice moving/walking around if you are not sure what comes next, and train yourself to do this on stage. To review the notes on this, see the section in this chapter titled: "The Secret To Never Being Stuck For What To Say Next."

Practice using different "body language" styles to communicate your message more congruently: If you tend to always clasp, or wring your hands, practice something different; if you tend to pace around, try delivering one section from one place for effect.

Before standing up to speak:

Take a big deep breath, let it out and expand your **Presenter Bubble**: this time feel that your vocal bubble is expanding along with it.

During your presentation:

Make eye contact: linger a while on individual audience members and smile as you speak. (The exception of course, is with very grave or upsetting content where it's not appropriate to smile.)

Deliver frames and notice your audience's reactions. Which ones work well for you?

As per "Before you present," where I recommended practicing moving while presenting, you should also be doing it during your next talk. Move around with deliberation. Avoid being stuck to one spot. Ask an observer or someone in the audience you trust for feedback about your movements.

Vary your vocal delivery: have some loud and soft moments; vary your pace; enunciate clearly.

Use variations on your body's physiological communication to enhance your content. Where possible, minimize or stop distracting habits in the moment.

Post-speech:

Immediately after: keep up the eye contact!

Review your design: how did your framing work for you? Any that need to be changed? If so, note those down while you are fresh. Inevitably the best ideas to improve your talk will come in the moments during and after.

Check in with your assistant, or trusted audience member (or watch your video recording): what feedback do they have for you regarding your use of varied vocal tones and "body language"? So much of this is out of our awareness (and should be, once your *Presenter Bubble* is maxed-out), that it can really help to have someone else tracking it.

How was your audio projection? Did anyone towards the back of the audience look as if they were straining to hear? How could you project more next time?

CHAPTER 3: FOOLPROOF TECHNIQUES FOR STRUCTURING YOUR PRESENTATION OR SPEECH

3.1 The Sophisticated Way To Structure Your Presentation That Makes It Easy

WOULDN'T IT BE NICE TO think you never needed to worry again about "what comes next" in your presentation?

Here's the really good news. I'm going to teach you something almost no presenters know anything about, and even those that do, either don't use it, or mis-use it. In this section I will teach you how to use this elusive planning and structuring tool correctly.

If you plan your presentation or speech by following a structure designed to help educators attend to a range of "learning styles," not only will *you* find it super-easy to construct your speech, but there are two huge pay-offs:

1. You will use the structure to help you know exactly where you are at in your presentation—and what comes next.
2. Your speech will always move smoothly onto the next "logical" topic, which your audience will experience as highly professional.

Even more fascinating is that this method allows you to *nest* elements of your presentation. So if you have a longer talk that requires *"chunking"* (coming up later in this chapter), then each chunk takes on the wireframe of the structure I will outline for you—to the degree that you'll know exactly where you are and what style the next "chunk" of your talk will require.

Even if you have a two-day workshop to present.

This methodology will revolutionize your planning and design process, and set you up with a better system of presenter's notes.

But first, we need to talk about the outcome(s) for your speech, talk, presentation or training session ...

3.2 A Crazily Named, But Key Design Tool

OUTCOMES: WHY ARE THEY IMPORTANT?

After all, if you've been asked (or told!) you need to give a speech, or make a presentation, then you don't really have much of a say in the outcome, do you? Isn't the outcome just "getting it over with"? For example, if your presentation has to do with your job, or constitutes something perfunctory that may not be something you are passionate about.

That's possibly true, if viewed only from your perspective.

But what will make a major difference to the ease with which you will present, and the reception you will generate, is when you begin to consider your talk from the perspective of your *audience's* outcome.

Let me ask you these questions:

- Why are you giving this speech? (Even assuming you've been told you must, there's still a good reason—and more importantly, why the audience needs to hear it.)
- Is it for entertainment?
- Is it to "move" your audience?
- Do you have to inform and educate?
- Must there be changes in "behavior" after they have heard your speech?
- How must your audience *be* after your presentation? Relaxed? Motivated? Energized? Reassured?

In my opinion, most presenters rarely stop to consider these issues, let alone use the detailed design and structure methods I will show you. Methods that in turn will help you discover the outcome of your talk ... for your audience.

So, I hear you say, "I already know what I want to say. How exactly do I convert that into audience outcomes?"

I'm glad you asked. Because we're going to start with something that has the most ludicrous name: *Index Computations*.

3.3 What You Must Know About Your Audience

WELCOME TO THE NEXT BIG key for your presentation success. For this exercise I want you to imagine that you have an audience and that audience arrives at your presentation in a certain "state." That seems very reasonable I know, and perhaps blindingly obvious. Let's deconstruct this in terms of basic needs.

Suppose you are giving your presentation just after lunch (do I hear your groan? This is a difficult time for audience and presenter alike). What state is your audience likely to be in? Lethargic? Sleepy?

So here we are talking about outcomes, yet we haven't even started with your content yet.

And that's because in order to think outcomes, we have to identify a "***Current State***" and a "***Desired State.***"

In much the same way you would plan a trip driving from City A to City B by understanding where you are leaving from, and the location of your destination, we must consider exactly where your audience begins—and your desired finishing "state." In other words, you (and your audience) have an outcome for your presentation. Both of you want it to be much more than just "getting to the end of your presentation."

Up until this point, I have only made passing reference to the "current state," and only in relation to how your audience's current state might be if your presentation followed lunch. Now we can drill down into how to better understand your audiences "state," and what to do with it. Thankfully, the most important part of the oddly-named "***Index Computations***" is not its name but its great practicality. It is a really simple way to describe any human being's *state*: what they are thinking, feeling and doing:

- Where what they are *thinking* describes their internal representations. (What they imagine. How they talk to themselves.)
- Where what they are *feeling* is a representation of their emotions, internal sensations and physiology.
- Where what they are *doing* is an indication of their body's movements, habits and (physical) behaviors.

We usually represent an "***Index Computation***" as a circle divided into three slices: one for each of the bullet points above. See the graphic on the next page.

Take a clean piece of paper. Draw two Index Computation symbols—each the size of a large coin—up the top of the page, as if they were heading two large columns.

As in the example image below, under the left-hand symbol write: **Current State**. Under the right-hand symbol write: **Desired State**.

Now, under "**Current State**," write down everything you know about your audience:

- What do they know about your topic? Anything at all? Very little? Or will there be subject matter experts in your audience?
- What reactions might they have to it? Resistance; excitement; shock; curiosity; indifference?
- Are they willing audience members? Have they been required to attend? Are they a captive audience? Will their attendance contribute to some professional development requirements? Are they wedding guests who are anticipating a speech?

- What state might they be arriving in? (That you are aware of.) Include times of day and days of the week. I once had to give a one-hour motivational workshop at 5pm on a Friday to a group of students who had already had a full week of workshops. Phew.
- What about their arrival state is under your control? The way they are greeted; your room set-up; lighting; tea/coffee. Is there somewhere to wait outside of taking their seat in the audience?
- What factors might be influencing their state? For example, if this is a wedding speech, has there already been significant alcohol consumption? Or at a funeral, is the atmosphere likely to be somber?
- Does your audience have any preconceived ideas about your presentation, or expectations of you personally? For example, you have to present a financial spreadsheet and it is widely expected to be boring. Are you known for your jokes? Or are you the CEO and the audience is going to be overly polite?

Make the list as exhaustive as possible. Eventually, as you use this method more and more, you'll have a good sense of their arrival state, and your audience's responses to your topic.

Now we'll focus on your *"**Desired State.**"*

This is what you want your audience Thinking, Feeling and/or Doing *after* your talk. Because if they walk out after your presentation thinking, feeling and doing exactly the same things as before, it's been a waste of everyone's time, and you could have simply sent an email.

Here are some prompts:

- How would their thoughts about your topic have changed post-speech?
- Would they now understand more about the subject, perhaps new information that they are supposed to use on the job?
- Would they have a new appreciation of your work or role?
- Would they know more juicy details about the groom?

Key to planning, but also key to good instructional design is knowing how your audience's thoughts need to change, *for your presentation to have achieved its outcome.* If certain elements of your information are critical to be remembered: If you need them to instantly pop into the thoughts of your audience post-speech, then you can design accordingly, and start to think about the use of mnemonics and other anchoring devices.

- How does your audience's emotional state change after your talk or training?
- Will they be re-energized?
- Will uncertainty have been removed or reduced?
- Will they be subdued or sobered?
- Will they be more aware—of each other, of themselves, of the workplace and/or customers?

There's also little point in making an impactful presentation with a rising climax, only to have your last five minutes covering admin and house-keeping. The emotional impact is quickly forgotten, and you'll miss taking advantage of the ***Recency Effect***. I believe this aspect of thinking about ***Current*** → ***Desired States*** is underplayed. Most of our decision-making and habitual responses are underpinned by our emotional states. Learn to influence your audience's emotional states, and you are already way ahead of the game.

You'll learn more about influencing emotional states throughout Chapter 4.

Finally, how will your audience *behave* differently after your presentation?

- Will they use different ways of communication with each other? With their customers?
- Will their guards be lowered with each other—or with you?
- Will they now expect more of themselves and will be more attentive to certain habits, for example, being on time, or something tangible such as leaving the toilet seat/lid up (or preferably down!)?
- Will they dress differently?
- Will they vote differently?

If you've been paying attention, you'll see how each of these three areas depend on each other. In reality, no-one is going to have *only* different thoughts post-presentation. Thinking differently could well be accompanied by feeling differently, and even *doing* different things. In my experience, the more changes you're able to create in your audience across all three areas, the more successful your outcome and more sustainable the change.

But the order in which we address them makes a huge difference. So we'll drill down a little further ...

On your left-hand column, arrange your list into three broad groups: a group of everything that relates to how they are thinking; another group for everything that relates to how they are feeling, and finally, a group for how they behave (or what they're doing).

The same with the right-hand side, which is probably already mostly organized this way after having tackled them by category as we did above.

Now step back and review what you have so far.

First: are there any obvious imbalances?

For example: your audience arrives with lots of thoughts about both your upcoming presentation and the day they have already had, but on the right-hand side, you are expecting them to leave after a 30-minute presentation with deeply changed behaviors. This will take careful planning.

Or is there a great deal of emotional upheaval or reaction to your topic, yet you are planning for them to leave calm and informed? This is especially important to understand if your topic is controversial; see the section in Chapter 4 on How To Deal With Difficult Audiences

An obvious imbalance in *Current → Desired states* should ring an alarm bell, for several reasons:

1. The outcome may be too difficult to achieve in the time frame, and must be revised. You may even need to change your speech, or postpone it.
2. Will you need to work heavily on changing an emotional state? In which case, no amount of logic, reason and appeal in your speech will make any difference. No, you're very likely going to need human stories, strong visuals, and an empathic delivery that comes from the heart.
3. Is the audience highly logical and full of academic thoughts about your speech? Have you made sure your speech addresses this need for technical content? If you're expecting this audience to feel differently about you, you may need to use appropriate "logic." For example, if you're addressing a roomful of doctors about spiritual healing methods, you may be drawing a long bow if you only use *emotional* means to try and appeal to their sensibilities.

A audience-focused balanced approach is needed ... but here's a question you might be asking yourself: Why do we care about "*Current State*" at all?

I mean, isn't it all just about where we get to? If I'm off on vacation, who cares where I started out from, as long as I end up in Hawaii (or wherever I wanted to go)?

Ask yourself this: Do you want your presentation to appear effortless? Isn't that why you're here, reading this book, putting these new skills (or enhanced skills) into action? Because when you understand how to design your talk to address both *Current State* and *Desired State*, you can do one very important thing extremely elegantly, and that is: **Build Rapport** right from the start. And why is rapport so useful? Because it gives us permission to lead. The ultimate test for rapport is to see if your audience will follow you ... in this case, all the way to your outcome, or **Desired State**.

To remind yourself about the specifics of building audience rapport, I recommend you review the section in Chapter 2, entitled: "The Skill Of Influencing Elegantly"

Once you have a keen idea of what your audience is thinking, feeling and doing, even before you open your mouth or show your first slide, everything is easier. From here you can build rapport by speaking their thoughts; empathizing with their emotional states, and acknowledging their routines, habits and behaviors.

They will feel—and *be*—understood. They will "get" that you took time to have an appreciation of their situation.

In my opinion, this is one of the most powerful pre-presentation planning methods you can have up your sleeve.

Of course, there are times you have no idea about **Current State**.

And even worse, your research (and sometimes your "needs-analysis" with the client) uncovers a deep resentment towards you or your content. What then? Sit back and relax, I have that handled in "How To Deal With Difficult Audiences." But we need to walk together before we run. First we have to connect **Current State** to **Desired State.** It won't happen all by itself!

3.4 What Walt Disney Taught Us About Designing Our Speeches

I WANT YOU TO PAY close attention to this section. Skip this, and you may as well resign yourself to being average. But take this to heart and use it, and you too, could join an elite group of the very best public speakers. I'm going to teach you the most ingenious planning technique and show you how to use one of our modern day accidental inventions: the PostIt note.

Do you know how movies are planned after the initial story meetings? A group gets together to develop storyboards.

What is a *storyboard*? A storyboard is a sequence of scenes from a movie, often hand-drawn, depicting visually what will happen, often with bullet-point style notes under each scene.

The storyboard becomes a central document for planning. Each professional who must contribute to the movie will use it to understand what will be required of them: scripts, cast, sets, lighting, props, costumery, special effects, music, sound and so on.

We're going to do the same with your speech—whether it lasts for two minutes or two days. And we're going to do it in a fun way, using PostIts.

Walt Disney had a unique view about the creative process, later distilled into three key "parts" that played critical roles in the development process.

- The first role is one we call **The Dreamer**. You might think of it a brainstorming—which it is— but, unlike most processes, it is completely unrestricted. Nothing judged, nothing excluded. The sky's the limit..

- The second role is **The Realist**. **The Realist** brings together what works. **The Realist** groups and arranges common threads. **The Realist** role is pragmatic and explores the content dumped by **The Dreamer** in a realistic fashion.

- The third role is that of **The Critic**. A word of warning: While this role seems self-explanatory, you need to *be very careful not to put **The Critic's** hat on at any other time*. Being critical is not the same thing as being the "judge and jury." If you use this persona too early in the process you will ambush your efforts and hamper your creativity (in both the Dreamer and Realist roles). You may have experienced **The Critic** rearing his or her head while brainstorming. You may catch yourself thinking, "this will never work." Even though this opinion may only be occurring in your head, make sure you park it until you get to the key role **The Critic** plays, which is *to throw out that which does not work*. **The Critic** questions idealistic or still unrealistic elements of your speech. **The Critic** is the one who will point out that you are trying to show 80 slides in 15 minutes. (Oopsy!) **The Critic's** role will be incredibly valuable in polishing your presentation and making it work. But keep **The Critic's** hat off until it is needed.

Now. How do we use these roles? This is where your PostIts come in.

Step One:

Please put your ***Dreamer Hat*** on.

Now, brainstorm all the content topics and subtopics in your speech or presentation that will help get your audience from ***Current State*** to ***Desired State***. Write each one on its own PostIt, and place it on a wall, or on an unfolded manila folder, on a flipchart, or on butcher's paper. Don't worry about the order. You can place it in chronological sequence after you have dumped all those content points on the sticky note pieces. One idea group per page, chunked well. Just brainstorm until you are done. Include everything:

- How to get from what they are ***thinking*** now, to what they *need* to be thinking:
- What you think your audience absolutely *must* know about, and what content you'd ideally want to cover.
- Address the ***feeling*** component of your speech: What stories, visuals, atmospheric elements, games, interactions and questions could you use?
- What behaviors will you be addressing?
- Are there any habits you'd like your audience to unlock or change? What could you include to physically demonstrate this? How will you have your audience move?

Dump out as many PostIts as you can. Don't worry if there seem to be "too many." That's only your Inner Critic trying to make his or herself heard, so just ignore it at this stage. Try to keep each PostIt to one topic or point. Often if I'm unsure, I'll get really granular, and drill down even further so that each PostIt is confined to one main idea, one bullet-point each.

And let the weird stuff come out. You never know—your unconscious mind often knows way more than your conscious mind about what should go into this talk. After all, every day we are besieged by sensory input, all taken in and filtered according to our needs in the moment. Who knows what you "unknowingly" picked up along the way that would be powerful for this talk, for this audience?

Step Two:

Now let's get to ***The Realist***. By now you should be staring at a huge jumble of yellow or multi-colored PostIts and possibly wondering, "what next?"

Give your body a shake out, have a large glass of water, and start organizing the PostIts.

- What naturally goes together? Link similar ideas by placing the PostIts in a group.
- Is there a flow yet? At this point you should feel free to shift whole collections of ideas around to link them in more logical or presentable ways.
- What would be some great rapport-builders (ie content at the state of your presentation that is close to the Current State elements of your audience)?
- What odd elements don't seem to fit anywhere? Park them to one side. But don't throw them away yet!

Be rational and objective, but not judgmental. Don't concern yourself at this stage if you don't see any way this will all fit into a twenty-minute talk. That's not your problem. Your job is to organize the topics and the order, and make what you have in front of you make sense. Maybe your five-minute talk is now looking like a one-hour lecture—at this point it doesn't matter. Why? Because the process will take care of this in Step Three. The clever part is that by *taking away* elements of your talk and leaving in the most brilliant parts, you make it *all* brilliant. Which brings us to ...

Step Three:

Enter the genius, with a sweeping flourish. (Just between you and me, you have to call *The Critic* a genius. He/she's sensitive like that.) *The Critic* is here, ready to tell you what will work, and what will not. But don't let her get away with simply passing judgment. Have your *Critic* make suggestions, polish rough elements, add missing—and important—content, perhaps review those items parked to one side for inspiration, or as previously mentioned, take sections out, until everything looks good.

Or not.

If it still doesn't look good, then I recommend you kick *The Critic* out of the room because you need *creative* input. It's time to invite *The Dreamer* back in to add new ideas, new content, innovate what's already there ... and so the process starts again.

Rinse. Repeat.

And now you have your content. Probably too much at this stage—everybody usually does—but that's okay. We're going to take your raw content and press it into a lovely baking mold (but be quiet as we do this. Don't want to make *The Critic* think her work was poor!).

How?

Chunks, my friend. Chunks. That's what we need next.

3.5 The Smart Way To Divide Up Your Presentation

SO WHAT ARE THESE "CHUNKS" and how do you "chunk" your speech?

Chunking is not some bizarre method for dividing up pizzas, but useful nomenclature for allowing us to group and qualify presentation content.

A "chunk" of content is merely a section. But hold your horses. It's not as simple as that throwaway sentence. Chunks and chunk *size* depend on context and categorization. A chunk could be a broad topic, taking up several hours, or a five-minute section about one aspect of your speech. We'll go over how to decide exactly what chunk size you should be using, and how to arrange them, later in this section.

So why are "chunks" of content useful?

For many reasons:

1. **They allow you to group and manipulate your content** to suit time-frames, audiences, learning styles, audience "states" ... and much more.
2. **You can "nest" chunks**, which makes your design job much easier. In the remaining two sections of this Chapter, I'll show you how to do that elegantly using a specific tool and proven learning methodology.
3. **Chunks have a visual component to them** (in your design). This makes them much easier to remember on-the-fly, and simplifying your presenter notes. You'll have far more confidence in knowing what's coming next.

It's time to identify your chunks.

You probably already have some from your storyboarding exercise, simply from grouping content together.

Now drill down into those sections, and divide up your content into obvious minor groupings. These will usually be your major topic chunks. See my example below:

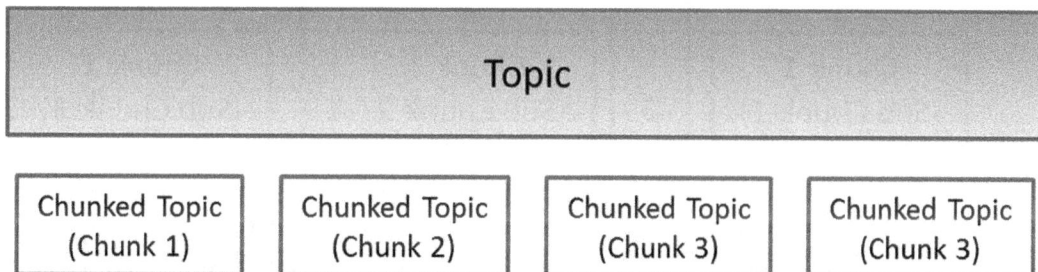

Topic			
Chunked Topic (Chunk 1)	Chunked Topic (Chunk 2)	Chunked Topic (Chunk 3)	Chunked Topic (Chunk 3)

The chunks effectively slip inside your main topic like this:

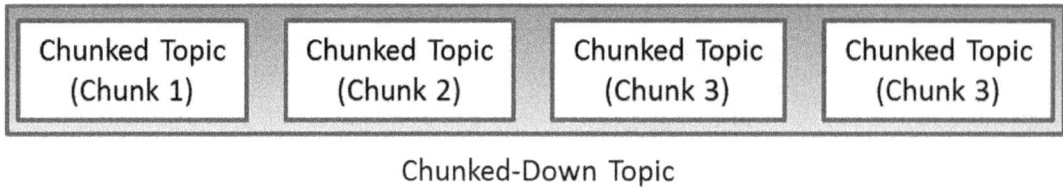

Chunked Topic (Chunk 1)	Chunked Topic (Chunk 2)	Chunked Topic (Chunk 3)	Chunked Topic (Chunk 3)

Chunked-Down Topic

Here's a real-life example:

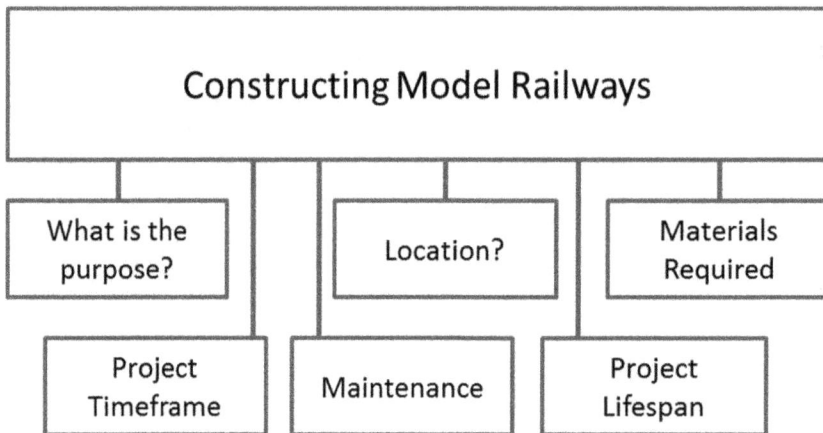

Constructing Model Railways

- What is the purpose?
  - Project Timeframe
- Location?
  - Maintenance
- Materials Required
  - Project Lifespan

Now we'll take just one of those chunks, and drill down to divide the chunk itself up into several sub-chunks (such technical language eh?). These will be obvious sub-groupings of that topic. Some may only be a two-minute section—but remember that the major determinant of the chunk is its comprehension and not how long the content takes to deliver.

A well-chunked presentation is powerful, and always easy to recognize, because it's easy to follow.

Take a look at a typical sub-chunk (shown below) using Chunk 1 from my example above:

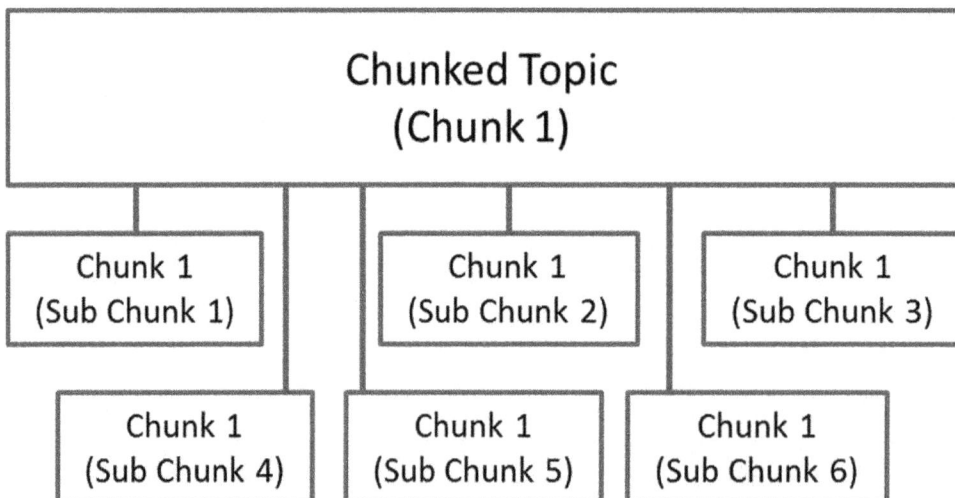

Chunked Topic (Chunk 1)

- Chunk 1 (Sub Chunk 1)
  - Chunk 1 (Sub Chunk 4)
- Chunk 1 (Sub Chunk 2)
  - Chunk 1 (Sub Chunk 5)
- Chunk 1 (Sub Chunk 3)
  - Chunk 1 (Sub Chunk 6)

We'll take another pass: are there any other remaining sub-chunks that still seem to be too big? Too much information in there? Let's chunk those down too.

Here's the real-life example again, this time showing one of the main chunks split into sub-chunks:

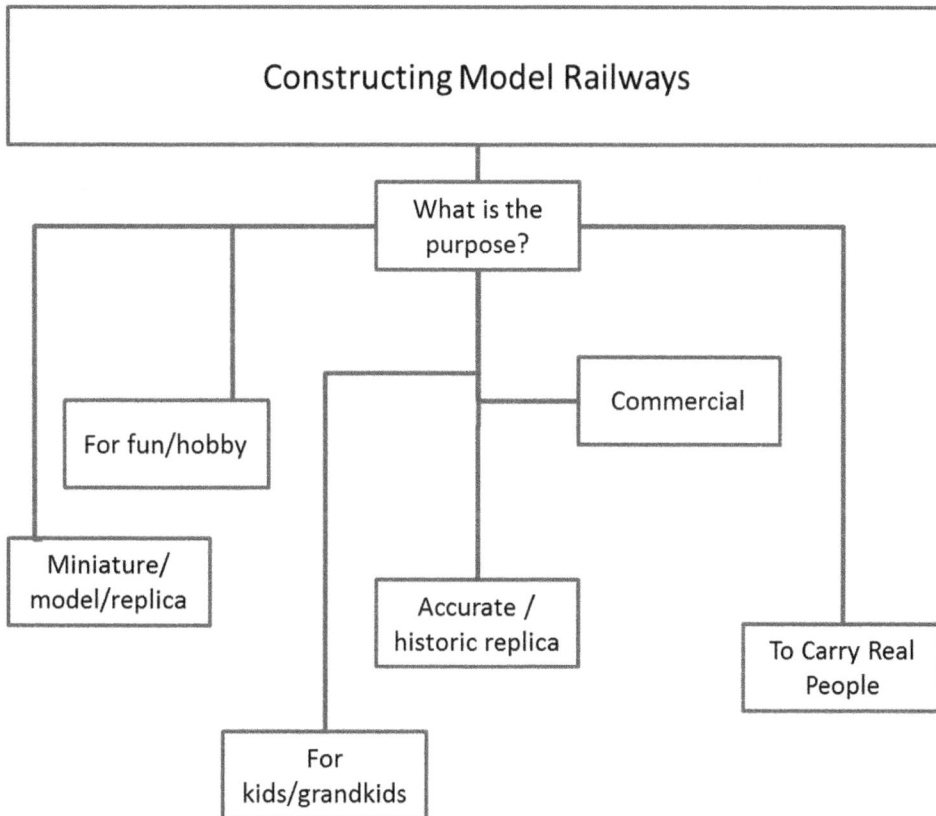

Showing One Sub-Chunk
Further Chunked-Down

Once you've filled this out completely, then you'll end up with something similar to my fully chunked example over the page:

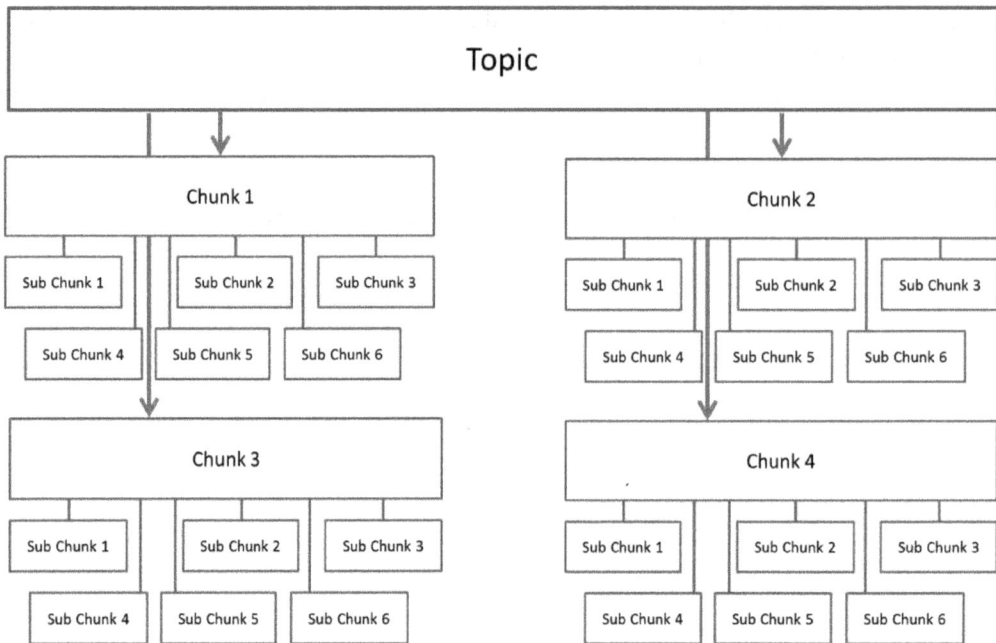

Fully Chunked-Down Topic

Now, if you use a writing software (such as Scrivener, which I'm using to write this book at this moment in time. In my opinion, it's an inexpensive and excellent design tool for writers, bloggers and presenters. See it at http://RobertScanlon.com/scrivener), then you've probably already spotted how useful this technique is. It will make all the difference in how you break down your presentation and get on with designing your content.

The power of this chunking tool goes beyond designing presentations. You will find it invaluable for writing books, blog posts, newsletters and more, but in order to extract the full value from your new tool you'll really want to read the next two sections before you jump right into producing content from your chunks.

So where were we? You're probably still staring at a big mess of chunks. And I was saying something about "chunk size" and audiences. We'd better attend to this right now.

In your outcome planning, you identified the "*Index Computations*" and both *Current* and *Desired States* of your audience. This will also provide information, or at the very least, strong clues, as to your audience's familiarity with your topic. And here's the easy bit:

If your audience is very familiar with your content or topic = **larger chunk sizes**

If your audience is unfamiliar, or will be grappling to digest your points = **smaller chunk sizes**

So the rule of thumb is:

Familiarity means you can "*chunk UP*" and cover more ground in less time. Doh! In other words, you can be more global and less detailed.

If your content is new to your audience, or unfamiliar, or is content framed differently to your audience's expectations, then you must "*chunk DOWN*". Which means drilling down, and presenting relevant and well organized details.

And therefore, during a presentation, speech or talk, you can *chunk UP* or *DOWN* depending on your audience's relationship to *that piece of content*. Why is this?

How about we let George Miller explain that?

3.6 The 7 +/- 2 Method

GEORGE MILLER? WHO?

As it turns out, Miller—a Professor of Psychology—carried out some fascinating research at Princeton. He investigated how we divide up our attention, and how many different "streams" of *conscious* attention we really have. Here is the reference: http://en.wikipedia.org/wiki/George_Armitage_Miller

If you've ever wondered why some things are hard to learn or understand compared to others, or why some people get bamboozled over a topic you found simple to understand, then this information will be a revelation. Then I'll show you exactly how to apply this methodology to your very next speech—you'll be amazed at how much difference it makes to both the planning and design process, as well as your audience's comprehension levels.

Miller's work became summarized and is often quoted as the "*7+/-2*" (seven plus or minus two) rule; meaning that humans can only (consciously) pay attention to between 5 and 9 streams (or "chunks") of information at the same time.

Although on the surface the notion of conscious attention seems easy to grasp, there are a lot of practical considerations for you to recognize, learn and apply. You need to know that chunks can present in different "sizes" that will vary according to the context, prior knowledge, environmental and emotional factors. However, once you know the outcome of your presentation, these considerations are easy to apply.

One rule of thumb I use myself and would recommend: If your content or information is new, the available attention quickly dwindles to between two and three chunks, or two or three different things anyone can pay attention to in that moment. Sometimes these attention streams are not even that new or different. For example (not that you'd ever do this): texting and driving at the same time clearly occupy too many chunks to safely pay attention to everything happening around us.

Here's an example from my own life: I have also taught yoga at my wife's yoga studio. Whenever we introduce new students to their first class, we're careful to limit the amount of things we'd like them to pay attention to in their first few classes. My wife likes to use an excellent metaphor. She tells new students that they only have $10 worth of "attention," which they must spend in $1 chunks, and in their first class, it's possible as much as $8 of attention might be spent just following what everyone is doing. But after ten or more classes, the same amount of attention might only "cost" $1.

Giving too much new information at once, or using chunk sizes that are too global, leads to audience overwhelm. Suppose the chunk size at the beginning of your talk was inadvertently too large. You may have already moved on to chunks two and three, but your audience is still digesting the first chunk and trying to piece together your information. This tends to feel overwhelming for your audience as they try to keep up. (We call it over-chunking.)

Equally, perhaps you've attended a talk where the presenter spent way too long explaining in micro-detail some aspect of their topic that the audience already knew. Boring, right? In this case, under-chunked, and perhaps even creating the perception the presenter is being condescending.

The first rule of chunking is to make sure every chunk does not exceed **7+/-2** different pieces of information. In my experience, I tend to aim for 3-5, and I recommend you do the same. This takes into account a neat aspect of human learning and memory-coding called ***Generative Learning*** (I'll be discussing how to harness the power of ***Generative Learning*** throughout Chapter 5).

Here's an easy way to understand how it works:

If you want your speech to be memorable, you'd want to make it easy to remember, wouldn't you?

Try this practical exercise:

Please read the following list. Read it at a pace similar to reading the words out loud—it should only take about fifteen seconds. When you've finished the list just close your eyes for ten seconds in an effort to remember the items. Then re-open your eyes and, without re-reading the list at all, read the next instruction under the list.

Pen, suitcase, love, your mother, a dream, Texas, plants, white, discontinued, water, tapping, short-sightedness, tables, weather, big banks, a fingernail, 100km, neuro-muscular function, bubbly, hairnets.

READ THIS IMMEDIATELY AFTER OPENING YOUR EYES: Now repeat the items back in the correct order, no cheating! Do it while you stay focused on this line.

If you are anything like me, you started to glaze over as soon as you started to read and tried to memorize the list. Perhaps you noticed some things that didn't make sense, or felt "jarring," or out of place. Then when it comes to repeating them back, some items have stuck, while others are lost.

What's going on here? (Actually what we're doing right now is chunking this exercise down for understanding.)

- Were there more than nine "chunks"?

Oh, yes.

- Were the chunks themed? (ie appropriately "chunk sized" or grouped)

Oh dear. They most definitely were not.

Now for our second practical exercise. Please memorize and repeat back:

String, paper, scissor, sticky tape, card, glue, permanent marker pen, box.

Much easier, yes? I bet you got them all, or almost all.

Not only was the chunk size easy (and consistent), but the chunks were themed. In other words, all eight of the chunks above would "fit" under a bigger chunk, such as "gift-wrapping," or "stationery," for example.

And how many items were there again? Eight, correct. So we're already seeing just how powerful this is, especially if you have complex information to get across in a limited time-frame, which for many people is the very definition of a corporate presentation.

So not only do we need to design each chunk to contain no more than **7+/-2** "pieces" (yes, chunks), and preferably less, we also must *theme* those chunks, and order them appropriately.

You'll also learn in Chapter 5 exactly how the combination of something known as ***Generative Learning*** and its iterative nature, lends itself to dynamic chunking, where chunk sizes can (and should) be varied according to where you are in your presentation. ***Generative Learning*** makes elegant* repetition and reviewing of your material with your audience super-easy.

* Elegant: meaning not just repeating yourself. You'll see what I mean.

Note: There are occasions when you deliberately wish to bombard or overwhelm your audience for effect. If you're selling the benefits of using a new resort for your sales conference, then perhaps you want to show an impressive list of leisure activities. That list doesn't need to be remembered. To make your point in this way, the deliberate use of "overchunking" is an excellent tool. If you know exactly what you're doing *and* how to recover, then overchunking is perfectly acceptable.

So let's get back to the basics of chunking, the theme of your talk, and its order. To do this, please review your storyboard that you completed earlier in this chapter (when we learned about Walt Disney and how to use PostIt notes). If you've followed directions and done a good job, then you probably already see some theming going on.

But what about the order? Well, I hear you say, don't you just start at the start, and finish at the end? Bzzzz. That might sound easy, but we'll use something way more sophisticated, practical and memorable.

Something that Dr. Bernice McCarthy* tells us will really win your audience over.

* Of *course* I will introduce her! She's in the next section.

3.7 How To Flow Your Presentation Perfectly For All Personalities

WOULDN'T IT BE EXCELLENT IF everyone in your audience was just like you? It would be so much easier to get your message across, wouldn't it?

Everyone would laugh at your jokes, too.

Happily, we're all different. That in and of itself, presents an additional layer of intricacy for us presenters. Your room will be filled with different personalities, with different learning styles and with many differing needs; some of which happen at different times throughout your talk.

Sounds really complicated, doesn't it?

But if you *don't* attend to it, believe me, things will get complicated!

Have you ever been in the audience (or worse, been the presenter), when a really left-field question is asked ... right at the start of the talk? To make it worse, the presenter goes on to answer the left-field question. Yikes. You can just about hear the audience mentally checking out.

That's just one example of what *could* happen if the presenter doesn't design his or her presentation or speech according to their audience's "learning styles."

We can pretty much divide up our audience into around one-quarter each of the four learning styles as described by Dr. Bernice McCarthy in her wonderful book, *The 4MAT System: Teaching to Learning Styles with Right/Left Mode Techniques*. Here is some more detailed information for those who need it (you'll see why there will be those who do) http://www.ascd.org/publications/educational-leadership/mar97/vol54/num06/A-Tale-of-Four-Learners@-4MAT's-Learning-Styles.aspx

And here is McCarthy's official site: http://www.aboutlearning.com/

McCarthy researched and developed this system predominantly for education professionals and teachers. She outlines how the presenter's content has to change in style during the course of the session, and points out that unless the presenter addresses *each* of the four learning styles, in the order to which they will likely "appear" (meaning: the time that learning style's needs have to be addressed), then their session is probably doomed! The term "*4MAT*" is used in this book by express permission from Dr. McCarthy.[1]

---

[1] The 4MAT® System is an educational tool developed by Bernice McCarthy for use worldwide in all instructional design needs. It is currently in use in education, corporate and government teaching and training programs. All references to 4MAT® and the 4MAT System are used by special permission of the copyright owner, About Learning, Inc. 441 W. Bonner Rd, Wauconda, Illinois 60084. Contact Michael McCarthy at http://www.aboutlearning.com

Robert Scanlon, Colete Pty Ltd and their associated websites, products and services are in no way endorsed by, sponsored by or affiliated with About Learning, Bernice McCarthy. For more information about 4MAT® please visit http://www.aboutlearning.com

When you learn the method for planning and delivering your talks using the *4MAT System*, and witness it in action, I promise you will never want to go back to your old ways. Even better, if you produce content in addition to presentations, speeches and talks, such as books, brochures, emails, blog posts and so on, you'll definitely benefit from using McCarthy's brilliant structure.

A quick aside: While we're certainly all different, no one sees the world purely through one learning style alone. McCarthy's work confirms this, and she points out that, although we all have elements of each style within us, every single person will have a *strong preference* for one style—and that is what counts.

The best way to for me to teach you *4MAT* is to first give you an overview of each style. Then we will use *4MAT* in the design and delivery of your presentation.

This book is designed to give you practical tools, so rather than approach this from an academic perspective, I'm going to cut straight to practical application. What this means is that if you want to learn how the styles were originally developed or evolved, or what dimensions or metrics were used in determining them, then you may want to read McCarthy's book (it's excellent). Take it from me that this approach works very well in practice.

McCarthy suggests that each of the four "styles" needs a "virtual question" answered in the audience member's minds, *before they will even let you move on.*

What's a virtual question? It's the one you have in your head. It's probably not in your conscious awareness, but it's there, being asked.

There is one dominant virtual questions specific to each of the four learning styles. They are:

Why?

What?

How?

What Else? / What If?

You'll often see this represented as a "cycle" of learning styles, beginning in the top-right quadrant as below.

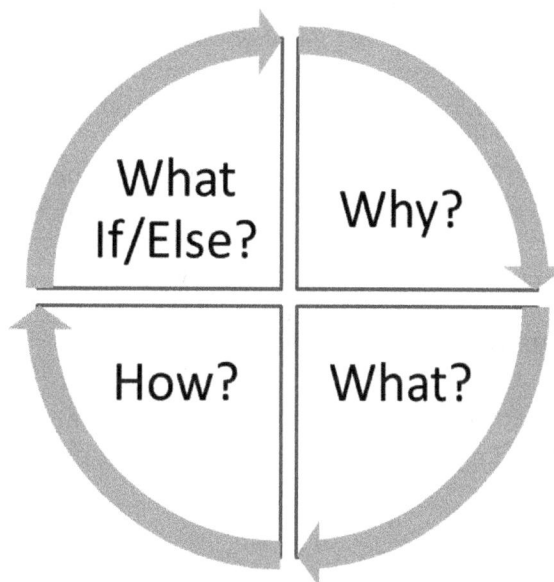

Once you know *4MAT* well, you'll occasionally hear a very obvious "virtual question" being asked out loud—a clear demonstration of an audience member's need for an answer. Whether this happens or not is irrelevant, and I draw your attention to it just in case you think your job is to make your audience ask these questions; it's not. However, in order for you to deliver an effective presentation, *every* virtual question must be answered by the content of your talk, whether it is asked out loud or not.

Let me give you an example: imagine you want to buy a new portable music player. You go to the store.

If you are a "*Why?*" learner, you will be desperate to be sold on the device that appeals to you the most. *Why* learners often make good sales people themselves, purely because of this. Listen to this pitch: "*This AudioTech Box will revolutionize your listening pleasure! It automatically enhances the emotional element of each dynamic element of the song you are listening too, and projects that directly to a unique binaural lattice, giving you a thrilling new experience from your music.*"

Oh yes, say the **Why Learners**, I want me some of that. And it's on sale, too? Here, have my wallet.

Meanwhile, the "*What*" learner has collared the salesperson and demanded to told the features, and requested to see the product booklet and the manual, before they even listen to the device. The *What* learner wants to know the specifications and guarantees. They want to know the product's functions: what it will and won't do. Does it have bluetooth for multiple devices? Simultaneously? How long do the batteries last before a recharge is required? What material is the chassis made from, and will it withstand a shock? Is it water resistant? What does the remote control do?

It's even possible they'll pull out some kind of consumer report and wave it at the salesperson.

The salesperson, usually being a *Why* learner themselves of course, will be completely confused by all of this and not understand why on earth someone would need to know all this. *Just listen to the damn thing, man! It's awesome!*

Meanwhile, the "*How*" learner has already left the building, having bought the first one that they could pick up, touch and get working, and are now at home, jabbing away at buttons, frustrated that the thing won't do what they want it to. The instruction manual? Still in the box. They'll get to know this thing through discovery, and sometimes frustration. (Their *What* learner partner will provide the instructions if needed!)

The "*What Else / What If*" learner is uncomfortable. Perhaps there are better options available. What if she spent less money? Or borrowed her sister's device? Isn't there some way of hooking this up to the existing stereo system and networking everything? More research required, and more questions to ask. There are a ton of options in this store, and maybe the music player was just an impulse thing after all. But, they *do* need a new washing machine, and there's one right over there being advertised at a discount. Maybe the money is better spent on that? In which case they might be able to sell their old washing machine and put the cash towards a new music player in the future. The salesperson by now has pulled out all of his hair.

Now hopefully, you've witnessed a glimpse of yourself in each of these, and identified more strongly with at least one.

These are the people you have in your audience, and in McCarthy's opinion their needs should be addressed in the order given. I recommend this exact approach for you, because even though very experienced presenters can become skilled at dancing around the learning styles, when you handle the foundational elements of *4MAT* well, you really don't need to get fancy.

Addressing the Why Learning Style in your audience

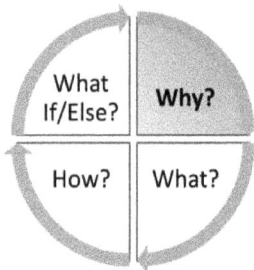

In order to win over the *Why Learner*, your presentation has to be relevant, motivational and inspirational. In short, you have to sell your talk. Don't just "*tell 'em what you're going to tell 'em, then tell 'em and after, tell 'em what you told 'em.*" Not good enough.

The *Why Learner* expects to be told why (implicitly or explicitly) it is even worth listening to your talk. The best way to drill yourself in the needs of the *Why Learner* is to use the well-known sales principle: WIIFM, or *"What's In It For Me?"*

You need to think about how the listener will *benefit* from your presentation. Both specifically and generally. The more specific the "why," the better it is. Here's an example:

"By understanding how your financial plan will change your daily habits, you'll be able to put cash back in your wallet you never knew you had. In this presentation, I'll cover the three key elements you must know before you begin."

Now the *Why Learner* is "sold," and you have implicit permission to move on. More importantly perhaps, the *Why Learner* part in *all* of us (or in your audience) is satisfied, and we're all 100% with you!

Addressing the What Learning Style in your audience

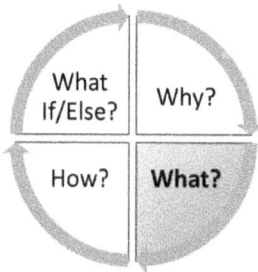

The *What Learner* is patient. But not very. Spend too much time "selling them" and they'll get annoyed. They're waiting for the background information. Your references. Your data. The historical analysis. Proof.

This is where your chunking is key, and arranging how you present the information needed by the *What Learner* without it turning into an info-dump will be critical.

"The latest research from Stanford has revealed 78.6% of all successful financial investors adhere to these 3 principles on a daily basis—and before you wonder about the remaining 22.4%, they go one step further, and integrate at least one other of the methods I will reference at the end of my talk."

Tip: You had better make sure your information is accurate and has no logical holes.

With the *Why* and *What Learners* handled, it's time to move around the quadrants to *How*.

Addressing the How Learning Style in your audience

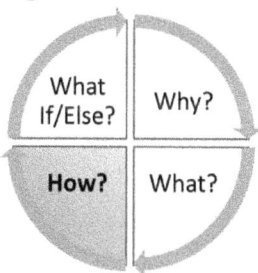

The *How Learners* are drumming their fingers and tapping their feet. This sales-pitch and seemingly irrelevant factual information is all very well ... but give me an example, already! How will I use this stuff in real life? What can I do in practice? The *How Learners* need to be coached in the *application* of your speech, talk or presentation. Here's a concrete "how" example:

"So let me give you an example. Sally takes $10 from her purse every day. She puts two dollars into a jar in the kitchen, and doesn't touch it again. She takes seven dollars and pays off her most expensive loan—I'll show you how to calculate that at the end—and with the remaining one dollar, she does whatever she likes!"

The *How Learners* respond best to examples, application and hands-on activities, worksheets and coaching. Questions about usage give you a clue that the asker wants to know "how" this will work for them.

Respond with more selling or theory and you've lost them. Give a neat concrete example, and all the **How Learners** will be grinning from ear-to-ear, and come up to give you a hug at the end. *"That was so useful! I love it when presenters use real-life case studies, it really helps me!"*

Then you get to the end of your presentation—but of course, the **What Else Learners** didn't bother to wait until the end to throw you those curly questions. Chances are, if you're asked a question at the start, such as, *"Won't this be too hard to implement for anyone who spends more than they earn?"* it's from a **What Else** learner.

Addressing the What If/Else Learning Style in your audience

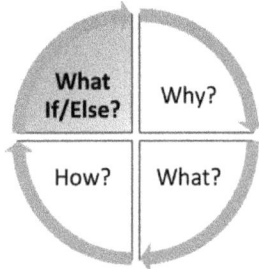

Questions from the "**What If/Else**" learner are genuine, and usually relevant to the broad topic of your speech—and may already be about to be addressed by you during your speech—but they've raised them at a difficult time.

Don't worry, we can deal with that.

Whatever you do, don't leave the **What If / What Else Learner** out. Or if you do, do so at your peril.

You can cover this in many ways: you can have a specific section in your talk where you take questions. You can have a specific chunk that deals with all the "what-ifs" (as long as you have it after the **How**, or you'll confuse everyone). You can even ask these questions of your audience (if skilled, you can do this at any time. You just better know how to get back on track!).

Defining some of the **What If** aspects of your talk are key to making it work for everyone—and especially if you want to be able to avoid that curly question thrown in right at the start. This is handled neatly with a technique called "**Pacing Out Objections**" which is covered in detail in Chapter 5, but here's a quick example for you:

"Now you might be asking yourself, 'What if I miss a couple of days? Do I have to back-fill my jar and pay more of the loans off.' Let me show you a couple of other options, for example ..."

... and boom. You have the **What If Learner** transfixed. *"He even came up with my own question!"*

A quick recap:

- **4MAT** is a Learning Styles metric.
- It identifies **four major learning styles** in any audience.
- Each learning style needs a "virtual question" addressed—and answered—in order to be satisfied.
- The preferred order is to move through each of the Learning Style quadrants, beginning with "**Why**":

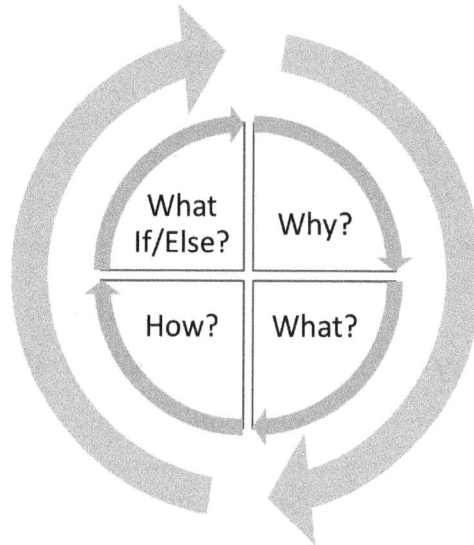

Start with "Why?" then cycle through

And this is what you do in each of the quadrants:

- **Why:** Persuade, sell, influence, motivate, inspire ... and above all, provide relevancy.
- **What:** Educate and inform; provide background (suitably chunked) and references if needed. Theory and context. But keep it all to the point. (Do you have a lot of theory to delivery? Is your talk information-heavy? There's a recommended way to help you structure and chunk this. I'll show you how to do this at the end of this section.)
- **How:** Provide concrete example. Allow hands-on interaction, if relevant. Coach and explain real-life application. Describe tangible steps, methods and structure (as long as not conceptual. That belongs with the **What Learner!**)
- **What If/Else:** Give options, alternatives, what works and what doesn't, traps and tips for young players and even what you may have learned from experience.

So what do you do next?

Let's revisit the presentation you've previously chunked. The next step is to arrange it into a **Why/What/How/What If** *sequence*. You may find now that you are over-heavy in one area, and too light in another. Go back to your storyboarding section and get creative. Then chunk and re-sequence.

What you are aiming for is balance across all four styles.

In a short speech the "**What**" and the "**How**" frames tend to blur together. We can start calling these "**frames**" rather than learning style quadrants. Makes it easier on us both, don't you think?

In any *training program*, the **How** sections must be clearly designed for the audience to acquire the skill(s) (the *how*), not just the knowledge (the *what*). Designing in practice sections, role plays, interactive workshopping, or coaching, will help bring these **How Frames** to life.

From here, you should be starting to see how much easier it is to maintain a memorable flow in your presentation, just from thorough design work.

And ... it will make it so much easier to remember where you are, and what comes next. Presenting inside the "**Why frame**"? You know exactly what chunks of content are supposed to be there.

Finally, you arrive in the "**What If**" frame. You'll know how your audience is likely to behave in this quadrant, and a curly question or two will be quite welcome. Because you are prepared for them!

Now this is where good, thoughtful design really comes into its own. Every single "chunk" you have in your presentation or talk can be designed to flow according to the *Why-What-How-What If* sequence. That's right, they nest into each other.

Take a look at the following diagram. It shows that each chunk no matter how large—or small—can be broken down, designed and delivered for optimum comprehension and buy-in of your audience so that it has its own *Why/What/How/What If* quadrant.

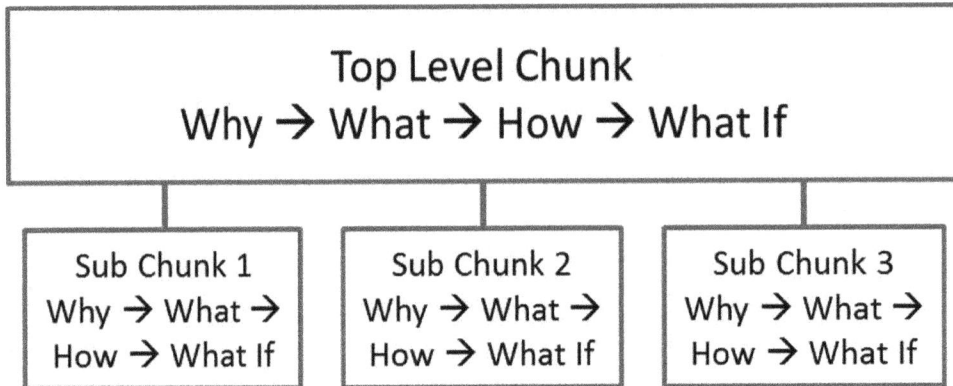

```
┌─────────────────────────────────────────────────────┐
│              Top Level Chunk                          │
│      Why → What → How → What If                       │
└─────────────────────────────────────────────────────┘
        │                   │                   │
┌───────────────┐   ┌───────────────┐   ┌───────────────┐
│  Sub Chunk 1  │   │  Sub Chunk 2  │   │  Sub Chunk 3  │
│  Why → What → │   │  Why → What → │   │  Why → What → │
│  How → What If│   │  How → What If│   │  How → What If│
└───────────────┘   └───────────────┘   └───────────────┘
```

Here's my real-life example again, this time with some *4MAT* quadrants sketched in for the entire top-level chunk of the topic:

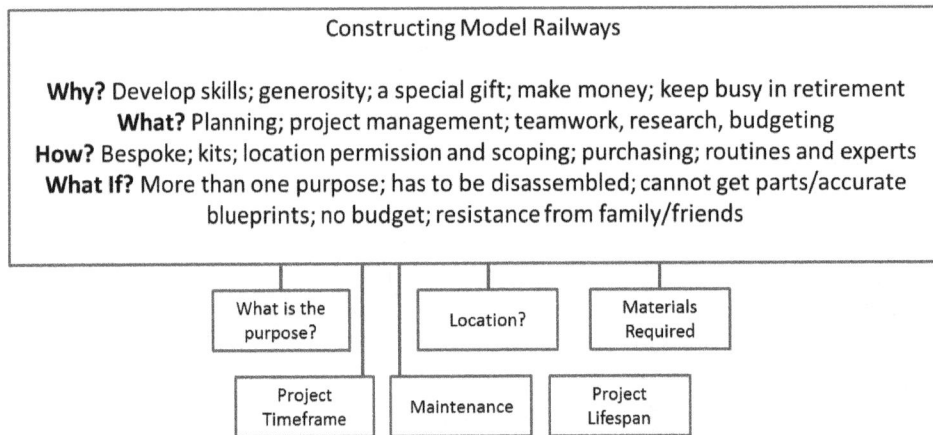

```
┌─────────────────────────────────────────────────────────────┐
│              Constructing Model Railways                      │
│                                                              │
│  Why? Develop skills; generosity; a special gift; make money;│
│       keep busy in retirement                                │
│  What? Planning; project management; teamwork, research,     │
│        budgeting                                             │
│  How? Bespoke; kits; location permission and scoping;        │
│       purchasing; routines and experts                       │
│  What If? More than one purpose; has to be disassembled;     │
│           cannot get parts/accurate blueprints; no budget;   │
│           resistance from family/friends                     │
└─────────────────────────────────────────────────────────────┘
        │               │               │
┌──────────────┐  ┌──────────────┐  ┌──────────────┐
│ What is the  │  │  Location?   │  │  Materials   │
│  purpose?    │  │              │  │  Required    │
└──────────────┘  └──────────────┘  └──────────────┘
┌──────────────┐  ┌──────────────┐  ┌──────────────┐
│   Project    │  │ Maintenance  │  │   Project    │
│  Timeframe   │  │              │  │  Lifespan    │
└──────────────┘  └──────────────┘  └──────────────┘
```

Every time you drill down to a smaller chunk of content, think to yourself: "*What are my Why/What/How and What Else frames here?*"

Eventually you'll find yourself thinking about every speech, presentation, talk or training this way, and even an impromptu speech will begin with some persuasion, followed by a reference or quote, then you bring it back to real life, and end with a couple of different options.

Here's how that might look for just one sub-chunk of the real-life example. for the sake of brevity and clarity, I've only shown a few *4MAT* ideas for each quadrant:

```
┌─────────────────────────────────────────────────────────────────┐
│                   Constructing Model Railways                      │
│                                                                    │
│  Why? Develop skills; generosity; a special gift; make money; keep busy in retirement │
│     What? Planning; project management; teamwork, research, budgeting │
│  How? Bespoke; kits; location permission and scoping; purchasing; routines and experts │
│   What If? More than one purpose; has to be disassembled; cannot get parts/accurate │
│              blueprints; no budget; resistance from family/friends │
└─────────────────────────────────────────────────────────────────┘

    ┌──────────┐      ┌──────────┐      ┌──────────┐
    │ What is the│      │ Location?│      │ Materials│
    │  purpose?│      │          │      │ Required │
    └──────────┘      └──────────┘      └──────────┘
    ┌──────────┐      ┌──────────┐      ┌──────────┐
    │  Project │      │Maintenance│      │  Project │
    │ Timeframe│      │          │      │ Lifespan │
    └──────────┘      └──────────┘      └──────────┘
```

```
┌─────────────────────────────────────────────────────────────────┐
│                        Location 4MAT                               │
│                                                                    │
│   Why? Determines cost; might require permission; involve kids; drives timeframes │
│  What? Planning; measures and scope; licenses and authorities; family discussion; surveys │
│       How? Scale models; accurate drawings/computer mockups; specialist help │
│   What If? Location temporary; railway to be gifted; cannot comply with regs and maintain │
│        integrity; access for maintenance may not be guaranteed for life of project │
└─────────────────────────────────────────────────────────────────┘
```

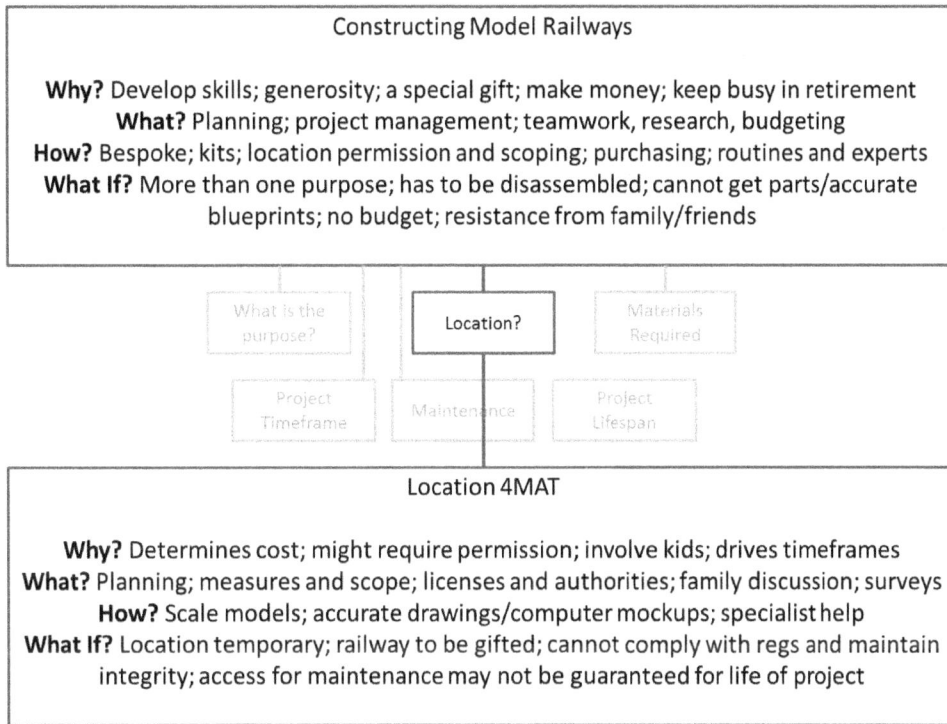

How to structure information-heavy content in the "What?" frame

I mentioned before that sometimes you'll be faced with a talk that seems to be weighted heavily towards a lot of "*What?*" In other words, you may have some significant concepts, theories and data to present. Here's how to structure that to make it easier for your audience.

The first step is to chunk your "*What?*" frames down: can they be further broken down into mini-why/what/how/what-if chunks themselves? Many presenters make the mistake of thinking they have to deliver the entire six-course meal in one sitting, so first ask yourself what can be made more bite-sized.

Once you've broken this down as much as possible—even using stories and examples to help break up your content—and you now know the exact information you must present within each "*What?*" section, then all you need to do is use a smart application of chunking and categorizing your delivery as follows.

Structure and chunk each "*What?*" frame accordingly into:

Concepts

Principles and/or **Methods**

Details and/or **Techniques**

Another way to think of this is to introduce your "*What?*" beginning with the Big Picture, then gradually drilling down into each section (or chunk) of information, ending with the detail.

This is a far less linear method for organizing your speech when it is theory-heavy. By starting with broad-based information *for every new concept*, then "descending" into the relevant methods then the final details, you'll prevent yourself—and your audience—from getting bogged down in that detail. Or worse, only delivering the detail.

Audience members need a "map" so they can understand how and where the background, history, concepts and theories fit.

Here's a quick example. My talk is about high-tension, high-voltage powerlines. I need to cover some detailed science before moving into some practical engineering solutions. It could be very dense. Instead, I'll do this:

"Let's quickly review the purpose of high-tension power distribution: to minimize energy-loss over long distances and maximize the effectiveness of our infrastructure expenditure." (**Concept**)

"In the past we've stuck with the low-cost principle: by using air as the main insulator, we save on construction costs, since our conductor cables need only be bare metal, and we've focused on making lines as straight as possible to avoid the extra costs of the supporting structures required to take the stress of making turns in the line." (Some **Methods** and **Principles**)

"New scientific methods for power transmission—such as wireless, magnetic resonance—along with a decentralized delivery methodology, and the growing social awareness of the indirect environmental costs, have led us to develop a new formula for the evaluation of the real cost of supply—and bear with me as this is quite complex. I'll explain each part as we go through it and demonstrate the theory behind it ..." (**Detail** and some framing up of more **Big Picture**—>drilling down to **Detail** chunks coming up)

This method, which we tend to refer to as a *"CPT Hierarchy"* (**C**=*Concept*, **P**=*Principle*, **T**=*Technique/Detail*) makes it much easier to lead your audience into some very dense content.

The far-reaching power of using 4MAT

4MAT is an intensely practical technique; both flexible and scalable. As your skills progress, you'll find yourself weaving into each quadrant the techniques presented in the rest of this book; enriching the *4MAT* sequence, and wowing your audience.

That's it. It's as simple as that. Yet as powerful a method you'll ever come across. Every presentation, you'll begin with persuasion (*Why*). Then your reference (*What*). Returning to the practical (*How*), and ending with a couple or more different options (*What If*).

4MAT works, and it will make every single one of your speeches and presentations memorable, flowing and appealing.

Even better, you'll be asked back.

***

Assignment: Read this section again, and pay careful attention to how it is structured. Yes, I follow my own advice (hopefully!).

***

Now you've got the basics to practice over and over, how about we learn how to polish, tweak, sharpen and improve every aspect of your public speaking?

Great, because that's what's coming up in the next chapter.

3.8 Drills

Before you present:

What is the *outcome* of your presentation? How will your audience be different as a result?

What will your audience be thinking / feeling / doing (***Index Computations***) before your talk or presentation?

What should they be thinking / feeling / doing *after* your talk or presentation? (From your ***Ideal Outcome*** or ***Desired State***)

Take your next topic (or any arbitrary topic you already know something about) and run it through the ***Dreamer / Realist / Critic*** storyboarding process. What additional material did you create? What did you learn about your own speech-design process that you can incorporate from now on?

Take your next topic (or any arbitrary topic you already know something about) and chunk it down into under seven chunks. What sub-chunks work for each section?

Knowing your audience, what chunk size would be too small for them? (Talking down to them.)

Knowing your audience, what chunk size is too big, and still would need chunking down?

Check your next presentation: Does it fit into the ***7+/-2*** rule? Are there less than nine (and preferably less) broad chunks?

Take a PostIt pad and storyboard your next speech off the top of your head. Now place each PostIt into one of four ***4MAT*** categories. Where are you missing content?

Tip: In my experience, many presentations are light in the "***Why?***" frames, or missing them altogether. Be tough, if this is the case for you. Ask yourself: Why should your audience listen to you? Why is this topic / chunk going to be beneficial to them? Use the "So what?" test—run your presentation opening lines past a colleague or good friend and ask them if it passes the "So what?" line—are they motivated and persuaded that it is worth listening on, or is this just another "So what?"?

Before standing up to speak:

Practice having a great opening "why frame" ready, to use within in your first thirty seconds, and notice what a difference this makes to audience engagement.

During your presentation:

Make quite deliberate transitions and links back / forward to your presentation chunks.

Practice weaving a neat structure between your topic chunks to give your audience a solid grounding: in an ideal world, they should be able to recite your chunks back to you. Note: Advanced presentation skills and training techniques do allow us to mess with this. For now, expect that your audience should be able to follow your chunking strategy.

Post-speech:

Review your impression of how your audience's *Index Computations* appeared to be post-speech. Do you think you hit your expected changes in thoughts / feelings / actions and behaviors? If not, what changes in chunking or *4MAT* could be needed?

How was your audience's current state when you started? Did it seem to match how you had approached designing your outcome? If not, how might you adjust your planning process?

What chunks seemed to flow really well, and why?

What chunks can you redesign for better audience reception?

Where can you improve any missing "*Why?*" frames for better audience buy-in?

CHAPTER 4: HOW TO POLISH, SHARPEN, TWEAK AND TRANSFORM YOUR TALK

4.1 Stirring In The Magic

WE'VE COVERED A LOT OF ground already. We've explored how to create personal confidence; using your voice and body to great effect; we've looked at planning and structuring outcomes and how to address all the learning styles in your audience, and how to ensure your talk flows easily.

Now it's time to stir in some magic.

In the rest of this book, I'll share with you the exact methods and techniques that have the ability to turn you into a highly skilled presenter—possibly one of the very best. Many of these skills build on the preceding chapters—they are the foundational elements mandatory for you to succeed—and many are tips and techniques that may seem like the icing on the cake, yet will be the precise reason you will to soar to new heights.

I'll show you:

- How to make dry and boring content come to life;
- How to make your talks much more appealing than others, to ensure you stand out from the crowd;
- How to guarantee a memorable impact;
- How to be FUNNY! (Tip: You don't need to learn any jokes, or study books of gags. Actually that's possibly the worst thing to do. Unless you really want to be a comedian. And an average one, at that!); and
- What to do if you have a hostile audience, or a controversial topic.

Some of the tips and techniques in these coming sections are what many people think public speaking really is, but in truth, the real gains are made in all of the previous sections, where you've already laid all the groundwork. Master the fundamentals of Projection, Rapport, Voice and Body, and Presentation Structure, and you will have an extremely strong foundation on which you will grow, make more distinctions and constantly improve. With practice you will discover a natural flow to your work.

But everyone has to start somewhere, and these fundamentals underpin *everything* we'll discuss in these next sections. So if you notice me repeating something, or refer back to a previous section, just know I'm gently reminding you what's best to practice *first*.

Now, Dear Reader, it's time to pull up a metaphorical chair, and put your figurative feet up, because I'm going to tell you a story ...

4.2 How To Take Your Audience On A Journey

I WAS ONCE LEARNING TO train adults in Neurolinguistic Programming Skills, at Practitioner and Master Practitioner level.

My own teacher and mentor had asked me to prepare and deliver a one-hour section of her Practitioner Program, as well as debrief and facilitate the participant experiences after they had applied this particular technique.

I was confident in the specific topic I was asked to teach, and although a little nervous and apprehensive, I got up on stage and engaged the group with a bright smile.

The stage wasn't high, and the group was small—about 20 or so participants—all of whom I knew to some degree from being one of the assistant coaches on the program, and some had seen me present at other events.

They were all seated in a semi-circle around the stage, and the room was bright and airy: a reasonably intimate setting.

Two crisp-white flipchart boards stood behind me as I stood center-stage.

Confident I might have been, but I was about to face a humiliating situation.

Now before you think, "*Oh my God, he's left his fly undone!*" or something similar, no, this was not one of those trivial embarrassing moments. Quite the opposite: it turned out to be one of my most profound learning experiences.

By this time in my career, I'd learned to master my nerves and deliver entertaining programs and talks to a variety of audiences; I'd prepared and designed my session accordingly.

So I began to explain the topic (with some great "**Why frames**" thrown in, of course!), and the way it worked. This particular NLP (Neurolinguistic Programming) technique is reasonably complex. There were some mandatory elements in the setup that I had to make sure each participant "got," or the quality of their learning (unknown to them) might be affected.

I thought it went well, although it seemed to take a little longer than I had planned to get through the basic concepts, and to make sure all the glazed faces were eventually nodding assent. I sent them off to practice the technique in pairs, returning in about 15-20 minutes for a debrief.

Which they did.

With questions. Lots of them.

Ones that I didn't expect.

Some couldn't even get the technique to work. (It should have been a breeze with my detailed ramp up.)

Answering the questions felt like pulling teeth. The glazed expressions returned for some, but I persevered until the audience was satisfied.

I sent the group to lunch. I was a little tired, but elated that I had delivered an important part of the program, so I returned to the back of the room to meet my mentor at the trainer's table.

Oh dear. I could see the fierce look in her eyes as I approached. What did I do wrong?

Actually she was seething.

Turns out I'd taken over an hour *just to explain the technique and set up the activity*! (**Why** and **What frames**, as you no doubt recall.) Why had I not tracked time?

But that wasn't all she was seething about. The poor use of time could have been forgiven, if I had been more thorough.

"Those questions," she asked me. "Why were there so many questions at the end?"

She waited.

I scratched my head. I didn't know. They didn't seem to "get it," did they? Why was that?

She insisted I should have known better, and waited for me to respond.

I looked at her blankly.

She then added another barb. "Why did you let them off the hook at the end? Why would you ever do that?"

Good grief she was angry. (Rightly so, in case you think I'm painting a terrible picture of my deeply caring mentor. She holds the bar high and expects the best from her mentees—and I wanted her to.)

I stuttered. "I ... I told them they might not all get it, and that was okay. I thought I was building rapport."

"No. You gave them permission to fail, and I will not have that."

I looked down at my shoes.

"And ... do you know why it took so long to set up, and why you had so many questions?"

I looked back up at her and shook my head. I knew I was about to find out.

"Way too conceptual. Not one single example. Just lots of repetition of the concepts and frameworks."

I opened my mouth to speak, but she silenced me by holding up her hand.

"You should have known better. I expected more. *And* you let them off the hook."

Then she softened. "Here's what I want you to do."

I nodded, wondering where I'd gone wrong.

"I want you to drill yourself, every single time, every single session you present, to say the following phrase, even if you don't know the answer yourself: '*Let me give you an example.*' And wait. Your unconscious mind will find one. Always."

I nodded, stuck for words. She was right. In my head, as I reviewed what I'd delivered, I realized it had been the most beautiful, conceptual, theoretical, abstract delivery. No wonder they had questions. No wonder the technique didn't work for some of them—they had no idea "*How*" it was supposed to work.

She was still talking. "And whenever you are asked questions like those in your debrief, those are signs that you did not deliver sufficient concrete examples before the activity. Here's how you respond to each question. You say—"

"Let me give you an example?" I said, ashamed at how obvious this was.

"Yes. And next time, don't let them off the hook. Don't ever tell them that 'maybe something won't work for some and it will for others.' Or that they'll 'get it' later. Assume there is no 'later.' You have one chance to influence your audience. Assume you'll never see them again. Get it right the first time."

I nodded again, red-faced. I'd been a star student up until now.

She stood and smiled. "Now give me a hug, and go get some lunch."

Tail between my legs, lesson learned, I joined the others for lunch and put on my bravest face.

So what did I do wrong? I'm sure you've already picked some things up—the very poor expectations of my audience for their success in the "**How frame**" for example, but what else?

Let's go through it, because some of what I'll teach you here should stay with you forever, as it did me. And not just if you present a talk that is "too theoretical." It can also happen the other way around, for example if your speech has no obvious theme or concept, and is *too* concrete.

One more thing. By learning from this example, I'll show you how to get your audience fully engaged—and you'll love it. It's super-easy.

I'll start with a question.

Are you being too conceptual? Is your topic esoteric? Too "heady"?

It's a common affliction for "ideas people," who get excited about their idea, then when presenting to others, struggle to bring it to life for their audience.

Consider that phrase for a moment: *bring to life*. What does this really mean? How does a concept differ from something living and breathing?

We know that something is "real" because we can see, hear, feel, taste, smell and touch it. (Yes, I know. Technically "feel" and "touch" can mean the same thing sometimes. Stay with me here.)

Yet a concept cannot be literally seen, heard, or felt. I like to think of it this way: if you cannot imagine buying this "thing" off the shelf at a supermarket, then it is probably still just a concept.

Let me give you an example:

Love. A concept universal among humans.

Can you buy "love" from a shelf at your local supermarket? Silly question (and please don't write in with lewd answers!). Of course not.

What about a rose? Can you see, hear, touch, taste, smell it—and purchase one from a supermarket? No question: of course you can. Although I'd refrain from listening to the roses the next time you're in the shop. Not a good look.

What about something big though, really big? A huge idea. The International Space Station for example. Could you buy that from a supermarket? Yes, assuming there was one big enough. The ISS is still a real object.

So we're dealing with two "things" here: concepts and objects; imagined and real, intangible and tangible.

Your talk, speech, presentation or training session is likely to (and indeed should) contain both, yet humans tend to have a preference to express themselves more in one of those domains (ideas or things) than the other.

Perhaps you have heard of the Myers-Briggs assessment tool. If so, you may already recognize these preferences as two extreme ends of the measurement scale: *Intuitive* (or "*N*") vs *Sensate* (or "*S*"). For a quick review or introduction to the tool take a look here:

http://en.wikipedia.org/wiki/Myers-Briggs_Type_Indicator

http://www.myersbriggs.org/my-mbti-personality-type/mbti-basics/

Ideas, concepts and abstract elements all appeal to the "*N*" tendencies in your audience's personalities. This type of information can leave the others—who relate strongly to what they see, hear, taste, touch and smell—struggling to make sense of the ideas, unable to make it real.

Those with "*S*" type preferences respond strongly to descriptions, examples, case-studies, stories, live-motion visuals, demonstrations, objects and samples. That's right, anything that is "real," even if it's presented as a mock-up, appeals to the "*S*" tendencies in your audience's personalities.

You'll notice from defining "*N*" and "*S*" people that I referred to *preferences* and *tendencies*. Why? Because while everyone will have a mix of both elements in their personality makeup, we all express a stronger preference for one or the other: to receive information in *either* an "*Intuitive/N*" or "*Sensate/S*" fashion. But just because we have a preference, like *4MAT*, it doesn't mean we don't understand, need, use or enjoy the other side of the spectrum. We just don't want to spend all our time there.

In the story at the start of this section, I recounted how I had been overly conceptual.

When I noticed my audience's eyes glaze over, I persisted in explaining my content again, in even more conceptual detail. What I didn't realize at the time was that the real reason for the lack of comprehension was almost certainly the lack of sensate material. I should have used examples, stories, steps, methods and demonstrations of a concrete technique. Just one story—one example—and I could have saved 30 minutes, *by bringing my topic to life*.

Here's a powerful method to guarantee your presentation will be understood:

- By all means introduce your concept *conceptually*. By the way, at this point in the text, all the "*N*" readers are nodding, and feeling tremendously wise. Even though they have no idea how to apply this wisdom. Yet.

- Make sure to **chunk down** your concept into something that can be seen, heard, touched, tasted or smelled. If this means using a case-study, or telling a story, relating an example, or passing around an object, then do it.

- You'll find the **Sensates** will perk up and start to appear engaged. But just as interesting is watching the faces of the **Intuits**, who can experience a significant "ah-ha moment" when they see an idea translated into reality.

Giving tangibility to concepts is a powerful technique, and one you should practice until you can perfect it every time. Remember what my own mentor said: **drill yourself to be able to give an example for every idea you introduce**.

The Referential Index Shift

That's a grand piece of jargon, isn't it? It's actually the correct nomenclature for what happens when you put yourself in the shoes of the person or people in the story. We *shift* ourselves and imagine it was ourselves experiencing the event in question.

Why is this important?

Have you ever been to a movie where a good part of the "action" was narrated? There may have been action being shown on screen, but the voice-over is only describing it. (For a good example, watch the opening minutes of the first installment of The Lord Of The Rings: The Fellowship Of The Ring. It consists entirely of a narrated sequence of events, showing us what happened leading up to the current time.)

It's not very immersive, is it?

Imagine you are watching a thriller, and you are in the shoes of the hapless victim hiding in a dark alleyway, being stalked by some ugly villain. You *feel* the action. Viscerally.

It's this human ability—to pretend to place ourselves in the mind of another—that has set us apart from almost all other species and led to our dominance. Yet many presenters ignore this power: The power to involve and engage their audience by bringing dry topics to life; by animating concepts and ideas; by illustrating theories with great example and stories.

It's super-simple, takes little effort ... and there's one more thing this does that when you realize what a no-brainer it is, you'll concentrate on doing it every time!

A really well-told story, example or case-study is also effective not *just* because it translates a concept to something concrete, but because it has the potential to engage *all* our senses.

Visually

Auditorily

Kinesthetically

Gustatorily

Olfactorily

The best movies have all that happening at once, don't they? They'll even try to have us imagine tasting and smelling food, or other atmospheric elements by clever use of visuals and sound.

And so does a good story or example.

- It engages our sense of sight: we can imagine in our mind's eye what the presenter is describing. Not just a building, but a towering skyscraper. Not a mere plant, but a water-laden tropical fern, glistening green in the forest sunlight.
- We hear the dialog; we sense the atmosphere in our heads.
- We can almost imagine what it might be like jumping out of that plane—we *feel* the air whipping at our jackets.
- We lay our hands on the cold stone of the cathedral's ancient outer wall.

The art of storytelling should not be underestimated for any presentation.

I once had the pleasure of critiquing a group of corporate managers. They were experienced folks who had already been well-trained, and were looking for an extra edge in their presentations over their competition. We talked about humanizing our speeches, about stories, about the *Visual*, *Auditory* and *Kinesthetic* (*VAK*) elements.

Then it was John's turn. He got up, sat on my presenter's stool, and fired up his single slide, the only one he showed in his five minute session.

It was a spreadsheet. Black text on white background. Tiny numerals in a busy grid of cells.

I groaned. On the inside. How would I temper my feedback? John was a really nice guy; I didn't want to destroy his confidence.

Then he began.

With a story. He pointed to a number in a specific cell, and asked the group about the month and year the number referred to, and who was on the team at that time. The group—sitting in a semi-circle of chairs in front of him—exchanged knowing smiles. They remembered alright. He went on to remind them about some of the politics in the office at the time, and the crazy sales targets—and that guy. The one who got fired that we can't talk about.

Suddenly his numbers were not disconnected metrics on a boring background, they had come to life in a vista of strong memories.

His entire talk continued in this vein. Every financial point he made was accompanied by some story, some example, carefully targeted to the audience he knew well. His outcome? To persuade the group to consider current results in context, and to recognize that their next sales opportunity is still an unknown figure waiting to fill a cell on a spreadsheet somewhere.

No fancy props. No fancy slides. No huge production.

Just John, his stool, one slide ... and stories.

He finished and expected us (especially me!) to tear him apart.

Instead we applauded.

Sometimes the simplest ideas can be overlooked. We are, after all, just human beings presenting and talking to other human beings. Bring your speech to life, show your human side, let your audience relate to your examples, and there won't be a dry eye in the house (as they say).

John knew how to spin a story. But there are those whose stories go on.

And on.

And on.

Until you want to tell them to "get to the point."

Fortunately, there's a perfect way to structure every one of your stories that will make sure you don't make this mistake, and that will be a great addition to the tools you can use to help your audience stay fully engaged, especially in your "*Why?*" frames. I'll outline it first, then I'll show you how to use it with *4MAT*.

Dale Carnegie—famous for the book, "How To Win Friends And Influence People"—had a formula for telling a story when public speaking, one that still stands today:

Incident. The bulk of your story. You should spend about 90% of time here.

Point/Action to take. Every story told in a speech or presentation has to have one. It can even be "the moral of the story." If it doesn't have one, don't use it, no matter how "funny" you think it is.

Benefit. This is the bit almost all presenters leave out. What's in it for the audience? Why is this powerful for them to have heard? If you want to see it done well, then Google the phrase "motivational keynote speakers" and watch a few videos. These women and men make big money by telling stories, but unless they can translate them into a benefit for the audience, they won't get re-hired.

http://www.dalecarnegie.com/communication_effectiveness_-_present_to_persuade/

Your story must relate to your topic, have a point, and be of use in illustrating your ideas. By structuring it in this way, you won't be tempted just to "throw one in" to liven up your concepts.

You might be wondering exactly how this fits into *4MAT*.

The answer is, *almost anywhere you want it to.* Sometimes I've used a single story as my "*Why?*" frame. In this instance, it must be an impactful story. Stories and examples are fabulous in the "*What?*" frame, as long as they don't obscure the information that the *What Learner* craves. My best tip for placing stories in this part of your presentation is to have your references, theory, key concepts and hard data up on your flipchart or slide. Then bring each one to life with a quick example or story.

"*How?*" frames lend themselves to great case-studies—but beware, this is not a substitute for the audience members actually *doing* the how, especially if you are training people. A case-study is still only you explaining it, and merely the beginning of the coaching process. Changes in behavior only arise when that behavior is *practiced* (the "how").

As for the pesky "*What If/Else learners*"? Curly question thrown at you? Ha! Answer the question by running right into a story. "*Great question! That reminds me of the time when Aunt Jean ...*" (and so it goes).

Stories and examples are particularly powerful when it comes to answering questions; holding debriefs, and facilitating understanding and integration of your topic. I'll show you how to do that in Chapter 5, "How To Create Brilliant Flashes Of Insight"

One word of advice about stories: calibrate your audience. If you've got a high-powered group of time-poor CEOs gathered for a breakfast meeting, don't pull out that 15-minute epic about the time you were working as a consultant in the tropics and your best friend was your assistant, and who would have thought he'd be the one who caught malaria ... you get the idea. Structure your story to suit the personality of your audience. Don't be vulgar at the Community Hall Neighborhood Watch Meeting.

Embellish a little and disclose personal facts if you want to build rapport.

Use your stories and examples *first* as bridges to building rapport with your audience. Then polish them via great delivery to also make them excellent entertainment.

You'll have your audience eating out of your hand.

Which brings us nicely to using metaphor and analogy, don't you think?

4.3 How To Avoid The Black Hole Of Misunderstanding

IF STORIES APPEAL TO OUR senses, then it stands to reason that they should work best with more "***Sensate***" audiences, doesn't it?

To some degree, this is true. If I had a roomful of "***N***"s (highly intuitive, ideas-type people) as my audience, I would dial back the volume of stories.

But what to replace them with? What can appeal to an audience as effectively as a story?

The answer still lies in our ability to illustrate our content: To make the light go on; to create those thunderclaps of understanding; to generate the blinding flashes of the obvious for our audiences, for your audience is a blank slate, waiting to be written upon; and we are the artists, drawing upon our creativity.

There's no doubt that speeches become more lyrical with the use of analogy.

And even though the ***Intuits*** soak them up like a sponge, if the analogies and metaphors are sufficiently strong, *everyone* responds to them.

So what makes an analogy or metaphor strong?

When they are *relatable*.

When they are not so obscure that they make us think, "huh?"

Analogies are powerful because they help us connect what we already know (the first part of the analogy) to something we are still seeking to understand.

Here's an example (I really hope you are getting this example thing down by now):

He moved through the hallway, as quiet as a mouse.

This analogy illustrates how quiet someone can be, by comparing them to how quietly a mouse might move.

Analogies compare *something we know* to *something we might not know*. This is incredibly helpful to assist your audiences in making connections to *new* content, by comparing it analogously to something *they can already recognize*. Especially if you cannot give a direct example.

Here's another example:

Our new paint is whiter than the whitest snow.

This will no doubt be far easier for an audience to grasp *quickly* than:

Our new brilliant white paint reflects light at over 5,120 Kelvin.

(Note: If your audience is a group of photographic studio lighting engineers, the second example works fine, of course!)

So find something comparable to your topic point and use it as an analogy:

This new system is more secure than encasing your documents in concrete under your house.

The new technology makes high-definition video look as old as a TV show from the 50s.

What is a metaphor?

A metaphor is a type of analogy where the comparison is like with unlike. They usually make no sense if taken literally.

For example:

He ran down the street like a bat out of hell.

Huh?

But what they can do is pack a lot of imagery into one sentence, which is very stimulating for the audience. Compare these two phrases:

She walked into the house, carrying the bundle carefully. I couldn't tell what was inside.

She walked into the house, carrying the bundle like it was a newborn. I couldn't tell what was inside.

The second example only changes a few words, yet is far more evocative. Metaphors help us assimilate strong messages more easily—as long as they can be understood by your audience.

Here are some common metaphors that work (and many of them are clichés, so use with care):

Don't judge a book by its cover.

It's the elephant in the room.

Which came first? The chicken or the egg?

It's raining cats and dogs.

It never rains, but it pours.

In a nutshell.

All the world's a stage.

Her heart was broken.

A lame duck.

A level playing field.

Walking on thin ice.

Cross that bridge when we get to it.

Avoid like the plague.

Now here are some not-so-good metaphors (a metaphor should never need explaining):

Her expression collapsed into a broken pretzel.

His love was dangling on a whim.

His look was stained coffee.

I fell into a deep washing machine of depression.

And be careful of the "mixed (or wrong) metaphor"!

It stuck out like a sore throat.

We'll burn that bridge when we come to it.

You need to stop and smell the coffee.

I think you get the idea.

So where are analogies, metaphors and similes useful?

- If you have a large proportion of Intuits ("***N***"s) in your audience.
- If you have 80% or more of your content that is brand new to your audience, and you need to help them grasp an important point, or make a more personal connection in their mind to something they can quickly grasp.

And at this point, I should stop, or I'm in danger of flogging a lame duck that bolted. I mean, it's not exactly rocket surgery*.

* Please don't report me to the Society for the Prevention of Abuse of Metaphors!

4.4 You Won't Believe What She Did!

WHY DO TV SERIALS USE cliffhangers?*
*Answer at the end of this section.

Most of us move through our lives in a trance. In buses, trains, elevators; watching TV, movies; reading books, papers, texts.

After a certain length of time watching your presentation, if nothing significant changes, your audience is likely to fall into a trance-like state, dictated by sameness.

Humans are programmed to track difference: it's a survival thing.

Was that flicker in the corner of your eye the curtain flapping in the breeze, or a tiger about to burst into the room and devour you? That's why you feel compelled to look.

We can use this tendency to bring our presentations and talks to life, simply by switching up the tempo from time-to-time (or slowing down the tempo!); varying our vocal delivery (volume, pitch, tempo, timbre, cadence); introducing new visuals—in fact anything that tends to reset our audience's attention.

Even pure physiology gets in the way of our attention:

- Uncomfortable chairs.
- Too long before a break (bathroom needs arise! Attention is distracted).

The presenter themselves can be blissfully unaware how they too, create sameness:

- The presenter remains in one place (eg. lectern).
- The slide or visual never changes, or is slow to change.
- Every slide or visual is simply a line or bullet-point of text.
- And many more things that contribute to your presentation being too "static."

SO HOW DO WE WAKE THEM UP?

To help bring interest to our presentations or talks, we can use techniques such as:

- *The Primary / Recency Effect*, where people tend to remember what came first or last. I first referred to this back in Chapter 2, and I'll touch on it again below;
- The *Zeigarnik Effect*, where people remember interrupted tasks better than contiguous ones.

(For a refresher on both, please review the section "How To Make Any Speech Memorable".)

How do you do this?

Read on ...

The Primary / Recency Effect

Because we (humans) have our attention setup to respond to *difference*, we tend to remember or pay more attention to any time something *changes*.

This is why beginnings and endings make a huge difference: we tend to remember what happened at the start (The Star Wars opening rolling narrative, "*A long time ago in a galaxy far, far away*"), along with great finishes, (The airport scene and memorable dialog in "Casablanca").

And so it should be for your presentation, talk or speech. Plan to make your openings memorable, as well as practicing the delivery and design of your finish. (You'll find more details and more techniques to help you with openings later in this chapter, in the section called How To Make Your First Two Minutes Super-Strong.)

There's nothing worse than what I call a "dribble ending," where the speaker pretty much says, "*Well, that's it. Oh wait ... I did want to say you can grab copies of my slides—just come on up to the stage* [cue two things: a mass exodus of those who don't want the copies of the slides, and a smaller group heading up to the stage to collect their copies. Meanwhile, the presenter is valiantly talking over the noise] *and I'll give them— but not now please. I wanted to mention you can also find out more about* [now he's having to shout] *THIS AT MY WEBSITE ...* [now he's given up, and turns his attention to those gathering and pestering him for the slides].

So make your endings definitive. Sharp. Allow room for applause or thanks. Take a grounded stance; don't move; look the audience in the eye.

Anchors

Another use of ***Primary / Recency*** is to anchor your audience's experience with music.

Music helps build anticipation and sets a mood. So use it to start or pre-start your presentation. Use it to send people off to breaks. Use music to bring people back from a break. My tip here is to use music tracks that have a strong start, that don't take time to build in volume or tempo. Rhythmic tracks are the best.

Another tip: You can use *the same piece each time* to bring people back to their places. You can even use the same piece as your opening (pre-presentation) track. In this way, you'll train your audience that "it's time to assemble again." Then once you're ready, slowly lower the volume to settle your audience in anticipation of your talk re-commencing (at the same time as showing a new slide or flipchart if you wish. Timing is key here). If you are holding a workshop over several days, then change the "call-in" track you use each day.

A word of advice: If you choose to use music, make sure you have permission, or the venue has an entertainment license, or similar official sanction to use music in this fashion.

Task interruption

Comedians do this brilliantly, by nesting story within story, sometimes seemingly unconnected, until eventually, when we return to the main "joke," the punchline is super-satisfying. See any Ronnie Corbett chair story (notice how many tangents he goes off on *immediately* after introducing the topic! https://www.youtube.com/watch?v=lFsuDlCFm4Q), or some Billy Connolly live shows (warning: might not be safe for work!).

These pros appear to lose their way in a very deft manipulation of story endings and beginnings. Why? It holds our attention, as well as serving as a clever build to the main punchline.

But we're not pros like Corbett and Connolly.

We have to *design* what we interrupt—to take a short detour—in order to *shift the audience's state*.

- This might mean showing a short video.
- Demonstrating something on stage.
- Having your audience move somewhere.
- Running a short activity (stand up and stretch is as simple as it gets).
- Recounting a story (ah-ha!).

Our aim is to interrupt the current theme, *in order to return to it more powerfully.*

And if you are really courageous, you can leave them hanging: *"After the break, I'll be discussing the single most important thing you can do to affect your long-term health."*

Who wouldn't come back?

* So why do TV serials use cliffhangers? It's memorable; plays to the ***Zeigarnik Effect***, and keeps us engaged. I bet you see why it's such a powerful technique (even if occasionally a tad annoying!). Here's a reference for you: http://www.spring.org.uk/2011/02/the-zeigarnik-effect.php

In the next section, I'll be showing you how to maximize the single most important part of your talk.

4.5 How To Make Your First Two Minutes Super-Strong

WE KNOW FROM THE ***PRIMARY / Recency*** effect that people pay attention to, and remember, strong openings.

But if you've ever felt nervous before a presentation, then you know that it's the beginnings that are fraught with peril!

Usually by the time you finish, the nerves and tension have abated enough for you to ease into your speech, and the ending feels less daunting (though still important to get right!).

However, as you've no doubt heard: you never get a second chance to make a first impression.

So your beginnings need to be one of the areas most thoroughly designed, and most thoroughly practiced.

That first thirty-seconds is crucial, because:

- It will make that all-important first impression.
- It will build your own confidence (when done well).
- It can be used very effectively to build audience rapport.
- You are already starting your "***Why?***" frame, and hence gaining audience buy-in, which in turn gives you feedback you've got them engaged.
- You'll have a small number of markers to get to, that you can reach before you need to refer to any notes, change a slide or focus on anything other than your audience. That way, it can be all about you and establishing your presence.
- You get to set your ***Presenter Bubble*** in place with confidence.

So this section of your talk needs to be the content you have practiced and know very well. For some speakers, this "intro time" becomes a standard set of frames that they always use or adapt (which you might only need to change if you have the same audience over and over). This repeated practice means your opening moments get polished over time, in the same way the humor of your favorite jokes improve with each delivery.

If you do have the chance to deliver and re-deliver an intro, it is a great learning vehicle, because you come to understand what is landing well on your audience; what really engages them, and what falls flat. Tip: don't repeat the stuff that falls flat! I know that sounds silly, but I've seen many a professional presenter fall into that trap.

I believe that creating a significant marker, that you want to get to in the first thirty-seconds to two minutes, is crucial to your confidence. This could be where you turn to introduce your first slide, or where you propose a toast, or where participants move to an activity that you set up.

Practice that run up to the first marker.

Then, at your first marker, while your audience's attention is directed elsewhere—to your slide, a video, or otherwise occupied to another in an introduction exercise—you'll often have an opportunity to cast an eye over your running notes.

This, for many nervous speakers, is a real lightbulb moment: That you don't have to either memorize hours of content to appear slick, or appear unprepared by constantly referring to notes. All you need to do is know each marker to hit, take a moment to regroup, and you're off again.

I've had participants at training programs come up to me and exclaim that they did not see me refer to any notes, ever. Yet sitting on my presenter's table are a couple of pages of running notes in bullet-point form.

Why didn't they notice?

Because I never referred to them in view of my audience.

But is it okay to make a mistake, and *have* to refer to your notes? Even in the first two minutes?

Yes, of course!

Remember your ***Presenter Bubble***? What do you think happens as soon as a mistake is made, or you're not quite sure what was next?

That's right, you adjust your attention to disappear onto your nose. Or at the very least, it will shrink back to being focused on your notes.

This is why your recovery skills are another string to your bow, if this should ever happen.

Simply take a deep breath, expand your ***Presenter Bubble*** back out, casually regain your position from your notes ... and resume play.

What if you have no obvious marker point?

If your audience is not interactive, or is very large, then there may not be a point at which their attention is NOT on you. Especially if you have no slides or other props. So how do you ascertain a suitable marker point, or find a place where you can consult your notes during your speech?

The answer is that it may not exist ... yet. You're going to have to engineer it. But if you've been following my design process so far, then you'll already have the solution right in front of you: chunking.

Each element of your talk is already "chunked." Chances are that your first two minutes *already* includes several chunks of information—and even if it doesn't, you can easily drill down into it and create them.

Here's the magic: Your "markers" become the *transitions and links* between your chunks. Memorize those and you will have your opening nailed. Think of them as the signposts and junctions on a long car trip. Each time you "take a turn," you transition to another chunk of content. In my experience, this is a powerful skill to develop: Remember all your links, and you remember the presentation.

I believe this is because of the self-contained nature of each chunk, and the fact that this respects the **7+/-2** rule. As soon as you move from one chunk to another, you're off again, and the **7+/-2** will take care of itself , both for you, and for your audience.

Of course, being this well-planned means that spontaneity is thrown out of the window ... or does it? Hmmm.

4.6 Being Fantastically Funny!

WHAT'S THE WORST WAY TO be funny or spontaneously funny?

Delivering it from a script.

There may be an exception to this, if you are a professional stand-up comic who has, over time, carefully honed their act. Perhaps even refining the gag after repeated performances to eventually draw a reliably maximum audience response. Even these pros would likely have experienced some disastrous fall-flat-moments. As a presenter, you probably don't have the opportunity to test the waters with a joke dozens of times ... and still get invited back to talk.

We're not comics, neither are we improvisation artists, and we're certainly not predisposed to be naturally funny while quaking in our shoes on stage ... so how do you do it? How does one become more spontaneous—and even hilariously funny?

Time for some straight-talk: It's entirely possible that in the first few talks or presentations you give, you simply won't have the attention on much else other than your **Presenter Bubble**, and getting through your talk.

Which is absolutely fine.

But as you get more stage-hours under your belt, you will want to know some of the best methods for enhancing the delivery of humor, being genuinely spontaneous, and even spontaneously funny.

You'll notice that you'll be building on the foundational principles of presenting. These skills become an extension of what you've already learned. Let's take a look at them:

1. The first method is to perfect your delivery over time, and enhance the body language that makes something funny (a gesture, a facial expression, certain tonality. See Chapter 2.)
2. Tell more stories. You'd be surprised how often your story grows and grows (make sure they get better and not just longer).
3. When telling stories, go the extra mile and bring them to life. Warning: When you first start implementing the following actions you will probably feel self-conscious. Knowing that, just jump right in and start experimenting.

    - Act out each character in your story. Portray and even embellish their movements and idiosyncrasies.
    - Act out the dialog of your characters! Many storytellers completely overlook this opportunity to make an audience laugh, reverting to passive voice description (she told him he was behaving like an idiot, then proceeded to list his faults) rather than bringing your speech to life, by bringing your characters to life (Spoken by the presenter: *"Barb of course, was furious.* (imitating Barb's voice) *'You great big idiot! How did you manage to get me into this? First you make promises you've no idea about, then*

you back them up with lies, and then you tell them it's all down to me!'").

You'll find when you do this that you totally get into your story, and this alone can really generate humor.

4. Practice the art of "***accepting the offer.***" This is a technique borrowed from improvisational acting methods, and involves taking any contribution from anywhere (the audience; the environment; a freak event), *accepting* it and using it in your content, or to illustrate your content. I've emphasized *accepting* to help you understand this is different to ignoring; carrying on regardless, or shrugging it off with a laugh.

    For example: A phone rings somewhere in the audience. You stop in mid-sentence and mime answering it: "*Hello? Yes, this is he. Ah, I see, that is a significant sum. Would you please inform Mr Gates I'm busy in a presentation at the moment, and I'll call him at home later. What's his number again?*" You mime hanging up and look out at the audience with a mischievous grin. "*Bill will have to do better than that to prevent me sharing my secrets with you.*"

    Or someone from the audience makes a wisecrack: "*Yeah, that's just perfect. For my mother-in-law!*" The crowd laugh, as do you, but you retort: "*I know, I know! I've had to hide this from every single mother-in-law I've met so far!*"

    This applies to anything that happens during your presentation: something clatters to the floor, ("*Another idea dropping into place!*"); a door opening and closing (You look at the door. "*My point exactly. An open and shut case.*"); a noise over the PA system (You peer up at the loudspeaker. "*I told you this topic is hot property. That's the Russians trying to hack in again. Nobody say anything incriminating!*")

    There is no question, this will come more easily when you have a few stage-hours under your belt, but that doesn't mean you shouldn't be practicing it from day one. Accepting the offer is a fantastic **recovery skill**!

5. Good stage work. If you are acting out a part, or dialog, then exaggerate *everything*. Audiences are generally in some state of inertia, and so treat them as a heavy object that takes some pushing. What you do on the stage often feels overdone, but hardly ever looks that way from the audience's point of view. What you think is a giant, beaming smile, they may think is barely a grin. So don't be concerned about being over-the-top. You can always pull back.

Then again, you might have an audience who is in far from good humor. In fact, they are downright hostile.

What then?

I'm glad you asked (*rubs hands together in glee*).

4.7 How To Deal With Difficult Audiences

WE'VE DEALT WITH THE FRIVOLOUS audience, and have been lighthearted about it ... but now things have gotten serious.

Quite out of hand, actually. And your audience is mad. Mad as hell, and they're not going to take it anymore.

You've been called in to give a presentation. What now?

Well actually, let's dial it back a little. I'll assume your topic is merely controversial. Then I'll build up to handling an audience who is not so happy. Baby steps.

I'm going to take us back to those pesky *Index Computations* again. Right at the start of designing your presentation, you probably had a good idea about your audience's thoughts and feelings concerning your topic. For now, we'll deal with it as merely "controversial," or has elements in it that your audience may well be resistant to, or object to.

These thoughts and feelings are a giant clue.

How do we build rapport with an audience? We show sameness. We demonstrate empathy. *We join the conversations in their head.*

Then when we've walked in their shoes sufficiently—or "paced" alongside them (to use a metaphor)—we can start to coax them our way, or begin to "lead" them. Not surprisingly, this is called *Pacing and Leading*.

But this audience has (or you believe they will have) an objection to something in your talk. So how do you build rapport in this instance?

The trick is to *Pace Out the Objection,* or *P.O.O.* if you prefer the humorous (and memorable) acronym. How? By alluding to your controversial elements. That's *alluding* to it. You don't call it out for a conversation here and now. Sometimes this is a simple as a short phrase, such as:

"I know some people here might find a couple of aspects of my presentation today a little challenging ... but stick with me, because later I'll show you just how to overcome that."

This immediately does a couple of things:

1. It builds rapport. They know that you know what they know. Of course, you have made some assumptions, and you have to tread a fine line between what "knowing" really means, and demonstrating genuine empathy. Framing is the key, and I'll show you how to do that shortly.
2. It takes the sting out of any resistance, and more importantly, gives you time to build more rapport, and make a good case for your content (in other words, to deliver a "*Why frame*"). In many, many cases, you might well find that the topic you thought might prove to be difficult, is no problem at all.

Put simply: If you show that you know something of their objections, *and* that you will cover it later, then 99% of the time, it will never *be* an objection.

Naturally, the above really only works if the objection to your content does not run too deep; that you genuinely address the issues, and that you genuinely empathize with their thoughts and feelings, and can help them move on. You must also deliver on your promise, or risk dis-creating rapport and creating further alienation.

We might think of the above as a surface-level "hostile audience," where the objection or controversy is in most cases, manageable.

But what if they really are furious?

This can happen. If it does, then no amount of logic will convince them, and you will not be able to truly shut the anger and aggression down. Instead, in order to go forward, you are going to have to find an outlet for it. In any case, this doesn't change the fact that you:

A. Still have to build rapport with your audience;
B. Must acknowledge the underlying issues, or they won't let you move on; and
C. Need to compartmentalize their possible questions. This process requires very careful facilitation (which I cover in these rest of this section and deepen in Chapter 5) because if you don't present a suitable process for handling these questions, the underlying issues could very well derail your entire talk.

Once again, our old friend, "*framing,*" goes a long long way to helping manage an agitated audience. Here's an example, which would probably be best delivered after a brief introduction and short personal rapport-building story:

"Now there's no getting past the fact that some people here are pretty angry, and rightly so. I'd like to hear your concerns and take any questions you have, and I'll take as long as I need to, to do this, but at the end of my presentation. My session does contain some things that I hope will address your situation, so stick with me, as I'll do my best to make that plain. Then at the end, if you still have questions ... please fire away. Does anyone object?"

99 times out of 100 this will get you *permission* to carry on. And that's all you need: permission. Once a hostile audience grants you that, then the ball is in your court, and all you need to rely on is a great presentation design, and your now-finely-tuned presentation skills.

But what if you're facing a barrage of questions at the end of your talk and don't know how to handle them?

That's an excellent question, and one that we'll handle in considerable detail in the next chapter. When you learn how to take any question graciously; enhance it so that it becomes valuable for the entire group, while simultaneously continuing to drive your points home ... everyone wins.

Which has the added benefit that when you check back with the original asker, they feel proud at having asked such an intelligent question that benefited the entire audience.

And guess what. It's easy when you know the steps.

But for now, it's time to pause a moment (you'll see why, coming right up) ...

4.8 Drills

Before you present:

What stories and examples can you already list? If you don't already have a journal of these specifically for public speaking, I recommend you start one now.

What stories and examples from your current repertoire can you use in your very next talk?

Think about what happened to you today (or yesterday, but make it recent). Note down anything that triggers a thought. For example, today I was in the coffee shop, writing some of these drills, and the owner was meeting with two other people about using social media to run a local cooking competition. What story or analogy could I draw from this? Plenty. Perhaps how social our meeting places have become; the typical places where business is now conducted; if you want to discuss social media, do it in a social place ...

Try turning three of your recollections into an example or illustrative story.

The next time you are at the dinner table and one of your friends is regaling everyone with a story, note it down for later use.

Practice for a whole day at work replying with *"Let me give you an example"* anytime someone asks you a meaningful question.

Design some analogies and metaphors that help illustrate your topic. What is your topic "like"? What are some of the chunks "like"? For example, you find yourself presenting about timeliness. You could offer this metaphor: *"Continually turning up late is like the supermarket continually trying to sell fruit clearly past its use-by-date. Pretty soon you start avoiding the supermarket."*

What "cliffhanger" style links can you already use and design into your speech?

For hostile or difficult audiences, try to ascertain what the potential objections are and design some early pacing-out statements. Ensure you address the whole objection later in your talk if it is warranted, or at the very least, have that up your sleeve ready to present if it rears its head.

Before standing up to speak:

Mentally rehearse your first two or three sentences. They'll help get you to your next marker.

During your presentation:

Practice using plenty of stories and examples to hold attention. As you become more skilled, you'll be able to notice and calibrate your audience's feedback (and later refine what you are doing). Start tracking micro-responses: whether they smile back at you; nodding of heads; general murmurs of acknowledgment; laughter, and use this to refine your story or example to really hit the mark next time.

Post-speech:

What did you notice about the responses to your examples, stories, analogies, frames, cliffhangers or tension-inducing moments? Note down things that you can use, re-use or fine-tune. I recommend noting them down as soon as possible, before the live event fades from memory. It is helpful to have someone to debrief with (whether they were present or not).

How did you fare with your difficult audience? Did you deal with objections authentically, or were they left superficially answered? This can be a fine line to tread, so don't beat yourself up if you think you didn't handle them well: it takes skill and plenty of hours under the belt to do it well. Because, as you know, there's always something you can learn.

CHAPTER 5: HOW TO BE ENGAGING, ENTHRALLING AND ENTERTAINING

5.1 How To Create Brilliant Flashes Of Insight

Time for a breather and a pause.

Feel better? Good. We've covered a lot of ground, and there's a ton of techniques, methods and tips of the trade I still want to share with you.

But for the moment, I'd like to review some things with the express purpose of reviewing, building on and deepening the "magic number" *7+/-2*.

The interesting thing about your conscious mind and its ability to pay attention (with the use of *7+/-2*) is that it is not static, but rather dynamic and contextual. What you can place your *7+/-2* attention on right now will be different to what you place your attention on tomorrow.

Here's an easy example that I gave at the beginning of the book: most of us learned to drive at some point (and if you haven't, or don't plan to, this is still a salient example, so pay attention!). At first, this required an incredible amount of attention—it took all of it, and then some—to keep an eye on the road, manage the steering, deal with other vehicles around you, check your mirrors, brake, change gear (if you are driving a manual shift), indicate, check your mirrors again, listen to the instructor's instructions, do head-checks—

Are you getting the sense that you have you overshot your *7+/-2*, that you've got simply too much to do and to focus on? This is where you feel so overwhelmed that doing the task (whether it's physical or mental) becomes nigh-on impossible.

This is what I refer to as being overchunked.

Fortunately for most of us, we each possess an amazing tool. So amazing that no matter how we abuse and mistreat it, it still manages to turn so much of what we learn into easy routines and automated actions. You guessed it ... it's your brain.

Your brain—or perhaps your mind—takes those seemingly-impossible tasks that required way more than nine chunks and learns the sequence. With repetition, tasks that used to be discrete get compressed and merged, so that what was nine (or more) chunks, becomes five, then the next time around two or three, until eventually, *the task is not something you need to pay any conscious attention to.*

Think of it this way: when was the last time you really had to think about driving? Again, if you don't drive, or don't plan to learn, perhaps you have an example of your own where you were learning something complex that seemed really overwhelming, that you can now do without thinking.

Most people who drive can now not only drive without thinking (!), they can also do other tasks at the same time. Perhaps you've found yourself engaged in something complex such as driving, and happily singing, or listening to a philosophical talk-back conversation, or even thinking about something completely unrelated.

And so it is with your audience. New content you present may feel unfamiliar to them at first, but they will quickly grasp your subject because of your clever layering of *chunks*; masterful design of *chunk size*, and use of empowering stories that help them relate and internalize your topic.

The same goes for you. You may not be able to do everything in this book in your next talk, but you will at some point begin to incorporate each element, until it moves out of your awareness (or as we say, has been chunked to "zero" and is now maintained unconsciously).

And if that doesn't make a good case for repetition, I don't know what does. Because each time you review something consciously from this book, you'll bring it back out into your conscious *7+/-2* attention capability, see it from a different angle, tweak it, polish it, fine tune it to suit you and your circumstance. Through conscious practice, your mind will re-work the chunks; coalesce and combine them, until eventually the entire improved process becomes internalized and out of your awareness again.

This is one of the key acts of *Generative Learning*, and one you can also use in your presentations.

What is *Generative Learning*? Merely a fancy name for the way human beings learn: We generate new knowledge, behaviors and expectations based on experience. A *Generative Learning* process is iterative. This means it takes place over time; it is often enhanced by repetition across modalities of learning (think visual, auditory, kinesthetic), and we may or may not be aware of what we are learning at the time we learn it.

Why is this?

Because our conscious attention won't always take in information and apply it, but our out-of-awareness attention can assimilate a massive amount of data. Think of the simple example of the hum of an air-conditioner, or the tick of a clock. We "know" it's there at some level, but pay no attention.

When your audience is first exposed to your content, the timing might not be right, or the chunk size not a good fit, or they simply zoned out.

But this doesn't mean the information wasn't gathered in some way outside of their conscious awareness. In the same way that you hear a song and it seems familiar, perhaps because you'd "heard" it in the background somewhere else but paid no attention, your audience will be more receptive to multiple exposures of the same chunk of content.

The trick is to present it in ways that is not simply repetition (though there's nothing wrong with reviewing what you've discussed from time-to-time).

If you think about the, "tell 'em what you're going to tell 'em, tell 'em, then tell 'em what you told 'em" principle, this is a crude attempt at making several passes of your content. By using your chunking skills, and weaving stories and examples, you can be far more elegant than that.

There is a whole raft of techniques and study into *Generative Learning*, but since this is not a text book on adult learning, I'll skip that here and simply state the following:

Find many ways, angles, stories and examples to get your message across, and layer them into each of your frames, and your audience will gain such multi-exposure to your topic that they'll go home thinking they already knew this stuff. Which in and of itself can be a problem, because sometimes it's so masterfully done that it's hard for them to realize that they have learned something new or taken on new skills. But that's okay, you just need to give them something called a "*conscious convincer*" that it was all down to your help.

What is a conscious convincer? A *conscious convincer* means you offer proof to your audience they can now act—or know how to act—on the knowledge you have just imparted. Occasionally this might mean you initiate an activity for them to prove to themselves that this is true. Some of your presentation may still be purely lodged at an unconscious level, and by bringing this back into your audience's awareness, you complete a loop for them. For example, if you've just spoken at length about how to make meetings run more effectively, you might ask your audience to split up into groups of 4-5 people and run a 5-minute meeting. By forcing them to be conscious of the processes and techniques you'd spoken about, you'll find them discovering their own learning—and connecting it with your help.

Conscious convincers are the architects of the "light-bulb" experience, or the "ah-ha" moment. The great thing about them is that no one argues with their own idea or brilliant mental flash, so you're more likely to have generated stickier content and true ownership of your material.

Generative Learning, Conscious Convincers and the "What If?" frame

If you have the capacity to introduce an interactive element of your talk; if you have a training session where there is a natural time for a "debrief" (or regroup for a discussion) after an activity or skills-practice session, then you have a golden opportunity to facilitate the "ah-ha" moment using stories, examples and questions.

Your goal is to bring to conscious awareness aspects of your previously delivered content in a way that your audience may not have thought about before.

This helps not only facilitate the obvious "*What If?*" learners, but also drives *Generative Learning*: the group experience your content in another form.

By using stories and examples, you force the audience to place themselves in the same situation. The same happens if you debrief what happened for participants in a previous activity: the rest of the listening audience will place themselves—not necessarily consciously—in this situation.

For example, to continue with the scenario where you had presented at length about making meetings more effective; sent the audience into a mock practice session, then had them return ... this is an ideal time for a combination of "*What If?*" and *Generative Learning*. You could begin by asking them general questions about their experience: "*What did you notice about your meeting process?*" Later in this chapter, I'll show you exactly how to formulate high-quality questions.

You could respond to a question from your audience by relating a personal story of experience of a really bad meeting you attended, and how it could have been made far more effective with some simple techniques.

Your aim is to create more connections to aspects of your content for each audience member. It will make your talk more memorable, and give them a more rounded understanding.

Even better, you'll help create those brilliant flashes and ah-ha moments.

So make everything you do—both for yourself, and for your audiences—iterative.

Get better each time. Come back, learn and review.

There, that's enough of a pause don't you think?

Normal programming can resume now.

5.2 "I Stopped ... And You Won't Believe What Happened Next!"

WHEN I WAS FIRST REQUIRED to speak in public, I was terrified. I did everything wrong: I wrote out my speech long-hand, word-for-word; tried to memorize it word-for-word; left the handwritten notes on the sound engineer's desk where I collected the microphone, and it was all downhill from there. With nothing to help me I had to rely on my memory. I didn't have the wherewithal to run off quickly and get my notes. That would have appeared unprofessional (or so I thought). I stood in front of the large crowd gathered and opened my mouth ... and nothing, and I mean absolutely nothing came out the way I'd planned. I motormouthed my audience. It was awful. I guess it had one good effect, and that was to motivate me to never repeat the experience. I resolved to get better.

Apart from the planning and design disaster, there was one thing I could have done that would have made a significant—and critical—difference to the audience's comprehension.

I could have paused.

Have you ever been forced to stop during a speech or presentation?

And have you noticed that the way you calibrate time in front of an audience is quite different. It feels as if an eternity is passing, when in reality, it's just a few seconds.

For the audience however, their perception of time is passing normally. Nothing is wrong, except you have stopped.

When you are presenting, whenever you pause, even for a breath, it's going to feel like it's taking forever, just because your sense of time is distorted.

This is one reason why speakers who are new to presenting can end up talking too fast and are scared to stop and take a breath. Which is exactly what happened in my example above when I turned into Mr. Motormouth, and is one of the traps for young players. You feel as if there's no "time" to take a deep breath, so each breath that you do manage to take becomes more shallow, and the vicious circle turns. Eventually you have to speak faster and faster with less and less lung-power, which in turn reduces projection, slurs your words, and increases pitch. None of which are desirable things to happen in a talk.

However, one thing will fix this.

Learning to *pause*. And breathe! (Oh, that's two things.)

You must practice pausing, and getting used to letting the time go by. Take a breath (or two), then resume. You'll feel much better for it, and so will your audiences.

Now here are many more things you can make a pause do for you:

Restoring the rhythmic pulse

Pausing during your talk will help restore a natural sentence rhythm and cadence; it helps reset the rhythm of your breath.

In addition to this, the pause will remind you to extend your ***Presenter Bubble***, which in turn adds yet more natural rhythm to your speech.

Restoring confidence

The opposite of pausing is to try to fill the air with words. This usually stems from a lack of confidence in your presentation, or a lack of confidence in your own ***Presenter Identity***. But learning to insert a pause, and taking advantage of the opportunity to take a deep breath, can be the very mechanism that turns this confidence around. It's somewhat counter-intuitive: You're using the pause to restore confidence, rather than thinking that confidence will enable you to pause with ease, which helps break the cycle.

Creating interest

Pauses help punctuate your talk. They give the audience time to assimilate what you've just said and make sense of it. It's also quite natural. Check out the top-rated movies: the action will always, always have a lull somewhere. If not, it's just too tiring to watch. This is counter-intuitive of course: stopping and leaving a gap to make things better can run against our instincts. Which is why you have to practice it, along with the breath.

Creating suspense

I'll show you later in this chapter how to engineer this more deliberately, but the ***pause*** can also be ...
... the dramatic pause.

For example, you say: *"Let's take a look at how understanding volumetric algebra will help you in your next engineering project."* [presenter turns to whiteboard]

In this example, there is no pause. Now the audience is simply waiting. They know the topic—volumetric algebra—and their attention may wander.

Contrast that with this example: *"Let's take a look at how this method will make a big difference to your next engineering project.* [presenter turns to whiteboard and begins writing a title obscured by his or her body. When finished, he or she turns back to the audience, and steps to one side.] *Volumetric algebra, unexciting as it sounds, will make a big difference. I'm going to show you how."*

This minor pause helps to reset your audience's attention, and continue to create a little suspense here and there.

The TV networks know how to do this to great (and annoying) effect, as do some internet sites that use subject lines and headlines in what is known as "click bait." So you do need to use the technique with care. Used well, no one notices. Used over-melodramatically ... you get the idea.

If you've seen those TV news items where right at the start of the half-hour segment they say something like this: *"... and coming up, how one man took on the might of the Russian army ... and won."* You have no idea what it's about—nothing is given away—but it sounds intriguing, so you stay tuned for the full half-hour (their goal, of course). Sometimes when you get to the segment in question, it's super-lame. But the network doesn't care: you've stayed to watch, and that's all they needed. They'll catch us with the same trick again tomorrow. Reality TV is absolutely jam-packed with these over-the-top melodramatic pauses. You're always being taken to a break after a huge build up. You have to wait until after the break (if you're lucky) to find out if the contestant got the answer right or wrong, if they won the $25,000 or if they are going to Hollywood for the next Idol competition.

A similar thing happens with the click-baity "blind headlines" you may have seen online. For example: *"This woman swallowed an entire set of cutlery. But you won't believe what she did next!"*

These link-headlines are designed to get you to click through, which enhances the site's visitor stats, which means they can charge more for advertising (and some of us will actually click on those ads, earning even more money for the site).

Nonetheless, we can learn from these techniques and apply them. You won't believe how ...

(Sorry! Couldn't resist.)

Here's how you do it.

Using either your flipchart, whiteboard or slide, build your intro to the topic. Keep stopping to address the audience and add more dimensions (or more "*Why?*" frames). Stacking "*Why?*" frames (layering more and more reasons for your audience to stick with you) is an effective way to naturally build more anticipation and desire.

Then eventually, you reveal what you are referring to, by writing it onto your chart or whiteboard, or by changing the slide.

Here's an example:

"Would you like to know how to avoid that mid-afternoon slump without resorting to coffee or chocolate? [audience nods and takes the "**Why?**" frame onboard.] *I expect you'd be interested to know a very simple technique that anyone can do at any time—and it works instantly?* [The presenter turns to the whiteboard seeing the excitement in the audience's eyes ... but freezes for a moment, then turns back.] *I'd also add that this technique looks normal—I mean that I'm not going to give you some bizarre dance* [presenter embellishes his or her point by making some silly moves], *or make you do a weird yoga pose* [presenter attempts convoluted pose ... badly]. *No, this is as easy as it gets* [turns back to whiteboard briefly, touches pen to surface, then stops, turns back]. *I'm not sure that you'll believe me, because it's so obvious. But I do it, and I can tell you, it makes a big difference to your day!* [the audience by now may be yelling at you: Yes! Just tell us already! The presenter turns back to the whiteboard and writes the answer—obscured at first—then steps to one side.] *I told you it was obvious*—now let me explain exactly how to make this work for you."*

* Answered in next section, just in case you were also curious.

More about *the pause*

Introducing useful pauses—as well as helping your audience digest the meal—will assist any introverts in the room to internalize your content. Introverts need quiet time (no one talking; no new data coming into their brains) to digest information. This is especially helpful to know if you are expecting your audience to do something with the information you just delivered—take it into an exercise or discussion perhaps. Extroverts don't need the pause, but may have to talk it through with someone else to fully internalize your point.

If you the presenter are extroverted, you may find pausing harder to do than the introvert. Just remember, creating space in your presentation is important.

The good news is that the pause also helps trigger the *Primary / Recency effect* (and to some degree, depending on the type of pause, the *Zeigarnik effect*). In effect, you are creating new beginnings and endings within your content delivery which facilitates your audience in maintaining attention *and* improving retention.

Phew. Now it's time to discover how to keep the audience on the edge of their—

5.3 How To Keep Them On The Edge Of Their ...

—SEATS.

YOU ALREADY KNOW THIS technique from the previous section all about "***the pause***," but for the sake of clarity, since it technically doesn't need a pause for it to work, we'll review and expand on the method here.

Remember those pesky TV News Networks and their "coming up after the break" teasers?

They work as mini-cliffhangers, and the TV networks are very good at them.

But you don't have to sound like a cheap TV station, or sleazy infomercial salesperson, in order to use this technique elegantly.

We talked about the "click-bait" headlines that fly around the internet in the last section. We're going to borrow from their technique and use it ethically.

You can also do this with the headline of your speech; the sub-sections or chunks, and any time you introduce a topic. It's called ***Setting Up Response Potential***.

The trick is to make your headline or bullet-point *blind*. That is, it hints at what is to come, but does not reveal it.

Here are some examples:

- The 3-point checklist for every graphic designer
- What you must know before removing a tooth
- A simple technique that makes you more productive
- ABC Corp launches new product range

I'd recommend you avoid using slides that are lists of bullet points (we'll talk about why in Chapter 6), but if you are stuck with them, then I suggest you suppress the bullets that have not yet been referred to while you present the current one.

The same with flipcharts and whiteboards, and to some degree, workbooks and handouts. If there is information on or in them that pertains to content you have not yet covered, then I'd recommend holding it back. Otherwise, the audience cannot resist running ahead of you, and you'll lose their attention.

You can also take a leaf out of the TV News Networks whenever sending your audience to an activity, break, lunch, or end-of-session/day.

"When you come back from lunch, we'll investigate the best ways to improve your study techniques."

Again, it's just another way to keep your hooks into your audience's attention. I recommend you make a habit of setting up response potential every single time you go to a break. Without fail.

In the next section, I'm going to show you techniques to automatically keep your audience thinking about your content, techniques that will probably generate questions from you.

But by the end of the next chapter, they'll all be answered.

Curiously, it all begins with me asking *you* some questions. Interested? Then read on.

* That technique to avoid the mid-afternoon slump I mentioned in the preceding section? Here it is, and it's especially helpful if you are often presenting or talking in public. Do this throughout the day and you'll be amazed at how your energy levels will remain high. Note: This is not nutritional advice, but based on my experience, and that of others who have adopted a similar regime.

The key is to keep hydrated, but not with water-only. Add a small amount (5-10% by volume) of diluted fruit or vegetable juice to your water. Use this throughout the day, and drink plenty.

If you ever used to suffer from a dry mouth when speaking, even though you drank a ton of water, or you avoided drinking a lot in case you had too many sudden urges to visit the bathroom, then this little trick is a lifesaver. I used to have both those issues: I drank a lot of water, but by the end of a day talking, I found my mouth felt as if it had been under a constant wash with too much water. And then there were those constant bathroom breaks.

By doing this trick with the water, the body seems to absorb it and hydrate far more effectively. I was told of the science behind it, but I won't share that here, I'd prefer to share what has worked well for me in practice. So well that I'm known for specifying the water and juice for my presenter table.

Be aware of stepping up the juice—you do not want to increase the amount of sugar in your fluid intake (actually you really want to minimize that), so use juices lower in sugar, and try to get down to that 5% level. Experiment with different juices and vegetable juices too. I was told it will even work with coca-cola, but I hate the stuff and couldn't bring myself to try it. Perhaps you will!

Let me know how it works for you—particularly when you're delivering a speech, or several speeches. It may just be the difference that makes the difference.

5.4 Can You Ask Your Audience A Rhetorical Question? Or, How Not To Sound Like A Politician

HERE'S A GREAT WAY TO make your talk super-interactive, drive audience engagement sky-high, and help vary the pace during your presentation.

If it helps, this is also a great technique for helping your audience take real ownership of your content, and for you to facilitate understanding, and removing the risk of delivering an info-dump.

What do you think could hook the minds of your audience like this?

Spot on. It's asking questions of your audience.

But why would we want to do this? Surely you are in danger of losing control—or worse, getting no response?

Yes, that is true, there's a tiny element of risk involved. But if you do it following my method, it's almost infallible. (I, of course, am not infallible. Only my techniques!)

The great thing about asking questions is that you *are* in control. When we're asked a question, our mind cannot help but try to answer it. Isn't that true?

For example, when you are browsing in a store, inevitably a salesperson will approach you, and after saying hello (if you're lucky), you're almost bound to be asked a question. Sadly, it's often a low-grade one: "*Can I help you?*" I currently live in Australia, and the best we seem to do is, "*Are you right there?*" Yes, I know. We're trying to change that. Some of the politest assistants are found in Europe, where you'll hear *Sir* this, and *Madam* that, as well as a very polite "*Hello, Sir.*" Then they'll wait before throwing questions at you.

Anyway ... back on track. Asking questions of your audience can be very helpful, even if you don't need an answer right there and then. Let's divide up the types and address why and how they are helpful, and look at some examples of usage.

The Rhetorical Question

Is this something that's overused or misused by politicians and media experts right now? You bet. My suspicion is that it's been reinvented by media and PR training companies as a way of helping deflect questions, implying knowledge of the subject, and taking control of the interview—by first asking the question themselves. (Or sometimes asking the question they wish had been asked!) A clever way to avoid being put on the spot.

Which is a shame, as in the right hands, it is a good technique to enhance audience engagement.

How does it work?

I'm glad you asked.

You simply pose a rhetorical question midway through your content. For example:

"We can surmise that elephants in the wild probably have a very similar behavior. Now, do we know that for sure? Of course not. But let me ..."

Whenever a question is asked, even rhetorical, our minds cannot help but be grabbed and engaged. It wants to search for the answer—just like those "Who Wants To Be A Millionaire?" shows. When watch a show like this, even if by accident when surfing channels, do you find yourself scanning the answers to see if you are right?

You'll notice in the example above ("... *that elephants in the wild* ...") that the question is phrased to invite a "yes or no" answer. This is called a "closed question." "Closed," in that it's unlikely to lead to much more than yes or no as a reply, thereby *closing* the answer.

You can also ask an *open* rhetorical question. How would that go, you ask?

Like this: *"Now that we have the data in from all our pipelines, we're able to conduct a comparative ROI analysis without worry of differences in local metrics. What do you think that shows? Exactly right. That we've been missing out on bulk wholesale opportunities all these years."*

Warning: Be very careful not to overdo rhetorical questions, or you risk coming across as a slick politician. As I've hinted, they tend to use them as throwaway lines to deflect real questions that could be posed, and appear to be (honestly) providing answers to the assembled media. For example:

"We've made huge dents in the positive social impact with these programs. Have we missed some people along the way? Of course we have ... etc and blah blah blah."

Fortunately it's pretty easy to avoid this: Make *your* rhetorical questions conversational and relevant, and don't overuse them.

Asking REAL Questions

It's possible to ask questions of almost any size audience, though it's far easier if your audience size is under a couple of hundred, and is an excellent way to stimulate interactivity and **Generative Learning** if your group numbers under twenty.

Why would you want to do this?

For many reasons:

- To check you've made your point correctly, or gotten your message across the way you wanted.
- To invite feedback and response.
- To stimulate debate.
- To pre-generate questions and/or responses prior to a session you have coming up.
- To help correctly contextualize the hierarchy of your next session (to help make the connections clear in your audiences' minds).
- To facilitate post-audience-activity debriefs, such as when they might return from an exercise or discussion among themselves.
- Any time you want to create more interactivity (games, quizzes, or just for the sake of the relationship with your audience).

Before I give you an example or two, some guidelines do apply. Remember that:

- It's almost always best to ask an open question.
- The exception to the above is when you *need* closure (*"Does anyone else need another example before we move on?"*).
- Make sure you use invitational and open body-language (I will cover presenter "body language" in detail in the following section. But for now, no crossed arms, clasped hands or frowns, please).
- Wait for responses.

- Even if you have asked a question, and nothing is forthcoming, this does not mean resistance from your audience. It may be that they are struggling to understand your question, or are still searching for an answer. Remember your audience moves at a different tempo to you, so give them plenty of time to respond. If necessary, re-ask your question from a different angle, or simply paraphrase it and ask again.

We'll review this by looking at some examples:

"How can you use the measurement system I just outlined to you?"

"What did you notice when you ran that first test?" [A question such as this is well suited to a post-***How frame*** activity—when your audience or training group returns from an activity.]

"Why does this make our first impressions so important?"

"What is your understanding of the 4-point licensing system so far? Let's get some feedback—who wants to go first?"

"Let me open by gathering some questions from you. What would you say are some of the most important elements of telephone-based customer service?"

As you can see by these questions, they tend to be more specific than general. A general question can be okay to start with, but I'd recommend that you get in the habit of drilling down. It forces your audience to search for a more relevant answer (to your topic), and you'll get higher quality responses as a result. Compare these two examples:

"How did you go?" The typical culturally-conditioned response? *"Good."* Or *"Okay, thanks."*

"How did you get on when you first examined the initial diagnosis? What did you notice first?"

The second example uses some "pre-frames," or "***hooks***," also in the form of a question, to help direct the response to drill down into a more specific answer. Far better.

Guidelines for responding to the answers

Beware of being critical or dismissive. Accept every answer you get—learn to roll with the punches, and learn to link anything to anything. Quite often you'll get left-field answers that don't have so much to do with your content, for example, imagine the presenter had just asked the example given above:

Presenter: *"How did you get on when you first examined the initial diagnosis? What did you notice first?"*

Audience member: *"When I looked at it first, John was making me laugh so much, I couldn't concentrate."*

(Presenter thinks privately: Thanks for sharing. But what did you really think? Throw me a bone here.)

Even if the response is lame, find a way to persist. If you dismiss responses, or appear fed up, your audience will refrain from giving them. Reward them all with a smile and a thank you, and link to something else, or re-ask the question.

Presenter: *"Yes, thanks for that, Lynn. Once you'd got a handle on it—and we'll have a word with John about his antics by the way—what did you discover?"*

Practice asking simple questions of your audience. You'd be surprised how often they enjoy getting involved. It often helps them comprehend or make sense of your content more deeply, and make sense of your speech—and that's a "good thing"!

"But, Robert," you ask. *"I feel great about asking the audience questions. It's when they ask me questions that I get stuck. Do you have any advice for me there?"*

What a great question. I thought you'd never ask.

How fortunate for us both that coming up next is an entire (and detailed) section on exactly that.

What good timing!

5.5 How To Handle Questions, The Right Way

HANDLING QUESTIONS FROM YOUR AUDIENCE is one of the most incredible ways to:

- Show your expertise;
- Deliver more compelling content (that you've deliberately held back for questions!);
- Build more rapport; reset everyone's attention span;
- Create some highly *Generative* "Ah-ha" moments, and
- Generally make your talk, speech, show or presentation way more interactive and interesting.

So why don't more speakers do it?

And why do those who do, often do it badly?

In the first case it's usually fear: Fear of loss of control; fear of not knowing the answer to the question; fear of drawing a blank.

In the second case, it's ignorance of a simple technique that I will teach you: A technique that engages, involves and delights your audiences. Not only that, using it will pretty much eradicate any of the fears I referred to above.

The lovely thing about this approach is that it really is a simple series of steps—a practical method—that is straightforward to follow and use. You do not have to be an experienced presenter to follow this structure, in fact it's probably much easier for those new to public speaking to follow and use, and make your own.

It's also highly *Generative*, and as you will likely recall, for your presentation to be *Generative* it means that your content can come alive in the minds of your audience; become a part of their own understanding; be an ongoing process of gaining understanding and awareness.

First I will outline all the steps of my process, then we'll deconstruct each step.

1. Make sure you have designed or have in mind a learning outcome (or just an outcome) for any formal question time.
2. Ask for questions correctly, using an open question. Note: You should not be asking, *"Are there any questions?"*
3. Listen carefully and show that the rest of the audience is included in this question.
4. Move to address the entire audience, if needed.
5. Repeat the question (sufficiently loud that the rest of the audience can hear you) by paraphrasing.
6. As you paraphrase, make sure you are addressing the entire audience again (not just the question-asker).

7.   Expand on the question, even if it seems to only require a simple "yes or no" answer. (In some contexts this is not appropriate, for example if someone asks a very simple question for clarification: "*Did you say we had ten minutes for this?*" In which case, a yes or no confirmation might be just fine.)

8.   Draw out an answer that involves a chunk up from your current topic-chunk. By this I mean making reference to the larger topic at hand: the context in which this question is answered.

9.   Include an example and/or story if possible.

10.   All of the above is still addressed to the entire audience.

11.   Summarize your response to the original question.

12.   Look back at the question-asker (you can name them in the next step, if you know their name).

13.   Confirm that you have answered their question. If not, repeat from Step 3.

14.   Ask for more questions, using more pre-framing if necessary. I'll show you how this works when we deconstruct these steps.

Let me step you through them one-by-one.

1. Have a learning outcome.

If you take the time to design your content well, you'll already be likely to have a good idea of the questions that might arise as a result. Accordingly, you'll also be able to define an outcome for this question and answer session: what your audience must have understood and taken away from your talk.

Many presenters (especially new ones) believe that the perfect speech is one where there are never any questions. But in so doing, they relinquish an opportunity to reinforce the content of their presentation by answering any question expertly and elegantly.

Remember the *4MAT* system that I introduced to you back in Chapter 3? If your session has a great deal of "*How?*" in it (ie with a practical hands-on application, or elements of your talk that are experiential), then an interactive "question and answer" session can form a significant part of your "*What If / What Else?*" frame. Make sure you have specifically structured your presentation to allow for this, and that you understand what questions are likely to surface from the activity. When you become skilled at this, you'll also start to use these question and answer sessions to provide links to your upcoming segment—something an audience loves.

Should you ever deliberately leave something out, in order to raise a question and stimulate interaction from your audience? I don't believe it's a smart tactic, unless you are totally transparent, and are using it with deliberate intent with your audience eg. "*I'm going to leave out an important element in this next segment, and I want you to tell me what you think it was at the end.*"

Most of the time, you'll have a good idea of typical questions that will be asked. So prepare for them.

2. Ask for questions correctly

Most speakers tend to ask for questions poorly, usually without warning (with no use of pre-framing or hooks), and using a closed question, for example: "*So. Are there any questions?*" or just, "*Any questions?*"

While this is fine if you *don't* want questions, it's absolutely the wrong thing to do if you *do* want them. You'll be standing there feeling silly, as the entire audience does an internal check: "*Did I have any questions? Let's see, yes or no ... mmm, no, not really.*" [cue return to blank look, or avoiding eye-contact]

There's another thing that tends to shut down questions, and that's "closed" body-language (or presenter physiology to be more accurate). If you stand there looking like you need to finish; ask "*Any questions?*" and clasp your hands together in front of you, then the message you're probably sending is, "*I don't want any questions, thank you.*"

Now remember, most of the time your audience is in a trance. So if you want questions, you'll need to wake them up. Which doesn't mean SHOUTING AT THEM!

How do we do this?

You do this by **pre-framing** and setting up questions. If you have designed your presentation well and you expect to answer questions at some point, then in most cases you will have framed this up at the beginning. That's your pre-framing. It can happen at other pre-determined times too such as directly after a break or when introducing a new segment; returning from an activity, or beginning a new day. The reason you need to set this up again just prior to taking questions is to get your audience's head around it—but what is even more important: you need to get your audience thinking about the questions by seeding some ideas. I call these **hooks**.

Hooks help you eliminate those moments when your entire audience goes quiet after you request questions. This is usually because the presenter has made a request of their audience that is too general; they don't know how to respond or search for an appropriate question. For example:

"Okay, it's time for questions. Who's first?"

While this may elicit a response, chances are, the audience will be on the back foot, caught unawares.

Here's an example of how to **pre-frame** using **hooks**, which I've placed in bold for you:

"So shortly we'll pause for some questions [that's the pre-frame]. *I've covered the topic in some depth, but I realize for some, this raises more questions. They could be in relation to* **our new bottle-design process**, *or specific to* **the new software** *we are testing, or perhaps you have questions about how we will* **change the structure of our teams** *and the* **continuation of self-managed quality control**. *We have about ten or fifteen minutes, so let's throw open the floor: what questions do you have?"*

These prompts set off internal searches in the mind of the audience member, and makes it easier for them to devise or remember a question they have.

They also help you direct the conversation, and facilitate your presentation outcomes.

That might seem a lot to think about, but believe me, it comes easily once you've seen how well it works. Here's the summary version:

1. Indicate that question time is coming up;
2. Seed some ideas about typical questions, usually taking a markedly different tonality to your recent dialog;
3. Move your body just as if you were still making your presentation, but adopting a different presenter "state" so your audience get that something different is about to happen;
4. Pause (to commence the question-asking process and allow your audience to rise to it).

You can see a lot of this is about audience "state management" which I'll be covering in even more depth later in Chapter 6, but for now, know that we have to bring your audience into an alert, question-asking state. This is what you are doing in your pre-framing. Sometimes, I'll even *pattern interrupt* my entire flow, for example, picking up and moving away the flipchart or whiteboard (or switching off the projector/monitor etc) then I'll move to a central spot on the stage, clap my hands and say, *"Right then!"* The marked change in my presenting style helps trigger a tangible change in the energy of the group.

3. Listen carefully and show that the rest of the audience is included in the question, and 4. Move to address the entire audience, if needed

You've probably seen this happen. Some presenters are drawn to the person asking the question like a moth to a flame. Imagine you're in the audience, all the way in the back, on the right. The question-asker is all the way at the front, on the left. The presenter takes a couple of steps towards the other person, starts talking more quietly and seems only to be talking to them. Do you find this infuriating too? The problem with this approach is that the rest of the audience can feel disregarded, ignored and completely cut out of proceedings. Some may be hard of hearing and are now totally lost as to what's going on.

Remember this: definitely look at and listen carefully to the question-asker. But equally important is to maintain rapport with everybody else. The trick is to look like you are happy to receive the question, and that you're going to answer it for everyone's benefit. This might mean nodding, and casting glances back to the rest of the audience. Try to avoid walking closer to the questioner. Keep your body open and facing the audience. You may need to adjust your stage position so you are not blocking any of the rest of the audience from the interaction, especially if the question-asker is directly in front of you. Adjust your position so you are inclusive of everyone.

There are exceptions of course: If you're asked a question, and you're already at the back of the room, behind your audience, you'll either want to wait until they turn their heads, or simply move to a position that is accessible to everyone's attention. In cases like this, it's polite to ask for permission to hold on while you get to the stage.

The audience need to "get" that you will listen carefully, and that you never appear to be impatient to answer; that you are "present" with the asker. This demonstrates professionalism and respect for your fellow human being, no matter what your official status as speaker.

5. Repeat the question (enough for the rest of the audience to hear you) by paraphrasing, and 6. As you paraphrase, make sure you are addressing the entire audience again (not just the question-asker)

Why is this so often neglected? How many times have you strained to hear a question being asked, and only heard the *answer* from the presenter, who is miked-up. A rookie mistake that's so easy to fix!

Get in the habit of paraphrasing the question first. However, the power of this is not just in making sure everyone heard the question, it's about control.

That's right, control.

Whoever asks the question has control. That's why it can feel uncomfortable as the speaker, waiting for questions. It can *feel* as if you no longer have control, even if you have your presentation meticulously planned.

But when you paraphrase the question back to your audience, who is asking it now?

Yes, you.

You have the reins again.

Even more helpful is this: who is having the question asked of them?

Correct. The audience. Who are at least attempting to answer this in their own head. Now the focus is off you, and back on the question. This can be a relief, and is usually enough to kick you back into "Presenter Mode" (and automatically extend your *Presenter Bubble*, of course).

Another advantage of this method is that by paraphrasing, you get the opportunity to re-frame the question being asked, and hopefully improving it so that it can be answered more *Generatively*. You can also *clarify* the question in your paraphrase. Note: Always maintain the integrity of the original question. I would never twist it to be more like the question I *wish* I'd been asked.

The person who had asked the question now feels like a real pro: you've taken their (important) question; rephrased it and repeated it to the entire audience, and taken it on ready to answer.

Two more things:

  A. You gain some time to think on your feet.
  B. It's now the second time you are hearing the question, and in a way, you are asking it of yourself as well. This is great "priming of the pump" for your unconscious mind.

7. Expand on the question, even if it seems to only require a simple "yes or no" answer

You may be tempted to answer a "yes/no" question with either yes or no. Don't. Of course there *is* a time and a place for the one word answer. For example: *"Please may I be excused to visit the bathroom?"* ... *"Well, that's a great question here from Michael. He'd like to know if there's any possibility that bathroom facilities are on hand, and that he might avail himself of them. Well, that reminds me of a time when ..."* LOL.

When you paraphrase the question, you may find it's possible to expand it out to include a longer overview of the context, to embrace what is being asked along with the issues at hand. The simple act of a thorough, detailed paraphrasing results in your audience feeling reassured of your authority on the subject and that it will be reflected in the rigor of your answer.

Another side effect of proper framing of question-*answering* is that it reinforces a positive question-*asking* culture. Everyone understands that asking questions is "a good thing."

It's a win-win-win. You get more time to frame up and respond; the process helps you to begin to explain the question to yourself, and helps your audience make solid connections back to the content that you're teaching.

8. Draw out an answer that involves a chunk up from your current topic-chunk, and 9. Include a story and/or example if possible, and 10. All of the above is still addressed to the entire audience

Now here's where you re-don your presenter hat. You've just been thrown an opportunity to speak ad-hoc about some aspect of your talk, so this is not an opportunity to squander. It's an opportunity to strut your stuff. Be the presenter and take up the mantle.

Start with **chunking UP**, ie to make it more relevant in a broader context, and review the key elements that will need to be considered in answering the question. Link back to any points you already made in your speech. Introduce a story and/or an example wherever possible. This helps bring you and your content to life, and helps your audience integrate what they might takeaway from your presentation. Make sure you don't keep looking back or nodding to the original question-asker. There's no need for that. Right now you're addressing the audience, and you are the professional public speaker, building rapport and engaging everyone.

11. Summarize your response to the original question

Occasionally an answer might take up to an hour, especially if the question and answer session accompanies a debrief in a multi-day long workshop. That might mean it's also harder for the audience to digest it because you may not have supporting visuals at hand. In any case, no matter how long the answer, if it's more than a few sentences, please take the time to summarize what has been said over the course of your response. Remember, it's human nature to zone in and out of attention. Never assume everyone can pay attention 100% of the time, even though they may want to know the answer to the question. Summarize the salient points.

Somewhat bizarrely, in my experience, audiences tend not to value Q & A sessions as much as the "content." This is precisely why you will always do better to take the question and turn it into a mini-presentation. That way you will always regain your audience. When you are closing your answer, experiment with adopting a more assertive stance and vocal tone. Not only does your state change signal the end of your answer but it helps zone-in anyone else ready to ask another question.

Now your original question-asker feels 100% taken care of. Not only have they been validated for asking an intelligent question, as is evidenced by your considered and thorough reply, but you've presented an entire discourse based on it; neatly summarized it and now, you're about to check in with them. Clarity for all is ensured and everyone else knows you'll treat their questions with the same respect and consideration. But you had better make sure your brilliance was warranted, and that you really did answer the question ...

12. Look back at the question-asker (name them, if you know their name), and 13. Confirm that you have answered their question. If not, repeat from Step 3

At the surface level, this is a matter of courtesy, but underlying this, there is a recognition that if you ask a question, you'll be regarded as important and you'll be cared for. Which helps encourage more people to ask questions, because they know they will not be ridiculed, no matter how "simple" the question might be.

And of course, if your answer has raised another question—from the same person, or another in the audience, then cycle back to Step 3, and repeat.

14. Ask for more questions (with more pre-framing if necessary)

Now you can sweep the rest of the audience back in, perhaps by moving to center stage, or by gazing around as you ask for more questions (again, using an open question, or simply, "*Who else has a question?*"). Again, if your response to the first or previous question was lengthy, you may wish to repeat some of the original pre-frames, or *hooks* to remind everyone of the context of your questions.

Here's what the entire process might look like:

"So in a couple of minutes, I'll be handling any questions you might have, in the meantime, let me outline the final steps in the preparation of this particular molecular assembly ..."

Finishes section. Presenter pauses, moves to central area of stage. Nods at audience.

"Now we have time for some questions—these could be in relation to my first session, where I presented the five formulas you should address in any molecular assembly, or perhaps you have a question related to how we use the micro-analysis spectrometer to zero in, or maybe just a general question about assemblies and their use in research. So ..."

Presenter pauses a moment.

"... what questions do you have?"

Notice this is an open question. It cannot be answered merely "yes or no," and forces each audience member to run an internal search (usually out of their own awareness) for a question. This can be difficult for someone in the audience to suddenly discover a question they'd like to ask, unless you've already given them some hooks to search with. Which, in this case, the presenter has done quite nicely with references to the topic. You only need three or four, and it will stimulate your audience perfectly.

Presenter stands assertively, hands open, palms forward, and looks around at the audience, allowing time for someone to formulate their question and (usually), raise a hand. Be prepared to pause, and remember, it may seem like it's taking longer than it really is.

Even if there's no obvious burning question, eventually the extroverts in the audience won't be able to bear the silence anymore and will ask a question ... which will begin an avalanche of more ... if you answer them the right way.

"Great, thanks Annie. Annie's question pertains to how we divide our assembly for analysis—should this be by periodic weights, or by using an arbitrary method. Or indeed, Annie, should it be completely random? It's a great question, and allows us to return to two things, the original research outcome, and the consistency of our rationale for the project ..."

The presenter has chunked up to the context for the question that will facilitate the answer (of course), and also broadened the application to the entire presentation and back to the audience.

"... which is why, given our current approach, I'd probably define the organization method before commencing the project. Unless of course, the outcome was specifically related to periodic table predictions."

The presenter looks over at Annie, or moves back across to be closer to where she sits.

"Does that answer your question, Annie? Great, thanks."

The presenter moves to center stage and straightens while he looks at the audience.

"Who else has a question?"

I hope you can see by now, it's a methodical process that has a sound basis for every step—and will win over your audiences like you wouldn't believe. It builds a huge amount of trust in your presenter-authority, and is a great way to make sure that interactivity is rewarded.

Wait.

Is that another question I see? Yes, you in the back. Go ahead please!

Ah. Great question from James. He'd like to know what the heck you do when you genuinely don't know the answer to the question. Should you just make one up? Promise to get back to them? Quietly creep off-stage?

Frankly, James, I have no idea!

Ha! Just kidding.

The real answer is tricky—it depends. One thing I do know, and that is, never make it up. You'll almost always be caught out.

But here's what you can do: be honest. [After paraphrasing so everyone hears the question] *"You know what, James, I actually have no idea! Who else would like to know the answer to this question?* [Turns to entire audience.] *Great. How about this then. I'll talk to my colleagues and get a definitive answer for you. I'll have that forwarded to Ms Anderson for you. How does that sound?* [Audience nods. You check in with James.] *Okay by you, James?"*

Job done.

Or ... if you have an easy or casual relationship with the audience, you can pose the question to the rest of audience:

"Great question, James, and one I frankly don't know the answer to right now. But chances are, someone here may. Let me ask: is anyone here able to answer James' question?"

Don't be tough on yourself. Not being able to answer a question every now and then won't be the death of you. It's unlikely, if you've prepared yourself using this book, that you'll be caught short, but if you are, you'll know exactly what to do.

Does that answer your question, James?

5.6 How To Handle Interruptions, Brilliantly

PICTURE THIS: YOU'RE JUST ABOUT to make a very sincere point, when a stack of chairs at the side of the room starts to sway perilously, distracting you, and definitely occupying the attention of the audience sitting close by. Those on the other side of the room start to rubber-neck, wondering what is going on.

Do you raise your voice, ignore the distraction and carry on?

Stop, and wait for your audience's attention to come back to you?

Rush over and start supporting the chairs?

Collapse into a nervous wreck?

The chairs by now are in serious distress, and just as someone in the audience is getting up to fix the imbalance, they fall to the floor with a resounding crash.

Luckily no one is injured, but it sure as heck has interrupted your speech.

How do we handle interruptions, distractions and the unexpected?

Outside of possibly physically harmful scenarios and emergencies (such as a toppling stack of chairs), the rule of thumb is simple: incorporate wherever possible, and act like it's all a part of the show. I know what you're thinking. How do you make a falling stack of chairs "part of the show"?

"Another solid premise comes tumbling down in a pile of disorder."

If the distraction or interruption is minor, then by all means ignore it. If someone's head pokes into the room and beckons an audience member out, it may be best to simply smile briefly at them and nod, but carry on with your sentence.

If the interruption is really pulling everyone's attention, you can ask to stop while it is handled. Or ask the people involved to take it outside.

Here's a question for you: What do you think happens to your *Presenter Bubble* anytime such a distraction occurs?

That's right, it tends to contract. So even before you resume, you'll want to first make sure you take the time—and breath—to expand your bubble back out. That will make it much easier to deal with whatever is going on.

To learn how to do this with ease, I strongly recommend you study improvisation techniques. Watching shows such as *"Whose Line Is It Anyway?"* is a marvelous education in how to incorporate anything thrown at you; a fundamental rule of improvisational comedy. Here's a not-safe-for-work starter: https://www.youtube.com/watch?v=tqR8131ae64) as these methods are based entirely around not knowing what is coming next, and having to *"accept the offer"* and respond to it.

I've mentioned *"accepting the offer"* before, as it's a fundamental skill that in my opinion underpins excellence in public speaking. Let's return to it again for another look.

There's a distinction made in improvisation ("improv") theater: when an improvised line is given to another actor, we determine whether the response was one that *blocked* or one that *accepted* the "offer" being made.

Person A: *"That's an interesting side of beef you have sticking out of your pocket!"*

Person B: *"No, that's not beef. It's a shoe."*

This is an example of *blocking*. It can even be funny (for a moment), but there is now nowhere for Person A to go because Person B has *blocked* their offer by making them wrong. We most commonly block others when we respond with, *"Yes, but ..."*

Contrast this with Person B now *accepting* the offer made:

Person A: *"That's an interesting side of beef you have sticking out of your pocket!"*

Person B: [Jumps in shock and tries to pull something out of her pocket.] *"Good grief! Where did that come from?"* [Looks at Person A suspiciously] *"You* put that there, didn't you?"

The conflict and disagreement is still there, but now Person B has *accepted* they did have a side of beef sticking out of their pocket, and has flipped the offer back in a re-blame to Person A.

The difference is in the flow of the conversation, and the level of rapport, *even when there is conflict.*

In any speech or presentation, when an audience member offers us something—a question, a comment, a joke even—your most useful response is to accept the offer, and do something with it.

The same recommendation applies for almost any unexpected occurrence, interruption, or unplanned event.

When you become proficient at this, you'll discover how much humor there is in being able to always "accept the offer," and your audience will never perceive you as being argumentative, even when you disagree with them (as you must, at times).

Never apologize

Unless you are hamming it up, never, ever apologize for any part of your presentation. It only directs attention where you don't want it.

And if you really have to apologize for something, make it short, sweet, and even funny if you can.

"I'm so sorry about the super-hard chairs. I had asked for the mildly torturous version just to keep you awake, but they delivered the full interrogation suite."

If something accidental happens (you drop your notes), or there's some issue with a slide (rows of tiny unreadable text), don't dwell on it. Just move on and find a way around it.

"Oops. One moment while I gather those up."

NOT: *"I'm so sorry! Oh gosh, how stupid of me, I'm such a klutz. I should have clipped them together. I'm really really sorry."*

Or: *"Hmmm. I must have asked the optician to make this slide. It's a bit hard to read isn't it? Let me draw your attention to the relevant parts with the laser-pointer*."*

NOT: *"Oh dear, that's way too small, I'm really really sorry about the small text, it's so hard to read. Don't worry, I'll get you all copies after my talk. We'll just have to squint."*

Take a leaf out of the theatrical actors' book: *"It's showtime, and the show must go on."*

* You'll discover later that I'm not too fond of laser-pointers. But this is one occasion where one could be useful.

So if someone arrives late (or several people arrive late), motion them to their seats while you're still talking to those who *did* manage to arrive on time ... and move on.

And occasionally, if you need to pause (while the fire drill siren goes off) ... then pause ... and move on.

Speaking of moving on ... shall we?

5.7 How To Flex The Funny Muscle Some More

BEING FUNNY IS A STATE of mind. End of story.

When you accept the offer and are *playful* with your audiences, the humor will become spontaneous.

Act out your stories, and occasionally ham them up ... and the humor will come.

Have some amusing stories up your sleeve; hone their delivery over time until you have your punchlines nailed ... and the humor will come.

You *don't* have to be a comedian. You *do* have to be prepared to be playful (if you want to be funnier).

Should you use jokes?

This is a matter of personal preference. In the main, I'd advise against it, but if you contacted any of my past clients, you'd discover I used plenty of them. Sometimes awful ones. But they were not my main modus operandi for being "funny," I was able to get away with this because I'd practiced being naturally cheeky, accepting the offer, and generally making sure my sessions were fun for participants.

Being "naturally funny" comes from relaxing; extending your **Presenter Bubble**; *accepting the offer*, being able to link anything to anything, and being willing to act the fool in front of others.

It's not about having the best joke or "lines." Most prepared jokes will fall flat, simply because you are not a professional comedian whose job it is to make these things work.

Concentrate on being a very playful version of yourself, and it will come.

And if it doesn't come easily, and you really want it to, I suggest you join a local improvisation group, and learn to flex your improv muscles; to build on anything from scratch and throw offers around; to take on board anything that's given to you and learn to make it funny.

And one more thing that is super-powerful: practice making *the movies in your head* to make things funny. It's the fastest way I know to introduce humor, and when quizzed, comedians say they do this. In short, you take the visuals you see in your head; twist, distort and change them until something looks funny.

I'll explain how to do this in a moment, but first let's answer the question: Why is this super-powerful? Why should you learn to construct humor visually?

To some extent, it's because when we're remembering jokes—and stories—we're trying to remember the exact words (the "lines"), which is very inefficient. In addition to this, if we're listening to someone else talk while we're also trying to remember words to say, the two audio tracks will compete for your attention. If you've ever been talking to someone on the phone and someone with you is also trying to talk to you, then you understand how difficult this can be. We can only pay attention to one stream of words at once: whether they are merely in our head or not.

Instead, try this: When someone is in front of you, and relating an incident or story, or asking a question, or you are listening in on an exchange as part of a group; let the movie in your head run riot. It's where our best creative imagination takes place, and we can process a huge amount of information in a very short time using imagery, especially moving images. If what the person (or persons) is saying starts to make pictures in your head, let that happen. You'll almost always be struck by some image that makes a unique left-field connection in your brain, and *boom*, you have something funny to offer, right there.

Note: If you've never paid any attention to "the movies in your head," or believed you don't have any, this might take some practice. We all have them, but for many, they've simply been out of awareness. You'll be amazed at how helpful it is for public speaking to develop this skill.

Keep a journal of funny stuff

One of my very first mentors in the corporate training world was a quite serious man ... off the "stage." But put him in front of a group, and he came to life as a funny man, brilliant teacher and full of great personal stories that he used to illustrate his points time and again. And the stories hardly ever seemed to be repeated.

I was curious to learn how he did this so effortlessly, so I embarked upon modeling his behavior, and grilled him about his routines.

Turns out, he was a keen observer of daily life, and loved to reflect on things—even what may have happened over the family breakfast table that morning.

For example, on the way to a speaking engagement, he'd think about his upcoming talk, and, remembering something that had happened that same morning—or earlier that week, or month—would draw a connection between the two.

Then what he did was both brilliantly simple and obvious, yet something I never did (until I learned it from him!). He wrote it down.

I asked him why he wrote it down, since he never seemed to refer to any paperwork when it came to these stories.

He grinned at me and said, "*Writing it down cements it for me. And in any case*"—he pulled a hardbound notebook out of his briefcase—"*I do refer to them. I collect them, in fact. Then I don't have to remember them for the next time.*"

Guess what I started doing from that day onward?

I recommend you do too.

You'll end up with a journal full of unique-to-you observations and "funnies" that you'll often remember in then moment, or look up to include in your next speech.

Occasionally of course, you'll use one of your most brilliant observations and it falls flat. It doesn't mean you should throw it out, it just means you may not have made the connection in a sensate enough manner, or that it wasn't made sufficiently strongly. Just review it, tweak it and try again.

Which is *my* cue to introduce a neat principle you should always follow ...

5.8 How Not To Have An Audience Like Oscar Wilde's

IN MY COMMUNICATION SKILLS CIRCLES, we have a saying that goes like this:

"The **meaning** of your communication, is the **response** you get."

For anyone who has to give a presentation or speech, this is a great philosophy to adopt.

You don't have to hold it as true, just as "useful."

Here's why.

Oscar Wilde was reputedly once asked how his play had fared (about a play that fell flat). His reply? "*My dear fellow, the play was a great success. Unfortunately the audience was a complete disaster.*" (I paraphrase the many versions of this found online. In fact Wilde probably never said this, though it was said *about him*, and the original idea of the quip came from George Bernard Shaw:

http://quoteinvestigator.com/2011/05/19/play-success/)

Obviously the reverse is true: whether our presentation or speech is a success or not is determined by the audience's response to it.

Your joke is only funny if people other than you laugh at it.

The *real meaning* of our communication is the *response* it generates.

Sometimes, a story you have related over and over before, and to great reception, falls flat. Your audience is giving you real-time feedback.

So don't blame them. Take a look at yourself: what did you do differently this time? What was different about the audience this time?

I often used to use a Michael Jackson song as a "call-in" song; one that signaled a return to our training session after a break.

I kept noticing that one of the more enthusiastic—and outspoken—of the group would often have a scowl on her face.

And the group members were not dancing in the way other groups often would, nor were the participants full of life at the start of the session.

I was soon to discover the reason for this. The woman I mentioned took me to one side, and very politely requested I swap the music. At the time (this was when Michael Jackson was still alive), there was a great deal of negative publicity about the singer, and the song I'd chosen was inadvertently generating negative vibes. The outspoken person had made it clear to everyone that she thought it was inappropriate, given the positive nature of our course content.

Me? I hadn't even considered it.

Needless to say, I changed the call-in song immediately. You'd have been amazed at the shift in energy of the group.

I actually chose to verbalize and discuss this issue at the time (with the permission of the lovely lady in question), as there was a real lesson to learn, relevant to the content I was teaching at the time.

When in doubt, incorporate.

Over time you will learn to **track** and **calibrate** your audiences with increasing efficiency: you'll come to know, or even intuitively pick up that something is wrong. You may not even know *exactly* what it is, but it will give you a chance to sharpen your ears; hang around at breaks; ask the organizer, or someone influential in the group if they too have noticed anything, or can shed any light.

Let me restate the opening principle: Your audience's reactions and responses *are* your presentation. Not what's on your slides or in your notes.

Knowing your audience—literally

Index Computations will give you an insight into your audience's beginning state, and allow you to plan. (Remember *Index Computations*? Review them in Chapter 3: A Crazily Named, But Key Design Tool)

But nothing works better than real life investigation. Who exactly makes up your audience? What kind of reaction and response can you expect?

There are a few ways you can ascertain this.

One of the best methods, but often one of the most difficult to gain agreement to carry out, is to run a full "needs analysis." This is beyond the scope of this book, but pretty much mandatory for designing any custom training program.

But if you do at least have the opportunity to *observe* the group you'll be speaking to beforehand, this is super-helpful. It may even be a breakfast meeting group you've attended regularly, and now it's your turn to make a presentation or a speech. You should already know the "culture" of your group; who the key influencers are; who the introverts and extroverts are; what they might resist or object to in your talk.

Then you can design appropriately.

So ask to go and observe your intended audience. Even informally if you can. Hang around their workplace. Stop people and ask them what it's like to work there. Maybe this is a different department to yours that you *have* to make a presentation to. Any prior knowledge will help equip you with the right anecdotes, the right approach to your design, and the most appropriate delivery style and format.

There is an excellent side-benefit to this work: you'll often be able to build rapport with some of your audience members before your presentation even begins. They'll already know you, and as a result, they'll most likely be a more friendly and willing audience member as a result. Remember—and use—their names, and you're already a star.

Which brings me to knowing your audience before your speech, and even knowing their names.

There is no better rapport-builder than knowing your audience's names before you even begin.

If you have under twenty participants, this is easily doable. All you need is a strategy for meeting them on arrival, and an attendee manifest.

Greet each person warmly on arrival (with a smile, already a rapport-builder), and ask for their name. Feel free to use the manifest in front of you to check against their name. Attendees will think it's for a roll-call. However, you know it's also so you can begin remembering their names.

My strategy is to look at my list, then look up and see if I can spot that person in the room (or outside the room). Then I imagine talking to them again, and using their name in my head a couple of times. Then, while beginning my "show," as everyone comes in and takes their seats, I count them off using their names—again in my head. Most times I am 100% correct.

It's not only such a great rapport builder, but when your audience realizes you've taken the time to learn each person's name, they increase their level of respect for you as a public speaker. Which is a great confidence-builder for *you*.

If you have a larger group (between twenty and seventy) then feel free to ask for names whenever someone asks a question, or volunteers information or an answer to a question of yours.

Funny story: I was giving a presentation to a group of lawyers on a Saturday morning. At one point early into it, I asked some questions of the group. One man kept giving me quite pointed responses, which I knew he was throwing out as bait, so I accepted his offer, grinned a lot, made fun of the responses (in a good-humored way that illustrated my point), and moved on.

Eventually, he offered up another idea, which this time I thought was excellent. I also thought it was about time I asked his name, which he told me (this is live, in front of the entire group of sixty during session).

I recognized the name. He was the CEO.

The group laughed at my reaction. (I hammed up a fake kow-towing response). It was a good moment, and one that I'm grateful I was able to incorporate, rather than be intimidated by.

You can bet I chose to use "Jim's"* idea wherever possible to reinforce the rest of my presentation.

* Not his real name. He's a high-powered lawyer for goodness' sake.

Managing More Detailed Reactions

Sometimes your audience's reactions actually do need managing: Either explicitly (where you need to split the audience up into subgroups, or decide a direction to go in), or implicitly (where you've picked up on something, and need more feedback).

Here's a trap for young players: avoid at all costs a "talk-fest" about what should happen next. You'll lose control, and your time will be eaten up managing twenty-four opinions in a group of twenty.

You need a couple of things up your sleeve:

1. Some efficient processes for collecting feedback.
2. A way to frame questions that helps weed out nay-sayers.

Efficient Processes

By "efficient processes," I mean mechanisms by which you can do things such as collect votes, estimate desires and group people accordingly. It sounds complex, but it isn't, and instead of spending forty minutes debating the next step (believe me, I've done that, and then some), you'll be done and dusted very quickly.

Here's a typical scenario. Imagine you have identified a need to review a particular point, as you sense from the audience's response that they may not have understood as well as you would have liked. You can ask, by a show of hands, how well they could apply, or articulate the idea just presented. For example:

- Arms held up fully vertical = very conversant: could teach it to someone else.
- Arms pointing fully downward = not confident that I "got it"
- Any variation from one to the other is on a sliding scale, as if the person's arm were a measuring pointer.

Very quickly you'll get a good visual sense of the proportions, and you'll be able to gauge their response to your question, without the need for counting.

If your assumption proved to be correct, given the audience response to your survey, then the next thing to do is ask a question. This next part is important to save you time. You must ask this question using a *negative* frame. Here's an example:

"*Is anyone* not *willing to spend some time adding more understanding to this principle? I'll give you some new tips and techniques to use.*"

Notice the "not" in there. It's far less likely in this scenario that someone will object, and even if they do, you've already got the rest of the group agreed on the next step, and time isn't wasted for twenty or more people to make their voices heard. All you now need to do is to deal with that one person—either clarify what you need to now, or gain agreement that it's okay to move on anyway because the majority are happy to do so. Note: I would never leave this hanging. I prefer to check in with anyone confused or not understanding something I've presented (later in the program, or after the presentation is over). Remember: *"The **meaning** of your communication, is the **response** you get."* This is my opportunity to learn what I can do better next time so *everyone* gets it.

Please note carefully: It's a trap to ask the question in the positive. If you say: *"Who'd be happy to go over this again?"* you are likely to be on the receiving end of many varied responses, or worse, inadvertently waste time by stimulating another long conversation with your group. With the question posed in the negative you'll be able to avoid vague answers such as *"Maybe. Sure. I'm okay with that. Don't know if I need it."*

Another method is to collect votes, for example:

You may need to work out which topics to focus on or review, from of a large number of topics already covered. Ask your group to fill out three separate PostIt notes, one for each of the three topics they want to prioritize (from the list that you've offered); or issue they wish to discuss.

These sticky notes become their "votes," and when tallied with the rest of the group's top three choices, will give you a clear understanding of where the group's needs are.

Here's how you do this:

- The entire group's PostIts are placed on a whiteboard/flipchart/wall, and any duplicates grouped together. The visual groupings of topics will give you a clear indication of the group's needs.
- If it's still not obvious which idea/issue received the most votes (by the number of PostIts submitted for each topic), then you can easily narrow down the group's requirements by extending the process. Tell your audience they are each allocated six points in total to use across three PostIts: The top PostIt/idea they vote for gets three points. The second highest priority on their list gets two. The lowest priority of the three receives one point. No more points are allowed.
- Have each person cast their points by writing the number (3, 2 or 1) on the PostIts already up on the board, for each of the three topics they have narrowed down. (You'll need to remove duplicates before doing this.)
- Ask an audience member to tally the points. Almost every time you'll have your priorities clearly identified.

Finally, you can split one larger group into smaller groups (up to five people per small group), and have each group either:

- Work on one issue/idea and present back.
- Present a case for which idea/issue to cover next, and why.

Either way, you've got the audience working with you to determine direction, as a result of their response, and from their subsequent decisions.

Using an efficient process is far better than a half-hour talk-fest where the loudest and most bullish people "win." I speak from the wounds of experience.

5.9 Drills

Before you present:

In Chapter 3 I showed you how to chunk your talk so that your audience experiences effortless learning. Take a look at the chunks in your presentation. What aspects of each chunk can you *layer into* another? This might mean a subtle revisit of a previous topic; building-on a topic (as I've done several times in this book); showing a new application of a previous topic chunk—the list is long. The idea is you *design in* the capacity for your audience to experience ah-ha moments when they experience some aspect of a particular content chunk again. By doing this, you deepen your skills in the planning and design of your presentation.

What pauses and / or response potential moments are there in your talk?

- Can you add more chances for your delivery to keep your audience informed "just-in-time"? Can you change slide bullets (I can't believe you're still using those old things!) into blind bullets;
- Try keeping flipcharts blank until you write on them, or just having a diagram drawn waiting for the text to be added;
- Structure pauses during your introduction to a topic for a build-up;
- Make sure your talk allows you to wait to distribute handouts or presenter resource materials until *after* your talk.

What questions have you introduced to help stimulate audience facilitation, interactivity and engagement?

Do you have an opportunity to take questions? If so, what is your learning outcome for this part of your presentation?

- Where will you need to lead your audience?
- Brainstorm a list of possible questions, and have a partner ask you them. Follow the process detailed in this chapter for answering the question(s), and ask your partner to check off each step.

Any time there is an interruption to your day, practice going with the flow. Practice **accepting the offer** by answering any amusing snip or throwaway comment from a co-worker or friend with "Yes ... and."

Design stories into your talk and/or examples that you know you can act out and make funny. Especially if these stories have characters you can act out, and dialog which you can speak.

Before standing up to speak:

Calibrate your audience while they are not watching you. What do you notice about them? Try to get a baseline **Audience State** calibration, that way, you'll be able to judge their reactions to *your* content more accurately for a post-speech debrief.

During your presentation:

Practice pausing before introducing something new ...

... and notice how it gives your audience time to assimilate, or to build anticipation.

Ask some questions (assuming audience size and available sound equipment is conducive to it) and notice how to get your audience engaged.

Take some questions and answer using the chunking method presented. Warning: It will take longer, so plan for this.

Try acting out more of your stories, and notice what gets a laugh.

Post-speech:

Jot down all the audience responses and reactions. Why do you think they reacted that way? What did you do that you could build on? What did you do that needs fine-tuning?

If you have a repetitive topic to deliver, note down any questions you were asked, and check how you can answer those more generatively next time. Also note if any questions should have been answered by your topic, if so, how can you pace out that question and make sure it's answered when you deliver next.

CHAPTER 6: DEALING WITH AUDIENCES, ENVIRONMENTS, PROPS, AND OWNING THE ROOM

6.1 Can You Have A Rigid Design And Still Be "In The Moment"?

WHAT'S THE ONE THING YOU should never give as a warm-up activity to a group of lawyers?

A debate.

Yes, that's right. Lawyers are used to arguing their case.

You're already familiar with the Saturday morning "professional development conference" that I ran for a firm of attorneys. I made the (potentially questionable!) decision at the start of the program to use an ice-breaker activity which was … a debate.

Oh my goodness. Did these guys ever stop? They well and truly let their hair down.

I wish I'd had a gavel to thump to shut them up at their allotted time. But it was funny.

The take home point for any presenter is this: It is the combination of your audience, the environment and their circumstance which dictates:

    A. Your initial design, and

    B. What you might change "in the moment" (for example, according to the presentation environment)

I'll give you a couple more examples to illustrate.

A change in the audience's *circumstance*

I had a short training program to deliver, which was designed to be quite upbeat, to a group of tele-sales staff. Together we were a good fit. Most of them already knew me and I knew their culture well.

The session involved seeking honest and serious feedback from the participants. The day before the training I was in a phone discussion with the senior manager coordinating the activity. She told me that over the weekend a much-loved, and fairly young manager of one of the teams had suddenly collapsed and passed away over the weekend, and many of the team were grieving.

Do you think this changes your approach and style, as a presenter to this group?

I think it is only human that it does, and that it should. It's part of your respect for the group.

For the record, the sessions went well, and personally I suspect what helped me was that I too, knew this man reasonably well, and had experienced similar shock at the news: therefore I had pre-existing empathy and rapport.

I cannot give you a formula for dealing with this type of situation, for I am not you, and you are not me. I would urge you to do your best to be authentic.

That was a change in the *audience's* circumstance.

A change in the *environment.*

I have re-organized rooms on so many occasions I've lost count. I've had to change the orientation of the space; taken away spurious and distracting furniture and audiovisual gear, and had to adapt spaces for my purposes. Most of the time these issues have necessitated many last minute changes. I learned to turn up early enough to handle the unforeseen, and most of the time I will have taken the time to visit the venue beforehand. I've learned to supply visual plans of how I want my room set up, which saves a huge amount of time explaining. If any re-arranging is needed, it's less extreme.

But one time, I had my room set up wonderfully—the night before no less. All the equipment was working as it should, and I really liked the room. My contact from the company—now a good friend—would be present at the back of the room to assist and observe.

The next day, the ten or so participants filed in bright and breezy, and we started. Or rather, I started the introduction. They were seated and I was miked up. If you think being miked up was overkill for a group this size, I'll tell you about using audiovisual gear later in this chapter, and why this can be a big help, even with small groups.

For some reason, every time I spoke, I kept getting put-off. The room was a long rectangle, and I was presenting down its length. The previous night, I'd tested my mike and small speaker system, set the volume and position, made sure I knew where the mike worked best on my clothing—but what had I missed?

There was a distinct echo to my voice—the kind that puts you off and makes you want to slow down. If you've ever had a similar echo on a phone call or Skype, you'll know what I mean. The amplified version of my voice was sailing down the length of the room ... and reflecting back at me from the solid wooden double-doors closing the conference room. None of the participants could hear it—it was accidentally and perfectly set up so it only echoed at *me*.

And all because I had tested my mike set up the night before ... with the doors *open*.

Lesson learned.

Curiously, it must have pushed my **Presenter Bubble** back, and since this was a presentation skills training program, one of the participants later that morning asked me (in front of the entire group) what had gone wrong, or what was different now, compared to the morning.

He had wondered if I had been nervous. I wasn't, and it was interesting that he'd perceived me this way. I told him what the issue was (quickly fixed at a convenient break by a simple change in the location of the loudspeaker), which in turn, triggered a discussion about whether audiovisual equipment was even necessary ...

Sometimes you have to explain *everything*!

How about I do that now?

6.2 How To Use Props, Visual Aids ... And Even Slides

SO FAR, EVERYTHING WE'VE REALLY talked about has been either about *you*, or *your audience*.

So many public speaking or presentation skills courses, manuals or books, will place undue importance on your equipment.

In the last section I gave an example where I had difficulties presenting because of an unforeseen problem with the set-up of my equipment. So it's not that your equipment is not important—it is—but unless your main focus is to handle *you* and *your relationship with your audience* correctly, then no amount of focus on your supporting equipment, fancy slides or super-duper multimedia production will help you. A chasm between the two will just show *you* up more and compromise your presentation and your message.

My recommendation is to make sure you could just as easily give your talk during a power outage, or without your slides. About the only thing I'm paranoid about losing are my presenter's running notes. I always have multiple copies of them and recommend you do the same too.

My view is that your equipment and props play a supporting role to *you*. Otherwise your audience might as well watch a video.

However, you can most certainly make sure that everything you do with your equipment, and use of props, lighting, audio etc will only *enhance* your speech.

Always ask yourself, *"How will this make my talk better?"* If you can't answer specifically, then leave it out.

Let's take a good look at what you can use, and how best to use it.

The Presenter's Best Friend

The Flipchart or Whiteboard, while ubiquitous, is a fabulous tool. Usurped these days (and quite unfortunately so) by the horrific "PowerPoint" or "Keynote" projection, the Flipchart is well worth considering as a great presentation tool if:

- You can ensure everyone in the audience can see it (I've attended four-day programs with 200 attendees where the only on-stage props were two flipcharts—used heavily—and a couple of tables with flowers. Simple, and effective).
- You want to build content organically (with or without audience interaction) as you go.
- You would like to keep each chart up on the wall, for you and your audience to refer to as you progress. (Hah! Try doing that with your fancy PowerPoint Slides.)

PowerPoint presentations can feel as if they are "set in stone" and do not easily allow any deviation from the planned framework, especially on-the-fly. Using Flipcharts (my preference) and Whiteboards, you can build your content organically. You also have the option to add responses from your audience onto the flipchart. This alone increases engagement and ownership: no one argues with their own ideas. If ownership and buy-in is important to you, then this is a powerful tool.

If you are taking responses from the audience and writing them up, you can do this two ways:

Take what is given, brainstorming style, where you write things up as offered.

Direct your audience to think about what you are likely to write next. Use a well-directed open question. For example: "*What else would you say is important when it comes to running an effective meeting?*" and facilitate your audience. Then when you write it up, it's virtually user-generated, and again, there's likely to be a lot more buy-in.

A few points to using flipcharts effectively:

- Use high-quality coated paper wherever possible, or at least low-porosity very white paper. This means your ink will stand out, and you won't be powering through permanent markers at a huge rate. Low quality papers absorb ink and are far more porous. Poor quality (yellowy and butcher style) paper also tends to transmit that poor quality to your presentation. It's worth paying extra for a crisp-white paper—colors will "pop" off the page, your presentation will look better and be more memorable.

- If you are able to lay your hands on refillable markers, this is well worthwhile. We re-ink our markers before each presentation, and after lunch. Your audience will always enjoy a bright and crisp flipchart! (Here are the best re-fillable markers I've ever used. They are a German brand called *Edding*. http://www.edding.com/professional-marking/products/permanent-markers/edding-500-permanent-marker/ You may have to search around online to find your local supplier.)

- Practice your handwriting. It does take a slightly different style to make things work on large flipcharts, but it can make a big difference to your professionalism.

Personally I think there's a lot to be said for the trusty flipchart. You don't have to darken the room, it's easily movable, the output can be pinned up around the room, you can still pre-prepare your content if you wish—partially for response potential, or in full. Just because they are handwritten and can be built organically does not mean they are unplanned or any less professional. The flipchart and easel is a truly interactive tool for smaller groups.

Projection: Slides (Decks) and Videos

The rule of thumb applies: does this media enhance your presentation? Could you do it without?

If you're in a large auditorium with more than 500 people, your choices are more limited. There is often the expectation that talks are accompanied by PowerPoint-driven slide shows (or slide-"decks," as they are sometimes called). I'd still make this your last resort. For example, take a look at any number of the famed "TED" talks. Here's a great place to start:
http://www.ted.com/playlists/171/the_most_popular_talks_of_all. So many powerful presentations *never use PowerPoint* (but they may use props!).

The first thing you'll need to know is whether there will be a camera trained on you, with the image projected to a larger screen (or two, either side of the stage). If there is, then you don't need slides. You can still use a flipchart—or two, one each side of the stage, or two placed side-by-side in the middle.

Slides *can* be effective for emphasizing authority. Whatever appears in print takes on an air of legitimacy. (Think of the internet.) Slide-decks also lend a more corporate and detached feel, if that's your aim.

Slides are perfect:

- For graphs.
- For high-impact visuals.
- For videos.

The problem is that 99% of all slides are poorly created, often using the basic templates provided in Microsoft or Apple's default suites.

Then to add insult to injury, the presenter simply adds bullet-points of text on each slide, and reads them out.

Aaarggghhhh! NEVER DO THAT!

Rules for slides:

- One idea per slide.
- Make each idea bold, unambiguous, clear.
- Wherever possible, make each slide image driven (a picture tells a thousand words).
- Diagrams and graphs must not contain tiny unreadable text. If you cannot do that, throw the slide out and use handouts instead.

The design and use of creative-driven slide-projections is beyond the scope of this book, but as I've mentioned before, I'd strongly recommend you get hold of a copy of Garr Reynolds' *"Presentation Zen."* You can find him at: http://www.presentationzen.com/ He'll teach you everything there is to know about using slides brilliantly (and has some excellent links to videos that have great examples of well-designed talks). Plus he's a TED presenter himself, so he knows the drill: get a succinct message across and make the presentation all about you, not your slides.

The same goes for video to some degree—if it doesn't enhance your presentation, then don't use it. Videos *can* be great as props. Use them to demonstrate something; to change your audience's state; to introduce humor. I have seen video compilations from the previous day's training sessions presented to huge hilarity.

But beware: humans are trained to go into a trance when they watch moving pictures. (It's a Pavlov's dog thing.) Anytime we watch a movie, go to the movie theater, watch TV, we tend to become more somnambulant. Have you ever fallen asleep watching TV or a DVD? I rest my case.

What that means is that you'll have to allow some time to wake your audience up after you've finished showing the video. That might mean bringing the lights back up; bringing up the energy of your performance; playing music; increasing your own volume and rhythm, sending them to an activity—even just having them stand up for a 30 second stretch where they are—any number of ways to "interrupt the pattern" and bring your audience out of their trance.

Microphones

For most informal speeches (weddings etc), you're not going to need one, but you may be offered a microphone.

For professional presentations directed at more than twenty participants, I'd wholeheartedly recommend getting miked up, especially if you're going to be doing this regularly. For a number of reasons, the most obvious being that you need to be heard.

Used correctly, the additional aural boost will stimulate your audience's attention and internal coding of your voice. Your voice should be under-amplified, rather than over-amplified. You want your voice to be supported; not to boom around the room.

You'll be able to speak more normally too. This has the added benefit of not only sounding more natural, but preventing the out-of-breath issue that can happen if you or your lungs are not super-fit. Constant use of your voice without a microphone can lead to a strained, higher-pitched and "weaker" voice, all of which will fight your presentation's effectiveness.

If you do a lot of public speaking, I would recommend investing in your own Lavalier-style microphone (a tie-clip style), preferably wireless, that you know works for you, and you know how best to wear.

It's not essential to use your own but it is certainly easier and less stressful. Just plug yourself into the audio system and you're ready to present.

Either way, you MUST run a sound-check before going live, or risk sounding terrible, and worse, ruining your presentation.

Many sound-desk operators tend to run the equalization too bright, and place too much emphasis on the higher pitched part of the spectrum. To prevent sudden howls of boomy feedback, they also tend to keep the bass down, which is fair enough, but in my experience, some of then take it too far.

I often find myself requesting less emphasis on the upper frequencies, and a litle more bass. Ideally you want a deeper, more chesty sound, especially when using tie-clip style mikes, to create the right responses in your audience. Your "aural projection" is as important as your visual projection. You wouldn't wear scruffy clothing to make an impact on your audience, and just because the audio is not visible, doesn't mean it has no influence. Think of it as how you "dress" your sound, and become familiar with what comprises good audio technique.

Tip: don't mount the Lavalier too high. You want to pick up the lower registers from your upper chest bones. Make sure it is angled towards your mouth, and doesn't move too much if you turn you head to one side (centrally located will always be better in this respect), and also make sure it has a good windshield (usually a small foam cap) to prevent the explosive noises than can come from your mouth or nose. These sounds are called "plosives" and "fricative consonants" (or sibilance) and comprise the tees, pees, kays, gees, bees, cees, esses and similar letters.

If you are using a handheld mike, then these are usually far better for the lower/deeper vocal registers, and you'll naturally sound more authoritative. Take care not to use a mike setting that booms out too loudly, and hold the microphone not in front of your mouth, but level with your chin (and close to it) for a better sound. If you struggle to maintain the right distance, or have a habit of waving the microphone around, it may help to rest the microphone on the front of your chin. Watch out for sudden exhales of air through the nose or mouth that can cause severe plosives. If you do encounter them, try lowering the microphone a few centimeters (an inch or so) and this will make all the difference. Handheld microphones are pretty straightforward, and you'll develop the techniques quickly if you use them on a regular basis. I recommend you run a sound-check, and make sure you know how to turn the thing on and off (if needed).

Lectern boom-style mikes. Yuk. I avoid them at all costs. Too boomy (pun intended!) and echoey, they also anchor you to one spot. They also require you to consistently angle your head in more-or-less one direction, and thereby restrict your ability to express yourself as easily as you could if you had complete freedom of movement. If you recall, I specifically mentioned the ability to move as being key to keeping your flow going, and avoiding the "blank mind." You can minimize the chances of this happening to you by avoiding being tethered to a lectern .

So as you can tell, I'd recommend not using them. Ask for it to be switched off, in case you do occasionally visit the lectern for your notes, or to drive a laptop or tablet. Having an additional live microphone suddenly in range can cause rapid escalation of feedback, or at the very least an unwanted change in the timbre, which could be off-putting. If you're a CEO who nearly always finds themselves placed behind a lectern at corporate functions, I suggest you ask for a Lavalier mike and move around the stage for greater authority. You are the CEO, after all.

All microphones take some practice, but learn to work them well and you'll find they can enhance your presentation, which is the golden rule. Ignore the need to learn about using them at your peril: a bad microphone set-up can destroy your presentation like nothing else. Bad sound can put you off—just like my own example before in the previous section, "Can You Have A Rigid Design And Still Be In The Moment?"

Laser Pointers

Please! Do you really need one of these?

If you already own one, I suggest you only use it for annoying the heck out of cats.

Most folks don't know how to use them, and forget that their sense of time is so distorted that what they thought was lingering on some key part of their slide with their pointer, was experienced by the audience as a fleeting race across the screen.

Then there are those that talk with their hands, now forgetting about the still-switched-on laser pointer, and wondering why audience members keep ducking for cover.

Work on being skilled enough to direct your audience's attention without the crutch of a pointer, and you'll have one less thing to worry about, and won't even encounter the fluttering, wobbly red things flashing over your screens.

What's that, you say, you need to point out something very small on the slide?

I refer you back to good slide design.

If you absolutely *have* to highlight something on your slide, then move to another slide that has the image/text in question magnified. Don't force your audience to play like cats with your new toy, and squint at something. Make it a rule: your props should always, or wherever possible, be easy for the audience to consume.

Stage Risers and Lecterns

Presenting from a "stage"—even if it's only a hired-in "riser"—does feel different. In the next section, we'll talk specifically about "knowing the room," but the stage riser has its own pros and cons.

For an audience of over sixty or seventy or so people, it's probably useful. I have had 120 in a room at banquet-style tables with no riser, and it was fine. I had the same group the next day in a more formal conference setting (still with banquet-style seating), with a proper stage setting, and that was fine too.

You'll just need to work the room a little differently if you are "up on stage." Most of us have a tendency to be "sided," or favor one side of the room over the other, and for some reason, stagework seems to emphasize this. Which means you'll need to work on balance: making sure you inhabit all areas of the stage.

Check the stage too—how to move on and off (gracefully!), and what noises, or even movements, it makes when you move. Especially if you are acting out a particularly dynamic story. Lots of creaks and bangs won't do you any favors.

You might find with stage-work, it is useful to have an assistant, or back of room spotter (who can also act as a coach and provide feedback). They can tell you how your stage-use is working, and help you correct, even in the moment.

Stages often come with lighting too. In fact, I usually request lighting for larger groups (there's a reason other than the obvious), so it's worth getting used to presenting under lights, as the force of the spotlights themselves can cause you to retract your **_Presenter Bubble_** (the solution for which is? Very simple of course. Expand it back out again). I'd always recommend some practice time in full-dress: miked up, and with full lighting. That way, you're already familiar.

That other reason for having bright lights in a larger group?

Shiny things.

We are attracted to bright shiny things. For an example, see your local supermarket's candy aisle. Lots of bright, shiny, metallic wrapping. Bright colors.

So when you have nice bright-white lighting on you, it can make you very visually appealing. Who wouldn't want that? Contrast that with dull, or dim lighting, and you'll get what I mean.

After all, who says, "We have a dim future ahead of us"?

Humans in general, and that includes your audience, associate brightness with positivity and success. So make sure you're well lit.

Lecterns

Oh come on. Really?

Unless you're a politician, media baron, high-flying CEO, or world-leader who feels the need to stay safe behind their protective lectern, then there's one rule: don't use them. Avoid a lectern like the plague. You'll be stuck behind it—which gives what impression? That your presentation is stuck.

You'll have to work *much* harder to influence the state of your audience, and to be animated.

You'll almost always be placed off to one side, which makes one side of your audience—the far side—harder to connect with, and may make it harder to present equally to all parts of the room.

You may even not be lit. Especially if there's a slide show running too. Heck, why not pull out your laser pointer while you're there. May as well commit all the sins at once.

Yep, you've worked it out. I don't like lecterns. They're a physical barrier to audience rapport, and to bringing your presentation to life. Many presenters can't help themselves, and hang on to the sides of the lectern (especially if nervous), which only forces them to be even more static.

Props and Open Loops

Now it's time for some fun, after having had to listen to all my complaints about PowerPoint, lecterns and pointers.

Because if there is one thing that can really enhance your talk, it's a good prop.

A prop (or several), can create interest, help build response potential, help demonstrate something, involve your audience, provide humor—the list is endless.

Even if your prop is a serious one, it can be made humorous.

I once saw Amanda Gore on stage talking about the health of our spine (among other things). She held up a mockup of human vertebrae stacked in a spine, showing its normal function. Then she let it flop over (melodramatically), showing what might happen if we don't look after our spinal health. The audience interpreted it in a risqué way (intentionally by Amanda Gore). Needless to say, it was a hilarious moment. (Amanda is a fabulous and funny presenter. Here she is *wearing* a prop in a funny clip about the differences between men and women: https://www.youtube.com/watch?v=sbF-4LOOC5c)

So what is a prop?

Simple. A prop is anything that supports your presentation or talk. Your flipchart is a prop. Your handouts are props. The way you dress is a prop.

Any of these can be made more creative: if it's a specific holiday period, perhaps you'd decorate your flipchart with holly, or tape small Easter eggs to your handouts.

But do these truly support your presentation?

Only in a trivial way. It doesn't mean you shouldn't do it, but don't let it detract from your speech.

Why? Because you're a pro-presenter! So I'm going to show you how to use props to *enhance* your talk.

You walk on "stage" holding a medium-sized pink teddy bear. You place it carefully on the table next to your whiteboard. You mention nothing about the bear, nor why it is there. You appear to forget about it, once you've placed it on the table.

What effect does this have on the audience? Where is their attention drawn?

We've now set up what we refer to as an "**open loop**": the audience may have had an expectation that you acknowledge the toy, or make some remark as you walked on, but you didn't. Now, some part of us needs closure. We must know! Your audience will unconsciously store mark this as something that still requires an answer. On the odd occasion, you'll stumble across someone for whom this is maddening, but that's okay, I'll show you how to handle that shortly.

Initially, your audience's attention may linger on the teddy bear. We can't help our curiosity! This means you'll have to work harder (initially) to pull their attention back to you, so you'll want to design in some strong elements, if you use a prop in this way.

At some point, for most of the audience, they'll forget about it. Assuming you have a compelling presentation.

But the open loop still exists.

You continue with your presentation for another hour.

Then just before the break, you summarize your session on our treatment of senility and our attitude to aging. You walk over and pick up the teddy bear and hold it in front of you.

You say, "*Just like this teddy bear was visible and possibly interesting to you when I began, after some time, like anything, it fades into the background once our attention is drawn away. It takes an effort to bring it back to our focus, and give it priority. This is why this program must be given a priority.*"

Now the open loop is not just about a toy, or a trivial story. It's helped you drive home a point from your speech.

You could have picked up the bear, and led into a personal story to close your presentation, where the soft toy was a prop from your tale. That would also have been excellent, and the open loop would close in a different way.

Props have a wonderful effect, they can help reset that attention span, and create clever open loops. But I'm sure you are thinking, "*What is the benefit of an open loop?*"

I thought you'd never ask.

Most presenters only focus their attention on the surface-level of their talk. You most certainly must get this right, but we can be smarter than that. The best books, the best movies, the most memorable plays, all have something extra that appeals. Or some hidden element that had us hooked.

Think about this idea: a hidden element that had us hooked.

Most likely this is out of our awareness, most of the time (and for some great stories, it may remain that way), yet when something happens in the book, movie or play, it triggers a series of connections in our minds where we recognize what *had* been happening, or we draw a conclusion about what *must have been happening* off-stage.

It adds richness to the story that goes beyond the surface-level entertainment factor.

This has to be done subtly. No one likes a murder-mystery where it's too easy to figure out "whodunit" early on. But equally, if it's a complete surprise, the story is extremely unsatisfying—there was never any way you could have worked it out. Foreshadowing—a form of an open loop—has to be carefully created in the right balance.

Done well, open loops reach down into your audience's unconscious processes and hook themselves there, until resolved.

This is why, if you accidentally create an open loop; for example you tell your audience you will handle a certain topic later on in your talk, but then you never complete it. You may have run out of time, or forgotten to "close the loop." Never fear, there will be those in the audience who have an uncanny ability to make unclosed open loops suddenly conscious, and you might hear this just before your grand-finale that will knock their socks off: "*Robert, you were going to explain why turtles prefer to mate in the shade?*"

(Hmmm. Did I really leave that bit out?)

Get in the habit of creating open loops in your presentations because they are a tremendous way to enhance your use of props. Still, the question remains, what do you do about that one person who is still being driven mad by the teddy bear? You can see them glancing at it from time-to-time, and then back to you, with a furrowed brow, quizzical expression, or even an angry scowl.

Open Loops, Nested Chunks and Stories

Early on in Section 2.2, "How To Make Any Speech Memorable," I suggested that stories could be interrupted, and another story or example could be related within the first story, *as long as you return to complete your first story.*

This is a more advanced technique, which also takes advantage of the open loop. Each story or example interrupted, starts an open loop.

When multiple stories are "nested" inside the initial story, this creates nested open loops. When these multiple open loops are all closed at ´nearly the same time—think of this as finishing the point of all your stories in rapid succession—the "ah-ha" effect on your audience is greatly multiplied.

Here's a visual interpretation of how nesting stories works below.

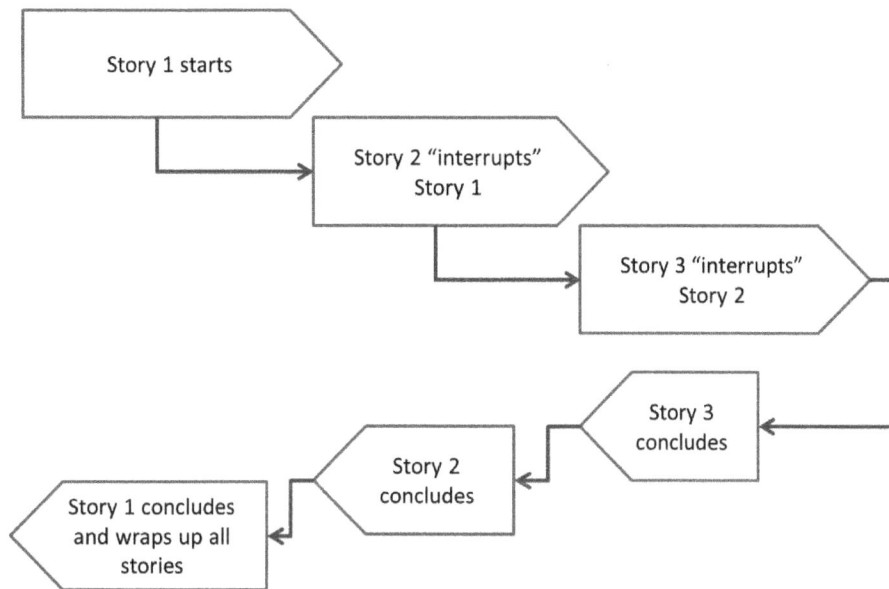

A map of nested stories

You can deliver nested open loops within chunks, stories—and of course with props—and the one thing they all require is careful design. What you must *avoid* is interrupting yourself and never closing the loops, so your planning of transitions and links is especially critical. As is reading your audience, because if loops are opened then you'll need to be super-aware of the attention your audience is paying you: there's a fine line between clever nested design and a big confusing mess of stories.

Tracking your Open Loops

Audience *calibration* is a key skill that you need in order to be a top shelf presenter. In your early stages as a public speaker, this will be harder, simply because your *7+/-2* attention stream is already full.

As you grow though, you'll start to be able to track how the audience's *Index Computations* are changing in real time.

You'll sense their discomfort.

You'll feel their excitement.

You'll track their anticipation.

And you'll spot that scowl, and possibly, very quickly, you'll rush to the teddy bear, pick it up and say, (while looking at the scowler), "*It's okay! I have a plan. All will be revealed.*"

And then let the new open loop fall away and out of general awareness until it is resolved.

In my experience, if you're following the *4MAT* system correctly, and are using the techniques outlined in this book, your audience—even if they are a relentless tracker of unclosed loops—will generally give you *permission* to continue.

They'll see you have a plan. They'll get that you're a professional, and that you wouldn't have done this just to be silly, or for good luck; that what you are doing is deliberate, and that there is a deeper meaning.

When you become skilled at this, you'll start to realize that you can open unconscious loops—when your audience thinks you've finished with a story or prop, but unbeknown to them you still have another use for it.

Perhaps the bear, now dismissed and back on the table, has more to say? You walk back to the toy and pick it up, looking fondly at your ever-smiling childhood friend.

"What I didn't tell you is that this soft toy is not just a prop. 'Timmy' has been with me since I was two years old. Most of have people, memories or items that in a way, become a part of us, or a part of our make-up. I believe that when we deliver this program well, it will become a part of every recipient's life; one that they will remember and treasure."

Remember: anything can be a prop. An item of clothing. A book you bring on, to read a passage from later. Even your own materials: your pen, your water. In the moment, that pen could turn into a prop as you're telling a story about when you wrote a really bad report about a colleague, if only to enhance the visuals.

Or do as I have sometimes done, when discussing a controversial topic, such as manipulation. Is it good or bad? *"I'm not sure,"* I say, moving to pick up my pen from the table and examining it. *"Is this pen good or bad?"* I look at the audience, who look baffled (mini open loop: they have no idea what I'm on about). I hold up the pen. *"A pen like this could be used to write beautiful prose."* I mime writing with the pen. *"Or it could be used to"*—I jump abruptly and hold the pen like a weapon, towards an imaginary adversary on stage—*"or stab someone's eye out!"* I make violent stabbing motions, then calm down and walk back to place the pen back on the table, resuming my previous state and turning back to the audience. I smooth my hair back into place. *"So what do you think? Is manipulation good or bad?"* (Closing the loop.)

The examples for using props are endless.

But the rule is clear: use them wisely to *enhance* your presentation and help make your points. And if you choose to use them to set up open loops, make sure you close them.

Speaking of which, I promised we'd talk all about "knowing your room."

6.3 A Critical Technique: But Don't Let Your Audience Catch You Doing It!

HERE'S A QUESTION FOR YOU: In which room are you most comfortable, or feel "at home"?

For most of us this might be the lounge room; a bedroom; an office, or workspace; a TV room; even the kitchen. It could well be a room *not* in our own house—your grandfather's study for example.

Now let's examine why this is so, before we take it into the context of any room in which you are presenting.

You feel comfortable, or feel "at home" because the room holds no surprises. It may also have pleasant memories and feelings triggered when you think of it, that tend to embrace you when you are in it, usually without any conscious awareness.

It's probably a room you know inside out. Every nook and cranny, right down to that mark on the carpet under the couch. How the doors open and close. Where the lights are. When the best daylight times are. How to stay warm. The most comfortable chair (and possibly the direction it should face!).

It's an easy space for you to be in. What's actually happening is that you have allowed your entire "bubble" to expand the space. You let yourself go.

Here's an important distinction: Most of the time, your intimate knowledge of this room is nowhere near your conscious mind. What portion of your *7+/-2* does it occupy?

Precisely none.

Contrast this with a room you are about to present in, or you've been invited to talk in as a public speaker.

- On many occasions this will be a room you've never seen before.
- If you have seen it before, you may not have been in it before.
- If you've been in it before, it may not have been as a speaker.
- If you've spoken in the room before, it may have been arranged differently for this occasion.
- If you've spoken many times in the room, it may still be differently arranged on this occasion.
- If you've spoken many times in this location, there might be something new about the room.

As you can see, I've just listed a few of the variables, the most likely of which are that:

    A. You've never presented, nor seen the room before

    B. You know the room, and may have been in it before, and possibly presented in it

    C. You present regularly in this room

We'll begin with scenario A., as it covers all the bases.

Your room at home occupies *none* of your precious **7+/-2** attention. It's a perfectly natural extension of your being. You don't think about it, because you don't have to. It just is. You can just be.

As a presenter, you want to reserve the entirety of your **7+/-2** attention to place on your talk, your audience, and your outcome. If you're new to this, then most of your attention will be on just getting it done with no disasters.

But if you are not familiar with the room, *some* of your attention is naturally going to be drawn by this.

Remember my example of the long rectangular room and the microphone echo? I was experienced enough to deal with it, and it still threw me. Probably because I thought I'd done everything I usually do to make myself familiar with the room. It happens sometimes.

Suppose a storm arrives just before your talk, and you have to close windows and turn on lights.

- Do you know how the windows operate?
- Do you know where the light switches are?
- Do you know how the lighting might affect your speech?

Or the reverse. You're about to show a video, and need to dim the lights. Where the heck is the switch? And if you find it, which one dims or turns off the lights at the front? What if you can't dim the lights, and the video is unwatchable?

All of this is easily solved, in almost all cases. And when you cannot, I'll tell you what to do—that's coming up later in this section.

I've heard that in some high-powered attorney training programs, they take the trainees to a real court of law when it is empty, so that they can familiarize themselves with the space.

But they don't just go in and stand around to "feel the atmosphere."

They are told to have the experience of sitting from every seat in the house. Including the judge's, jury's and from the witness stand.

- They are asked to strut in front of the jury's bench.
- To go to the back of the room, and plead their case.
- To bang on benches, slam doors, sit (dramatically) back down at their clients' table.
- To make entries and exits from all doors.
- To whisper, to shout, to sing; from anywhere in court.
- And to operate the lights, curtains, microphones: you name it.

Why go so far?

Because when these men and women are under the spotlight, they need their entire attention on defending their client and making the best case possible. If they're all of a sudden running dramatically to the opposite side of court to shout their point across, they don't want to be surprised by the wobbly floorboard and the strange reverberation from the nearby windows.

No. They should *expect* to find those things, because they already know the room (or type of room) well.

We have a saying for this, and that is: "***Owning the room.***"

And yes, you can do this without so much physical activity first, but that's for pros. I'll tell you how *you* can do this once we've covered the basics.

Here's what you need to know: The more familiarity you have with the room, the easier your presentation or speech is going to be. You need to make it *your* room, in the same way that the most comfortable space you have at home is your room (even if you share it with others).

And the best and fastest way to achieve this, is to do exactly what the trainee attorneys do. Get there early, or ask for access after hours, or the day before. Or, if it's a room at your workplace, just rock up when you know it's not in use.

Walk around the entire room. Go into the corners. Speak out loud and discover how differently your voice sounds from all parts of the room. Sit down in the participant chairs. Who has the best view? The worst?

How does the lighting work?

Will you need to pull a blind, because it will be too bright for some attendees? Or temporarily because you'll be using a PowerPoint presentation with tiny writing? (Of course it won't be with tiny writing, because you've been paying attention! LOL)

Will you have any chairs or equipment left over? Do you need *more* chairs?

Where will you put your notes/props/computer/tablet/water?

Where will you sit?

From which direction will you enter, if introduced?

What is the stage like? Ease of approach?

I think you get the idea. Make this room your own, as much as you can both mentally and physically, before you begin, and already your confidence will be increased.

This is even more crucial if your attendees know this room really *really* well. You might even sense this—that their own "bubbles" expand to fill the space. They could enter and simply take over, adjusting lighting, blinds and moving chairs—as they are used to doing. If you've not already taken the time to "***own the room***", this could throw you.

If you do ***own the room*** however, you're much more likely to gently and firmly request that it be set up the way you want it—and give instructions as to exactly how to do so. When you then go to the blinds and confidently rearrange them to how you want them, they will realize you've done your homework, and the level of respect will go up.

Before you've even started.

I also like to "zen" my rooms before starting. I'll give you a full explanation and instructions for "zenning" your room in the next section. I also consider this part of the ownership process. I love how the room feels once it's done, and for me, it creates that "***It's showtime!***" moment. I usually play music not only while I'm doing this, but also some specific songs once I'm done, to anchor *me* in the space. It's all part of *my* personal process to owning my space.

Now we should talk about those times where either you cannot check out the room beforehand, or there are people already there, and you can't exactly go running around shouting, "I'm just owning the space, okay?!"

Early on in Chapter 1, I introduced the concept of the "***Presenter Bubble***", and since then, I haven't stopped talking about it.

If there's one key skill that could underpin everything we do as public speakers, it's this one.

It will also be your savior when you come to a space you cannot "pre-own."

Here's my recommendation: *Before* you go on stage, expand your bubble to fill the entire room, and then some. If you don't get to actually be in the room before going on, then you'll need to expand your bubble *as you move to your presenting area*. This is something that is worth practicing until you can do it with confidence.

I'd also recommend you do what I do: have a trigger for your ***Presenter Identity*** that automatically kicks in your very best public speaker "state" and identity. If you need to, I suggest you review Chapter 1 in its entirety before going on to create your own trigger.

Here's what I do in addition, and before moving into the stage area or the front of the room. I like to imagine myself at the *back* of the room facing the front, and I see myself as a huge gentle giant, looking down at all my "kids" waiting for me to help them. I imagine myself to be super-tall and extending up to the ceiling; mighty yet unbreakable.

This seems to have the effect of completely removing any intimidation I had previously. If the audience are all highly experienced or very senior, that used to kickstart my nerves. Until I realized they were all human. And that they were like little kids inside. Perhaps we all are.

So find a great trigger. It could be some weird thing similar to mine. It might be something simple: a short phrase you utter to yourself. An image you have that makes you feel good. A memory of a time when you did something you never thought you would. Or several of those. Or *all* of these wrapped into one code word!

Whatever it is, I suggest you do it—and then every time you make a speech, or give a presentation—you stack onto it, as proof you can do this stuff: another metaphorical notch on your belt.

Own the space. And own what you're about to do with it*.

*Because sometimes, you'll raise eyebrows with your room setup requests ...

6.4 How To Set Up Your Room For Maximum Impact

WE CAN'T GET AWAY FROM it: the room setup will influence your audience, and to some degree, it will affect you. It depends on your style, and the outcome of your talk, but here are some typical setups and what I regard as their pros and cons.

Flipchart-driven presentation

Your flipchart will be central to your talk. In most cases that probably means it should be at or near the center of the stage, or not everyone will be able to see easily.

If you prefer a clear stage area, or if you also need to show videos or slides (or other co-presenters do), then you can also position your flipchart easels off to one side. Check that the people seated nearest to them can still see easily; that the angle is not too steep. Also if the easel is angled, check reflections from any overhead lights or spotlights are not appearing in any of the seating positions.

I will spend some time making sure my flipchart easel is well-lit, and that there are no shadows where, as a presenter, I will be badly lit from the audience's point of view. Both the presenter and the flipcharts have to be in optimal lighting.

My personal preference is two-fold: If I'm not using tables, I arrange the flipchart centrally, and the chairs in a gentle and unbroken semi-circle arc in front of it.

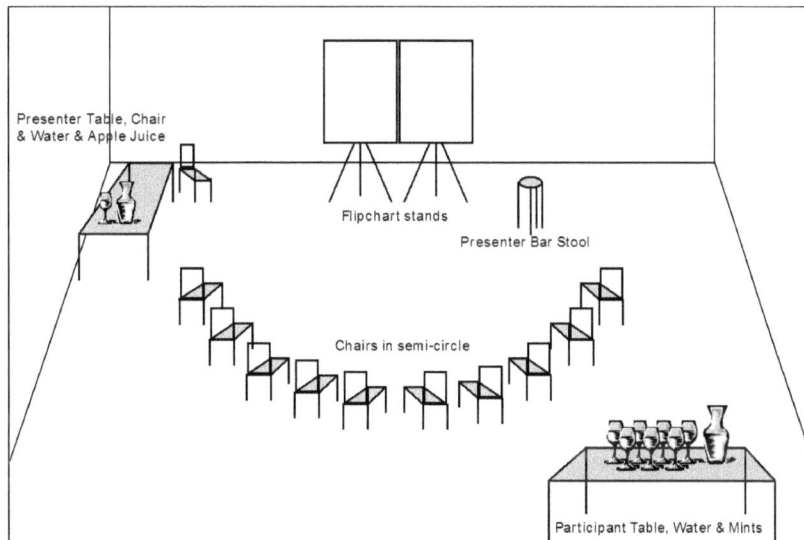

Presenter Table, Chair & Water & Apple Juice

Flipchart stands

Presenter Bar Stool

Chairs in semi-circle

Participant Table, Water & Mints

Any more than twenty or so chairs in the front row, and it does get tricky to use the flipchart for everyone, and you may need a different room set-up, or a stage, or screens with video on them showing what you are doing.

If your audience is larger, then arrange another rows of chairs also in a semi-circle behind the front row, with as many rows as you like going back, until the flipchart cannot be seen well, even if elevated. This could be as many as ten or twelve rows.

I usually make the center of the first row, and the central one or two chairs, six to seven strides from the flipchart. This does vary with your own height. I'm tall, and if the audience in my front row are too close, they might feel me towering over them, or worse, "projecting" past them.

Theater style

For a larger audience, you may even have to resort to a theater style pattern.

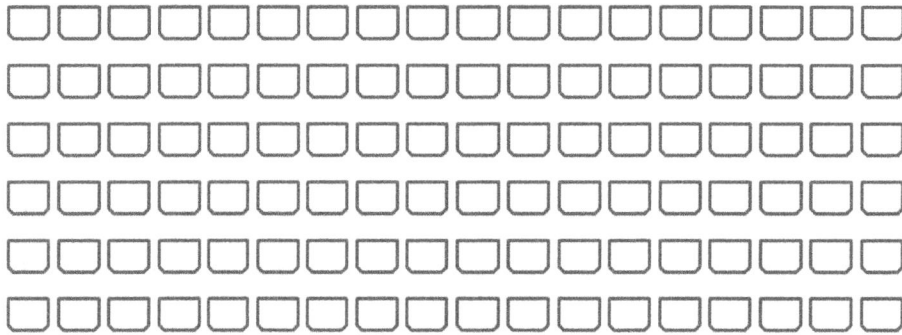

Theater style: no central aisle

Avoid splitting your audience down the center to create a left and right block. Instead, make the access aisles *between* the rows. If there is a central aisle, you'll just waste some of your presenter energy down the space. It can feel disconcerting; you'll find it harder, and you won't know why. Unless you know about the **Presenter Bubble** and projection, in which case, you *will* understand why. If you have a choice however, stack the cards in your favor and present to a block without a central aisle.

U-shapes, or hollow table

I recommend you avoid completely, and either refuse the job, or don't start until it's changed, the ubiquitous U-shape trestle tables.

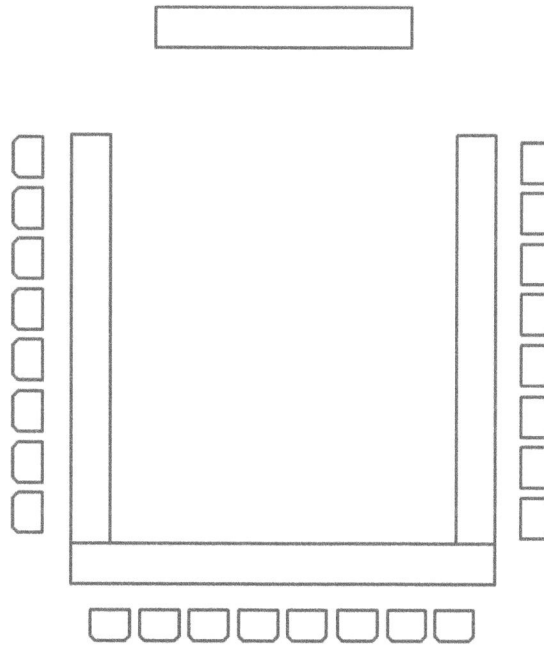

U-shape

The tables are already a barrier to rapport, and in the U-shape, you are the trapped victim, and you don't want to be that, trust me. It's a tough set up, and one to do your best never to encounter.

Banquet style

But maybe you do want tables (as do I sometimes, for workshops when there's a lot of planning and writing), or the tables are already a feature. Perhaps you are giving a breakfast talk, or a wedding speech—yes, I know, there's not much call for breaking out into planning groups at weddings ... In any case, the best set-up is the banquet set-up, with two or three places left without chairs at each round table, so everyone can see without continually twisting around.

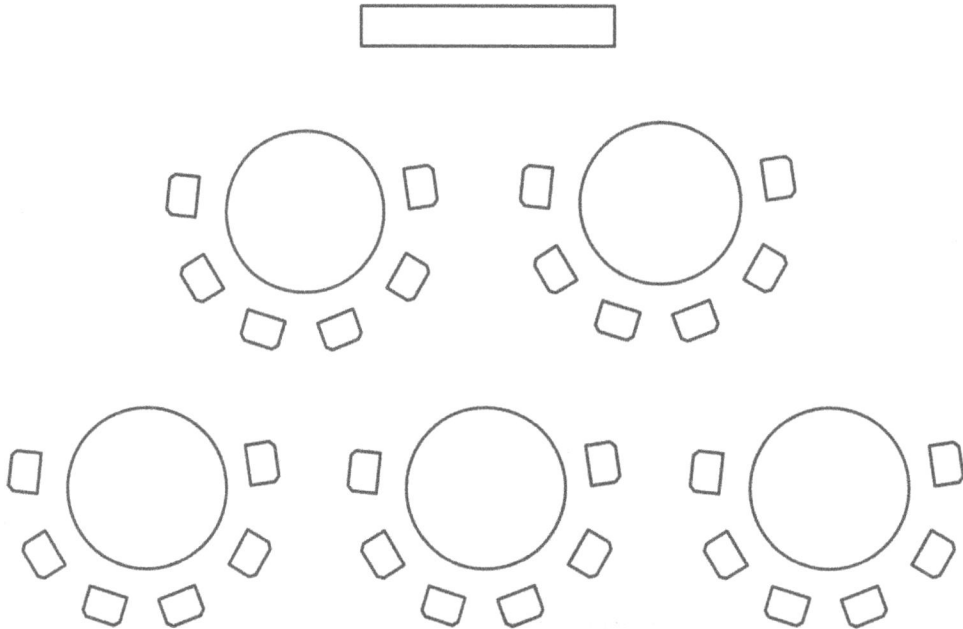

Open banquet style

This may not be possible at the breakfast or wedding scenario of course, but that's expected. In that situation, you can ask everyone to turn their chairs around so they are more comfortable. If you don't have round tables, then ask for two trestles put together side-by-side along their longest sides to make a wider, square-like table that participants can be seated around.

Conference and/or classroom style

I would also do my best to avoid rows of trestle tables (as is typical of a larger conference), often called classroom style.

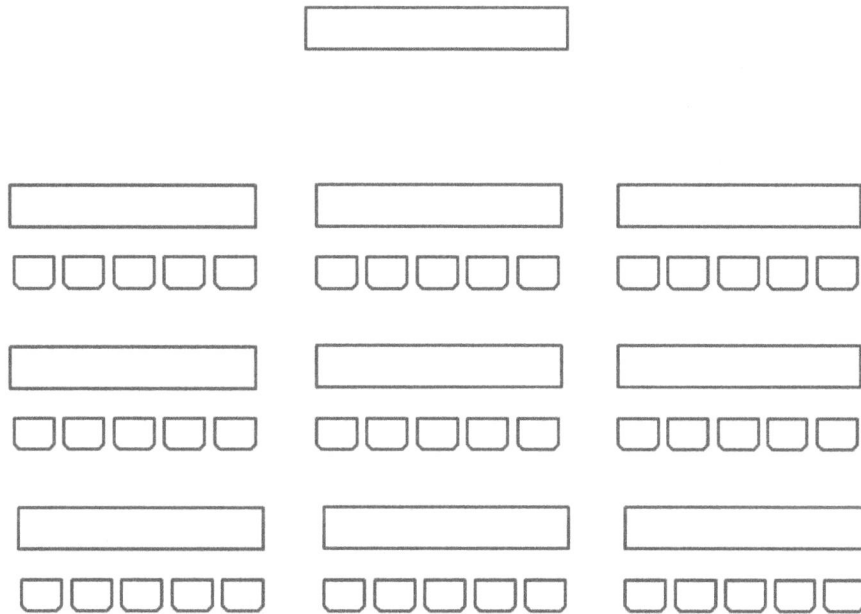

Classroom style

For the same reason as the U-shape, you'll find it harder to develop rapport, but more importantly, your audience will be much more limited in their interactivity *with each other*, and therefore in building audience-audience rapport. When you use the banquet set-up, you'll be able to watch the groups of six or eight at each table building rapport over time. They can also interact easily as an entire "team" or group of six if need be.

As always with room set-up, audience rapport (with you and with each other) is something you want your set-up to facilitate, not act as a barrier.

Larger groups and slide- or video-driven presentations

Over a couple of hundred attendees, and now you're in auditorium land, where the set-ups are harder to influence. Chairs may be immovable, and the stage is fixed.

One element you probably *do* have control over is the lighting; the equipment on the stage; the spurious objects that may be in the room, and any other distractions, right down to the things left on the stage by the previous speaker.

You should do a preliminary sweep of the room first (if possible), to determine what you will look like on stage, how the monitor screens look, and what the projection screen looks like from the back. If you haven't already designed your slides to be super-simple to digest, you might still have time to do this, when you realize how little will be easily seen from the back.

Make sure you request bright lighting for the stage, and also reasonably bright for the audience. Otherwise you risk triggering them to feel as if in a movie theater (cue the sleepy trance-like state), or simply in the dark (cue the nap). You want to do everything you can to help you audience maintain an awake state. Remember: you can design your presentation according to your venue. For larger groups and spaces make sure you include more changes in visuals, in your own performance state, introducing appropriate breaks—whatever you can do to influence your outcome, especially if you feel that the venue might work against you.

In a large venue like this, a sound-check is mandatory, so never pass up the opportunity. I have had a couple of occasions where I could not, and I was definitely aware of the increased discomfort and extra effort I had to put in to expanding my bubble to compensate for less than optimal audio conditions.

Also be aware that in a larger crowd and typical larger-sized venue, everything takes longer. They'll take longer to settle down, longer to be quiet before you to begin, longer to digest your content, and longer to react to most things outside of humor.

In a larger crowd, humor is your friend, as it is contagious. Large-audience humor is surprisingly fast at rapport-building. Imagine you've just arrived to hear a talk and you're seated somewhere in the audience. That guy you sat next to, that you thought was a bit offhand and unfriendly when you first sat down? Now you're both laughing your heads off, and his streaming eyes, and your knowing glance instantly break down the barriers. So even if you are not naturally funny, think about what you could include in your visuals to help break the ice, and maybe stimulate some ripples of rapport-building humor across your audience.

Check also that you are not being confined to a lectern, and preferably hook yourself up to a Lavalier or handheld microphone. Make sure you know what happens when you move across the stage, and that you are not suddenly blinded by the projector, nor covered in a mosaic of your own audiovisual presentation. Neither is good for you or your audience, who might see strange things appearing on your face. For example: that video of baboons you were showing? Unbeknownst to you, there's a baboon's backside appearing on your forehead, and you won't understand why your audience is suddenly in hysterics.

Lighting

I've mentioned this a few times over the course of the book, but getting yourself well-lit not only makes a difference to what your audience will be paying conscious attention to, but also it makes you appear crisper, brighter and well-defined. Which, if you think about it, makes an excellent metaphor for a successful presentation style: Crisper, brighter and well-defined.

Take the time to set up your lighting well, and you will find your audience will find it easier to take in what you have to say. Sounds silly, but once again, take a look at how the most successful high-street retailers use clever lighting to make us "want to buy." Contrast that with a shop with poor lighting, which can look closed. This is no different.

I once taught a three-day presentation skills program, where I had decided I was definitely uncomfortable with the hotel conference room lighting.

We'd got in the night before and set up the room. The carpet was dark red, and heavily patterned, so it didn't help "lighten" the mood, and it certainly absorbed the room's reflected light.

The lighting was all ceiling downlights (old-style incandescent with a narrow spread), leaving significant shadows around the room. I'd set up the two flipcharts under one downlight, so that was okay, but both myself and any audience members would tend to be either in or out of good lighting.

Since this was a presentation skills program, I wanted to get it right—because all of the attendees would at some point be presenting under the same conditions, in order to review their progress, provide coaching and give real-time audience feedback.

To fix the lighting issue, I'd ordered a spotlight to arrive and be ready in the room by 7:30am. The program was due to begin at nine.

The spotlight not only arrived much later than 7:30am (more like 8:30am), but it wasn't particularly great, so it took some time to set it up correctly, and we delayed beginning the program by a few minutes, until I was happy with it. I tend not to let participants in the room until we commence (usually with a pumped-up call-in song), so I'd already gone outside in the lobby to meet them, and to explain what we were doing.

Everything went fine after that. This was a great group, some of whom really took to heart the techniques I've outlined here, and totally revised their presentations since, and have gone on to rise up through the management ranks.

Towards the end of the morning of the third day, where we traditionally regroup for an extended "***What If***" session, one of the participants, a really sharp guy who didn't miss a trick, volunteered this gem:

"To be honest, Robert, when we were waiting to start on the first day, and you were fussing around with the lighting, I was thinking to myself, 'What kind of freakin' primadonna is this guy?', but you know, I can totally see not only why you went to the trouble to do that, but why something as simple as lighting could be the difference that makes the difference."

I love to hear comments like this. They are a good reminder that our environment *also* goes to make up the public speaking experience, and wherever you are in a position to influence it, you should do so.

One last point about lighting and presenting on a large fully-spotlit stage: You might find yourself peering up into the audience, and/or having a furrowed brow.

This is obviously not good for enhancing your speech. The problem is that we tend to avoid looking up to the back of the auditorium seating because it means we are squinting into the lights. I recommend you practice *relaxing your face* with all the lights on, and not just looking at the front row, but looking up and around. It's best to try to do this at the same time as the sound-check. Practice scanning the entire theater *and* speaking, under full lighting, and getting used to the lights. Address every seat. That way your mind already has an understanding of what it will feel like when you present for real and those seats are filled.

There's a reason the top theaters around the world have full dress rehearsals to get themselves ready: it leaves nothing to chance, and by the time it's "showtime," everything is familiar, because they've practiced it many times before. Similar to any high-stress event—fire-drills, emergency evacuations, accident and emergency admissions in hospitals—you'll be far more comfortable once you've run through in full-dress a few times.

Here's my philosophy for setting up your speaking room, whenever you are able to influence it in any small way. A practice that can be one of the ways you continue to up the ante on your level of professionalism, and make you really stand out from the crowd. I've already mentioned it once in the previous section ... and now I really think it's time to get into more detail.

Imagine you are taking some very important clients out to dinner. You've picked a fancy restaurant (or so you hear), and you're a little nervous as you meet your two clients at the entry, and escort them inside.

The front-of-house waiter seems a little harried, and shows you to your table. The place is full, but you expected that, given the reputation, and the fact that it's a premium destination.

You sit down together, and to your horror, you notice there are food scraps still on the tablecloth.

The cloth itself has seen better days, and you hope your clients, who are now engrossed in the menus, haven't noticed. Then you spot the food smears on the menu of the client in front of you. Her neatly manicured fingers are about to wipe through a particularly sticky patch, so you snatch the menu away. *"Here, have mine. That one is a little ... uh ... creased."* She gives you a strange look, but you force a smile.

Which quickly disappears when you see the state of the cutlery. It's untidily arranged, and there are water stains on almost all of the silverware.

Inside you are screaming.

What do you think the food would be like?

What would worry you about the food?

What are your first impressions?

Not good, I suspect.

I'll grant that I've chosen an extreme example for the sake of illustration, but it only takes one glaringly obvious thing to be out of place, and your mind's attention is drawn to anything that isn't right. Most of the time however, we're dealing with this at an *unconscious* level.

We call this "distracting the unconscious mind," which simply means that there are reasons why it's harder for someone to focus their *conscious* attention. They won't necessarily know why, because it's out of their awareness. If you've ever felt better about working after tidying your desk, office or house, you'll have experienced how this affects us.

Back to the restaurant: Contrast the previous experience with one where you walk in, are seated at an immaculately laid out table, with a fresh, crisp cloth and gleaming, perfectly aligned cutlery. The menus are so clean, they could have been printed just for you.

The smiling waiter delivers steaming hand towels, perfumed with rose water, and waits while you and you clients freshen up.

Your expectations about the standard of the food this time?

Probably way different.

Now let's take this into the speaking experience. You have to give a talk, and the tables are dirty, the chairs mis-aligned, your own presenter table is messy, the flipchart is tilted at an odd angle, and the room is dim.

Even if your content is scintillating, you're fighting an uphill battle. First impressions are not good, and there are so many things to distract the unconscious mind that you'll also be fighting the audience's competing attention. And before you say most people won't notice: I agree. You're right. But that doesn't mean it doesn't have an effect, or that you shouldn't fix it.

You bought this book to learn how to do this, not only with more ease and confidence, but hopefully to rise way above the average public speaker standards.

I recommend that you always do as I do, and those that I coach do … and that is to *always place attention on room set-up to an extremely high level of detail.*

I usually explain it's the level of detail we would expect from a silver-service restaurant: everything in its place, and nothing that shouldn't be there.

We call this: "*Zenning The Room.*"

Similar to a Japanese Zen Garden (see some great examples here: http://phototravels.net/kyoto/zen-gardens-index.html, http://en.wikipedia.org/wiki/Japanese_rock_garden), your room will work best when everything is perfectly set out, and in its right place. More to the point, anything spurious, *that does not need to be present for your talk and for the audience*, should be removed, wherever possible.

And in case you're wondering how far I go (and how far you should go), I have taken down paintings, and photos, removed phones from the front of the room, carted out extra chairs and tables, swapped wobbly chairs and dirty chairs, carefully straightened and tidied anything I could, asked the room's maintenance staff to replace non-working lights, taped down cords, and hidden anything unnecessary that couldn't be taken away.

It *is* going to an extraordinary extreme, but you *will* standout from the crowd, and it sends a clear (often unconscious) message: This guy is organized, meticulous, attends to detail, and is clearly ready. This is going to be good.

One thing you will need to pay attention to, especially for those who arrive early, is to make the room feel "friendly and welcoming." This may be necessary if you let your participants in the room before you begin, for example if they wish to deposit their belongings. When everything is so neatly arranged, some people may take it as "too perfect" or sterile-looking, or be frightened to disturb your arrangements.

You (and your team if you have them), can easily put this to bed and make it a non-issue in two ways:

1. Have some friendly music playing that is very informal. Soft jazz, or well-known easy-listening pop is fine. Not too loud, but just enough to take the edge off. Again, think like a restaurant: If you're the first in to the dining area, and it's immaculate, with all staff on stiff display, empty tables everywhere, and deadly silent … that could be off-putting, right?

   But if you are welcomed with a genuine smile, and there is soft music playing, then suddenly it's a welcoming place.

   You can do the same for your audience.

   One advantage of this is that you can then change the room "state" rapidly simply by starting your "call-in song"—a track that is loud, rhythmically different and upbeat, and obviously signals the start of something. If your attendees are still outside, then this, and your smile as the door opens to admit them, will have the desired effect.

2. Meet and greet your participants with a warm smile as they arrive in the lead up to your talk. As I mentioned before, it's also handy to find out their names—and even if you cannot learn everyone's name, it's still a huge rapport-building activity and will seed your audience with people you've already "met" by name. You'll need to plan to make time for this, and still have time for that last-minute glance at your notes, and to get into your *Presenter State*, but it's well worth the effort, and goes a long way toward relaxing *everyone*.

When you take care to make your environment inviting, as well as immaculately set up, you'll be blown away at how differently you are already perceived by your audiences.

This is one very clever way to start to influence your audience's "*state*." To find out why this is key, and what to do about it, all you have to do is proceed to the next section ...

6.5 What To Do When Your Audience Zones Out (Yes, They Will)

HAVE YOU EVER BEEN WATCHING a movie, caught yourself thinking about something else, and had to turn to the person next to you and ask them what happened?

Or had a similar experience reading a book, where you keep going back and re-reading the same paragraph or page?

It may not be anything to do with the quality of the movie or book.

It could very well be you are simply due for a "zone-out."

In simple terms, this has to do with personal energy states called "*uptime*" and "*downtime*."

An "*uptime*" state is when you are paying attention to everything, especially what you are currently doing. You might be very uptime when reversing a car into a tight spot. Any other distractions can be tricky. Try doing the same thing with the radio blasting away. Why should that be so hard? Because we've got all our senses dialed up for the highest level of sensitivity. Maybe our mind is telling us we should be able to listen for the slightest sound of a car fender scraping. Which still doesn't explain why the same thing happens—and by that, I mean the need to turn the loud radio down—when we're trying to read a map, or look at signs on the road.

A "*downtime*" state is more introspective. You find your mind wandering, or thinking about dinner, or wondering why that man over there is standing in the rain. You're easily distracted, and find it hard to concentrate.

In my opinion, we all need these moments of downtime. It's impossible to be fully-present for extended periods of time and maintain a consistently high quality of attention. It's why airline pilots rotate shifts, and why truck drivers are prevented from driving "all-nighters."

It's not just about physical exhaustion either. Take the movie example: We're often in a relaxed seating position, and the "zone-out moment" can happen even if you are fully alert and awake.

But before we divert into a discussion about the whys and wherefores of human psychology, we'll just assume that this is a normal fact of life.

Which means that your audiences will at times, need *downtime*.

In addition, and even when you are in full flight and regaling them with your best story ever, various members of your audience will plug into a downtime state. Not because of you, but because their mind and body requires it.

Luckily there are things we can do to make sure we take this into account, by managing our audience's "*state*."

Imagine the formal dinner has just concluded, and your turn on the podium has come. Some of your audience have clearly consumed a moderate amount of wine.

What is their propensity to zone out? Quite high, one would imagine.

So perhaps this is not the time to be presenting your discourse on the relative time-space issues affecting high-speed fiber-optic cables. (I have no idea if that exists. I made it up.)

But you can be humorous; risqué even. You can tell stories. You'll need good vocal variety and good pace.

To prevent your audience from going into a trance, you'll want to vary your pace; use the dramatic pause, and possibly have some props.

Avoid a twenty-slide PowerPoint show in the dark, unless you want to be the only one watching.

Right back in Chapter 3, we looked at *Index Computations*, which is simply a way of chunking your audience's "state."

So from a circumstantial point of view, if you know the venue, your audience, and the time of day you will be on stage, then you'll be able to design your talk to first meet, and then influence their beginning state.

But what about the downtime?

You need to assume that your audience will zone-out—on an individual basis—from time to time.

They'll also start to zone-out en-masse if you abuse natural physiological needs. For example, if:

- You run late when it's time for lunch.
- You go over time when it's time for morning tea or afternoon tea.
- You go over time when it's time for finishing for the day or shift, or when your audience would ordinarily be doing something else, such as picking up kids from school. Or anytime a routine is triggered.
- You go for too long without a bathroom break.
- You go for too long without a change in your delivery style.
- The chairs are uncomfortable to sit in for more than a few minutes at a time. (Yes, they make them like that. Why?)
- The air-conditioning is too cold.
- The room is too hot. (Yikes! That is *hard* work!)
- The lighting is dim.
- You've gone for too long without allowing your audience to drink (hydration).
- You're standing in the way of an alcoholic drink. (eg, at a conference, the bar is already open, and it's on the tab. Some attendees will have itchy feet.)

So how can you combat this?

First of all, you need to realize that *you* will be running on a totally different physiology. *You* might be hot, and *they* are cold. You are holding on for the bathroom because your adrenalin allows you to, but they are busting. Your sense of time is distorted, and theirs is not.

So you need to learn to **track**, and to **calibrate** your audience's **state** on the fly.

This is easier than it seems, mostly because you're doing it anyway.

What you need to do is to deliberately "read" how they are when you start, and while you are building rapport. That's your base state reading—a calibration.

Then, as you present, and certainly once you have more than a few speaking hours under your belt, you'll pick up clues.

- People squirming in their seats.
- Yawns.
- Fidgeting.
- Arranging papers.
- Looking around.
- Adjusting their seating positions.

Those are the obvious ones, but there are the individual non-verbals as well:

- Less responsiveness to your words and actions, especially in facial expressions.
- Blank faces, or flat expressions.
- Rubbing temples.
- Clearing throats (especially for hydration).

But you can design your presentation or talk to avoid this. And by being clever, you can introduce something different every twenty to thirty minutes to switch up the routine. This could be some interactivity; a video; a role-play; a story (if you don't tell many)—in fact anything different. Remember: humans track for difference. It's what keeps us from zoning-out and going downtime. So by introducing *difference*, you are influencing their *state*, in addition to what you have already designed into your talk.

Make sure you schedule regular breaks, or opportunities for comfort stops. I recommend ninety-minutes between bathroom breaks as a good rule of thumb.

Breaks can be simulated too: You can ask everyone to stand up and stretch if you really notice severe zoning-out. It makes no difference if it has happened because the air-con failed, or if it's the end of the day. Remember, most of the time, your state will be different to that of your audience. As you move and speak during your talk, your blood is circulating, your lungs are getting a workout, all of which helps you feel vital and active. By contrast, your audience is largely inactive and silent, and breathing is not likely to be deep or invigorating. So, have them move if you are speaking for longer than forty-five minutes at a time.

There is a myth perpetuated that we stop "learning" after fifty-minutes, and a break is critical to reset attention.

By now you probably realize this is perpetuated by people who have not studied *state* in enough detail. You *can* go longer than fifty minutes, easily, if you know how to keep your audience's state varied enough to stop the zoning out.

Never discount the adage: "*the mind goes numb at the same time as the bum.*" Some factors are as simple as physical discomfort. No matter how hard you try, if you're up against uncomfortable chairs, or your audience spends too long sitting, their suffering will win every time.

Then again, if the chairs are *too* comfortable ... it's a fine line to tread.

Your audience's state, and your introduction

Are you being introduced?

Did you supply the words for your introduction, and do they match the audience's state and your presentation outcomes? Or has your MC simply lifted your credentials from your online bio?

We've already discussed just how important those first thirty-seconds are—but what happens if they are delivered by someone else?

Yes, you are correct: your introduction is going to set the scene. You'll want to brief your introducer, or the MC, on what sort of "*state*" you'd like your audience to be in as you are welcomed on stage.

Mysterious?

Enigmatic?

A point of fame and/or authority?

Laughing?

Quiet and respectful?

Any of these and more can be requested. And don't think that just because you have a sobering story to start with that your intro should not be upbeat. That may be a part of your design—

Wait.

Your introduction *is* an integral part of your design, even if you're not the one delivering it. So be planned and thorough in how you would like that to happen. It can make such a huge difference in establishing you and your speech—and the best part is that, because it's being spoken by a third-party, it's often more believable.

For example: It's hard to stand on stage and say, *"I am the world's leading authority on the use of composite and laminated woods,"* and not have some people in your audience disbelieving or "mismatching" your claim, even if their cynicism is outside their awareness.

But when someone else says it, it's okay.

Assuming they do it well, of course. However, what do you do if your third-party intro is lousy?

You need to remember *you* are the star. Feel free to begin with another intro. *"Thanks, David. I should add that ..."*

You may also wish to do something quite quickly to distance yourself from the **state** they may have left the audience in. Remember, you are the presenter, you have control, so take it. You don't need to—and shouldn't—live with a bad introduction!

Here's a valuable tip that will help you distance yourself from a poor introduction: don't start by standing in the same physical spot on the stage where the person introducing you was standing. That way the audience are already *physically disassociating you* from your introducer *spatially*, which creates an unconscious expectation of difference.

In the same way, you might choose to be quite different vocally—to create a strong "contextual marker*" that your introduction is behind us, and it's now time for the real show.

* What is a "contextual marker"? Any shift in state or circumstance that denotes the difference between one context (or situation) and another. For example, if you've ever changed out of your work gear and into casual clothes at the end of a work day, this often signifies "the end of work." Or a family-room table changes to become "set for dinner." Or when you fire up your "call-in song" to flag the start of a session. Or when the lights go down in the theater to signify the play is commencing. All these changes dictate a change in *contextual state* to your unconscious mind.

When it comes to introductions, set your context strongly: Use your energy and influence; build rapport; pace and lead your audience to where your talk is taking them, and your introduction will be long forgotten.

Unlike you.

6.6 How Not To Address An Audience

WE KEEP TALKING ABOUT "THE AUDIENCE" as if it were a thing by itself. But an "audience" is a collection of individuals, so how can it have its own properties?

In my experience, it's easiest to break your audience sizes into two different types:

- Less than twenty or thirty
- More than twenty or thirty

When you have below twenty or thirty people in your audience, you'll still find it easy to address individuals by name, and the "crowd" doesn't seem to exhibit any real crowd behavior. Note: You can still easily address individuals by name in much larger groups—up to 200 or more—but it takes more effort.

Once your audience starts to grow in size, past thirty or more, you'll potentially see some crowd-like behaviors, and also you'll need to make allowances for longer time frames if you have much activity.

Larger audiences may:

- Take longer to warm up;
- Be very quick to warm up if you hit the right sweet spot;
- Take longer to get to and fro breaks; activity areas; forming subgroups, and almost any other organizational task;
- Pick up on hostility—or any audience reaction—and allow social proof to help it spread ("*Gee, if they think that, maybe I better join them!*");
- Take on a life of their own; back hecklers; cluster together in cliques; demonstrate competition between sub-groups of the audience ... you name it.

All of which takes more effort to control. Fortunately we have some tools that will make a big difference and help our audience *feel* as if you are speaking to each and every one of them, no matter how they behave.

Because, while it's true that an audience over twenty or so people may start to exhibit group behavior, one thing that sets a great public speaker apart, is their ability to communicate directly with each person, while addressing a group.

"*I felt like she was speaking to me!*"

"*He really made a lot of sense.*"

"*Didn't you just die when she told you about her son's first day at school?*"

Each person in your audience is exactly that ... a *person*.

Someone with their own hopes and aspirations; their own fears and issues; their own ups and downs, bumps and scrapes in life.

The more your speech can appeal to that one person, the more impact you will have. Every speech, every talk, every presentation, should be given as if to one person alone.

Just imagine you are presenting your talk to a friend, or supportive work-colleague.

How would that change your language? Your expressions? (Both your physical expressions and your spoken phrases.)

Practice delivering your speech, not to an audience, but to one human being.

In that situation, would you ever say something such as *"You guys ..."*?

Would you talk in general terms? Would you say, *"I'm sure you people understand ..."*, or *"When everyone here adopts this ..."*, or *"Employees must take responsibility for ..."*

Don't inadvertently turn us into a group of sheep, just because you used collective terms. Speak as if to one person. *"You may not have heard this before ..."*, *"If you haven't tried this before ..."*, *"I'd like you to think about it this way ..."*, *"You must assume responsibility for ..."*

And look individuals in the eye. No matter how big your group, we all *feel* it when you do that. Don't stare them out, and don't try to sweep across everyone. Just linger every now and then, and you too will *feel* as if you are speaking to a real person. Not to "an audience."

In turn, your audiences will experience you as natural and relatable.

Even if you forget what's coming next.

6.7 Drills

Before you present:

What environment are you presenting in? Can you check it out beforehand? If so, what will be the pros and cons? Make an extensive list. What things in the speaking environment can you take advantage of, or incorporate? What should you remove? Tape down? Move to make less visible/invisible? What switches and controls are in the room and how do you use them?

What contingency plans might you need to design into your talk? For example, if you need to go outside for an activity, but it's raining. Or if less people show up than you had set chairs out for? Tip: Set out exactly or less then you expect, and have a few spare chairs with easy access of to the side. Having assistants in the room will help enormously.

What will you do if the microphone stops working?

What will you do if yours is a speech likely to be heckled?

If using a flipchart with easel and paper, practice your handwriting, and on the very easel you'll be using. They all vary in stability. View it from a distance—preferably from the same distance as the audience member who is furthest away—make sure it is legible and looks professional. Many of us tend to write uphill or downhill when writing close up and larger on a board. Tip: If you need to build a diagram on the flipchart, or need to build up points you are speaking to, you can pre-draw or pre-write them smaller, using a soft pencil. You can even draw the full skeleton-outline of the diagram (or parts of it). Your audience will not be able to see any of this from their vantage point.

Design a presentation without slides, or, using slides but with no text. Practice this with a partner.

Run a sound check, at normal presentation volumes, whether you are using audio-visual equipment or not. Check if there are any echoes, or, if using a microphone, any areas where you should *not* stand due to acoustic feedback (screeching). Have the sound engineer test the position of your mic if clipped to your clothes, as this can change the sound a lot. Ideally have it closer to the top of your sternum for bone conduction of the lower frequencies. Have them reduce the sibilance (reduce the volume of some or all of the higher frequencies), and boost the lower end. Many sound engineers prefer it the other way around (less potential for boomy feedback), and also make your microphone too loud, so have someone you trust in the sound-check audience to confirm. You'll have no idea, since you are speaking. Make sure you test at normal speaking volumes—especially if you know you'll be raising your voice from time to time. Practice some or all of your introduction and don't use *"Testing one, two, one, two, testing,"* as your only check.

If you are going to be using a handheld microphone for the first time, practice speaking while *not* waving it around—in other words, practice keeping it closer to your face. But remember that the best place to position your microphone is not right in front of your mouth, otherwise you'll get an amplification of those "plosive" sounds. Position the mike at the chin, even rest it there. Many inexperienced speakers forget they have it in their hand and talk while it's pointed elsewhere, or get carried away with gestures.

Using a laser pointer? Put it on the ground and jump on it until it is smashed into pieces. Now move on. Nothing more to see here folks.

Using a lectern? Demand or order in a roving mic (Lavalier or handheld).

Props: Review your presentation design. What props would enhance your content? How could you use them to introduce open loops (if you wish)?

Know your room beforehand whenever you have the chance. Sit on the chairs from different points of view, go to the back, step up on the stage, speak out loud, use the doors (do they squeak?), check the lights (are all the globes functional? Anything that will cause glare for the audience?), check the natural light and adjust blinds if the sun is too strong.

If an assistant or engineer is supporting you, make sure your signals to and from each other are crystal clear, for example if you require any changes in lighting during your talk. What will the signal or cue for this be?

If you cannot get into the room prior to your speech, make sure you survey it well while waiting to speak. And if you cannot get any access beforehand ... your **Presenter Bubble** is your friend!

How will your room be set up? How do you *want* it set up? If you have plenty of access beforehand, practice **zenning** your room, then sitting in it as an audience member. How does this affect your experience of the room?

If you will be using music, plan out specific tracks, and test using them in the room (for adjustments of volume and cueing issues). If you have an audio engineer present, you'll need to practice this with them several times; have a playlist, and at the very least have some pre-agreed signals for start/stop and volume up/down.

Does your presentation include long periods of time where the audience will be in the same state? For example, if they are seated for over thirty minutes while you talk. How can you vary your presentation delivery so that their state is influenced? Can you design in activities that will break it up? Questions you can ask? To help break up a lengthy discourse, are there changes you can make to your media, or could you pass around a prop, demo or mockup, or some handouts?

Before standing up to speak:

If you could not get free access to the room beforehand, take much more deliberation over getting your **Presenter Bubble** working flawlessly, it will help reduce the "newness" of the space to your senses. Remember to tell yourself: "*I own this room!*"

During your presentation:

As you become more experienced, force yourself to track your audience's physiological state. Are they fidgeting around? Yawning? This doesn't necessarily mean they are bored, it might mean they need to move and get some blood flowing around their body. If you notice this while presenting, do something to shift the state—have them stand up and stretch for example; or introduce an on-the-fly activity ("*Tell the person on your left three things you have taken away so far, and ask them what they have gained*"). Note: If this is happening to you a lot, then I refer you back to your design and ask you to reconsider how you are approaching it. I'd also request feedback from a trusted audience member about your deliver—perhaps your vocal variety is not as varied as it might be, or perhaps you are only using one part of the stage, and not creating enough visual interest. Or perhaps you're still reading out those dratted slides!

Post-speech:

What takeaways do you have from this session? How did the environment help or hinder you? Would you use the same room setup again? How would you change the audiovisuals? Your design? The use of breaks to help shift state?

CHAPTER 7: WHAT TO MEMORIZE AND HOW TO USE YOUR PRESENTER NOTES

7.1 Your Audience Doesn't Care About What Happens On The Inside

WE'RE NEARING THE END OF our journey together in this book, and it's time to assemble all the pieces we've deconstructed, and put them together to create one "super-presenter."

Your goal should be to not only feel comfortable and confident, but to *appear* that way to your audience.

I would consistently find when coaching public speakers that the following things would happen:

Immediately after an excellent presentation, the presenter would metaphorically wipe sweat from their brow, and often drop their physiology, as if to communicate one giant, *"phew, I'm glad that's over!"*

When asked to debrief their own talk, they would immediately focus on everything they did wrong; the things they forgot, and the mistakes they made.

When asked to name what they did well, it would usually be tough to pull out more than one thing, and often it was trivialized. (*"What did I do well? I finished."*)

Why is this? I think because the fear of public speaking is so firmly entrenched, and because with that many eyes on us, it's tricky not to feel judged. Not only that, in many English-speaking cultures, it's considered egotistic to brag, so perhaps we're conditioned to avoid appearing smug, or boastful. And I would note that asking someone to name what they did well is not bragging or boasting: it's eliciting an observation.

However, I would then turn to the audience, and ask them a similar set of questions to gain their feedback. At which point I would have to stop the presenter dashing back to their seat in palpable relief, and ask them to return to take the feedback. I would typically hear the following answers:

"That was a fantastic presentation [because] *"* And they would go on to name five or more things they noticed. *"You looked so confident and prepared."*

They wouldn't usually single out mistakes (or even notice them, in some cases!), or correct anything.

They were generally impressed.

You can conclude from this that the speaker clearly tracks different information than their audience (obviously!), but the point I want to make is this:

What you feel on the *inside*, is often never noticed by the audience, especially when your **Presenter Bubble** is extended. You might be as nervous as they come, but follow the recommendations in this book, and your audience will never notice.

They will think you are being natural and authentic—and isn't that the goal?

After all, I never promised to *remove* the butterflies.

Just to make them fly in formation.

So let's conclude by looking at some ways you can appear more natural, and my best techniques to help you remember your speech.

7.2 How To Remember Your Speech; How To Use Notes

APPEARING NATURAL AND CONVERSATIONAL ON stage is made far easier by having "presentation hours under the belt," so your first goal should be to get as much practice under your belt as possible.

I was an anxious, nervous speaker, determined to be perfect. I spent many hours practicing presentations in front of friends (thank you!), gaining feedback, and getting up and doing it again.

It wasn't until some years later, when I found myself teaching other people to be effective and professional presenters, that the Blinding Flash Of The Obvious started to hit me until I got it.

Confidence and comfort in public speaking doesn't necessarily come from doing it over and over.

It comes from knowing how to *recover*.

The best public speakers are constantly using their recovery skills.

Stumbled over a word? No big deal: extend your **Presenter Bubble** and move on.

Joke falls flat? Make a self-deprecating statement and move on.

Someone interrupts? Manage the interruption and move on.

Microphone stops working? Talk louder and move on.

Notice how much "moving on" there is?

The professional presenter knows that their job is to capture the hearts and minds of the audience—or to re-capture them, if momentarily distracted.

And now you know the methods involved, you can do that too.

It's my belief that most audiences want you to succeed. They're happy for you to move on, even if there was a mistake. We're all human, and if you demonstrate this with great authenticity from the front of the room, you've already won them over.

Now you are ready to overcome the last hurdle: Appearing to be smooth and natural, while remembering your speech, and avoiding those "blank moments," and stopping that over-reliance on your notes.

The best ways to remember your talk, speech or presentation

Rule Number One

The first rule is never to memorize every single word. You're not an actor employed to memorize a script. Even if you could remember every word, it won't appear as natural as speaking "in the moment."

If you've ever been anxious about speaking in public, as I was, then I can imagine your reaction to the idea of speaking in the moment goes something like, *"But I won't know what I'm going to say?! Help!"*

Rule Number Two

The second rule is to always, always imagine you are simply presenting as if you are having a conversation with friends. What you say exactly won't matter, as long as you deliver the gist of your talk.

In fact, when you deliver your speech from your unconscious store of ideas, you may well find there are "genius moments," where you feel you could have been channeling your speech from Bill Clinton, Gandhi or Mother Teresa.

Relaxation helps, of course. And that you have to practice!

There are some things that I do recommend you practice word-for-word, not that they have to come out that way when you "go live," but it helps to code what you want to say at key moments. I personally practice these in different ways, depending on the situation. There's one part of your speech you'll definitely need to have down as pat as possible in your head, and that's the first two to three minutes.

What is the best way to get your first few minutes locked into your brain?

I remind you of rule one again: do not attempt to memorize every word. Work on the markers you wish to hit, and boil those down to a few key trigger words.

That's the precious tip right there: *a few key words*.

For example, I might have these notes:

Welcome. Me, English & Australian, don't speak proper. Why you are here. Perhaps you do this ... Whiteboard of the mind story.

As you can see, they are super-sketchy. But *I* know what they mean, and I know roughly what I'm going to say at each "marker point."

Have trigger words for each marker point. Practice delivering your intro to those marker points. It will make a huge difference to your level of relaxation when you understand just how easy that is. Even if you're a massive introvert, as I am, somehow the words appear in your mouth, and you can concentrate your attention on your audience (and not on remembering each word).

Rule Number Three

The third rule is to use your visual memory. This is a major clue. Why? Because if you try to "remember words" while you are speaking words, the two auditory channels compete. I mentioned this before: Try having a conversation with someone face-to-face while simultaneously having a conversation on the phone. It's impossible. The only thing you can do is rapidly switch from one to the other to give the appearance of carrying on the conversation simultaneously —but if both your conversation partners reply to you at once? Good luck with that.

You do not want to confuse your brain by having your internal words "jam" your external speech.

This is why using your visual memory (or developing it, if you're not used to using it yet) to retrieve your key triggers is hugely helpful.

How should you do this?

If you wish, you can color-code your bullet-points (for example, as per my notes above). You'll far more easily remember the order, and after that, connecting for example, "red bullet point," with "Whiteboard of the mind story," is a no-brainer.

Another way is with symbols. Color-code those too, if you wish.

Yet another way is not to have any color or symbols on your notes page, but instead, inside your head, you have a "visual map" that you've practiced memorizing. It might be pretty shapes; a "map" with stations; a series of small movies-of-the-mind—whatever helps you visually track what is coming up.

The beauty of the visual memory is its speed. An idea can flash up, then be gone in an instant, and you immediately have it to draw on. Whereas remembering words and sentences is slow. A picture tells a thousand words, so use pictures to help you tell your words.

That's the first two-three minutes. After that, your material will start to drive itself. Because?

You are using *4MAT*. You know exactly which quadrant you are in for your current topic **chunk**. You know what **chunk** comes next. You remember (visually) your PostIts.

From here, I usually bullet point each "chunk" (down to whatever chunk size you are comfortable with). As you become more proficient in a particular topic, or with a speech you've already delivered a few times, your list of bullets will shrink. That's *7 +/- 2* in action.

A warning: Somewhere, please log the full version of any bullets that have become shorthand. Otherwise you might find you've been asked to redeliver a speech you last made over a year ago, and you pull out your notes, remembering what a great speech it was ... but hold on ... you scan the bullet points for your introduction. What the heck does "tell cat story here" mean?

Particularly if you lean more towards "*Intuit*" tendencies, you might find some ideas will need more sensate language around them. "*Tell cat story here*" might be more useful as "*Tell cat story—unemployed, last dollar, no cat food, who wins—here.*" Use **sensate** trigger words to help you hook you own mind into retrieving your own stories and examples.

Once you start to know your **chunks**, and what's coming up next, what will really makes you stand out from the crowd is how you **transition** from one **chunk** to another. You'll appear more natural and authentic, and when you start to *link your chunks together*, you'll create a satisfying, complex matrix of ideas.

It is from this that more "ah-ha moments" will happen in the minds of your audience.

How do you plan for this?

You add specific speaker's notes (bullet points), for *the links and transitions you will use* at the beginning and end of each chunk. Take as much care in designing your transitions and links as you do your main content chunks.

I would also recommend practicing your transitions and links. I mentioned before that I memorize in a couple of ways. The first is as I've already illustrated: with bullet points, visual memory and chunks. I like to keep well inside my own *7+/-2.*

But I'll also construct my links and transitions in the moment, and may even say them to myself in my head if I have an opportunity. This might be in a moment of downtime for me when the audience is on a task. Obviously not all speeches have this. It depends on the level of interactivity. But you may have a moment when the audience is digesting a slide you've just flashed up, or are watching a short video clip.

Either way, I know what chunk I'm completing, and what chunk and outcome I'm moving to. Knowing beforehand what the transition and the links are (usually to my bigger chunks) means I'll have a bullet point reference or two, and because I'm now in the flow of my content, this is super-easy compared to presenting your first few minutes.

Keeping to time

Even with a lot of practice, you might find that once you have an audience and are presenting live, what was coming in well under ten minutes, is now looking like taking fifteen. This is not at all uncommon. There's something about the two-way connection with your audience that extends the time for each nuance: Maybe they laugh more, maybe they digest an idea more deeply than you'd planned, so you calibrate that and wait for them to be ready for you to continue. Maybe you get an unexpected question.

So along with your transition bullets, train yourself to have a running time-sheet. Know approximately when you expect each transition to take place in your talk. That way, you'll realize way earlier that you need to catch time up, or drop a content piece, or simply speed up.

The last thing you want to do is to discover you're out of time just as you get to your earth-shatteringly brilliant conclusions. You know; that ah-ha part where the earth moves for your audience. Start tracking it early on in your presentation. I use a stopwatch for some critical moments, but not everyone needs that, or is comfortable. You do need a timepiece easily visible though, because I'll remind you what I said before: your sense of time and tempo is running at a different pace to that of your audience, and the more you are "one with your content," the less likely you are to reliably track time.

Your endings

Just as critical to get right (and to practice) is your ending.

Back in Chapter 2, "How To Make Any Speech Memorable," I discussed the horrible "dribble" ending, where the speech just seems to fade-out; the finish is not obvious, and some of the audience are already leaving when the presenter suddenly remembers some key point they forgot to mention.

I caution you against ever telegraphing too early that the close of your talk is near. As soon as you do, you'll hear a rustle of activity as papers get shuffled, pens are put away, cell phones are pulled out and checked, and some people will grab their belongings and appear ready to sprint.

The only exception to this is when you sense a need for a break, and you flag it. "*Just a few more minutes and we'll be on a break, so stick with me.*" But avoid that too, wherever possible.

So you get to the end. Your finale. Your moment in the sun.

How to do this?

In a word?

Definitively.

Make it a **contextual marker**. A clear cut finish. So obvious that the audience know it's time to applaud. You can do this in a number of ways:

- Tell a story, with a key point or punchline, then say thank you.
- Summarize the main points of your talk, and restate a succinct version of your opening "**Why?**" frame(s). For example: "*As I stated, taking the time to do that extra five minutes of preparation, along with the three keys to making your work-day productive, will guarantee a measured 80% reduction in your stress levels ... and a healthier life.*"
- Future pace your audience into using your content: "*The very next time you encounter an angry person, I recommend you ...*"

Never end apologetically: "*I hope you found this useful.*" "*I'm not sure if you got all my points.*" "*I'm sorry I had to rush the last few minutes, but I didn't realize the time.*"

And wherever possible (and assuming it suits your designed outcome), end on a positive note, with positive body language.

You can even signal the positive moment coming: You move to the center of the stage and pause, assuming a confident stance, and look your audience in the eye.

<cue dramatic music>

It's been a wonderful journey together. One that began with us both believing that we'd rather die than give a speech; connected at different points in our lives by the same disabling thoughts: That somehow, this was something that *other* people find easy, and that we never would.

By now, you realize there are a ton of techniques and methods that will help you with the practical elements of designing your outcome, planning your show, and wowing your audiences.

But none of that happens until you accept the mantle, as I did, and truly believe that inside of you there lies a wonderful "**Presenter Identity**" ... and that anyone can do it.

It's time to thank your old fears and anxieties for bringing you to this point, and for forcing you to learn how to be a great presenter. In battling those demons, you've been able to place particular attention on the quality of your work, and on removing anxiety. Perversely, this intense focus is more likely to make you a better public speaker, perhaps more so than someone who has never had to face those anxieties.

My wish for you, is for you to take a deep breath, expand your bubble and go out into the world with your message ... because we need to hear it.

7.3 Drills

Before you present:

Never try to memorize all your words. By all means have a sense of your opening sentence, but this can be formulated in your head just before you stand to speak.

Use visual notes, color code them if you wish (this is much easier to remember), or use easy to understand symbols and icons.

Make your notes and what you memorize all about making it to the next "marker." This might be a transition to the next chunk, but it's just as likely to be another link providing relevance and context to the next piece of content. Memorizing your design chunks in isolation isn't always useful, though obviously helpful. Make sure you are also working on memorizing links and transitions.

Practice your first two minutes out loud! Allow the words to change from what you had bullet-pointed on paper, and allow them to change each time, until they flow naturally.

Before standing up to speak:

Have that first sentence ready ... and extend your *Presenter Bubble*.

During your presentation:

Remember to move. This alone will help you make the links to your next piece of content. Recent research suggests we are more creative when we move (specifically walking: http://news.stanford.edu/news/2014/april/walking-vs-sitting-042414.html), so the opposite is true: you'll be less creative if you stand still, or present from a chair.

Post-speech:

Focus on what worked—ask a trusted colleague for feedback. Remember after you finish to stack your *Presenter Identity* with all the positives, and jam into it all the goodness and improvements you make each time. You *can* do this. You *are* the fabulous and fantastic presenter you always wanted to be.

How do I know?

Because if I can do it, then you can too.

Robert Scanlon, August 2015.

Thank you!

May I ask you a question?

Did you like this book?

Then would be willing to post your review on Amazon?

Just use the link below and it will take you directly to the reviews page.

Thank you! Every review helps other people like you decide what books are worthy ... and your review also encourages me to write more!

http://RobertScanlon.com/publicspeakingreview

Check out all my books here:

www.RobertScanlonBooks.com

ABOUT ROBERT SCANLON

Born in Australia, Robert was whisked back to England where he spent his childhood. After many years complaining about the weather, he did the only sensible thing, and moved back to Australia. Queensland actually. Where he enjoys walks along the beach with his wonderful family.

(Pssst. He still complains about the weather if it gets too cold!)

Here's a bit more about him ...

Robert is an Author and Entrepreneur–but he wasn't always.

He's studied chemistry; worked in the music industry; sold handbags; taught yoga; raced motorcycles; and trained thousands of people in Presentations Skills, Train-the-Trainer, Negotiation Skills … and more.

Mostly though he loves to read.

And read and read. His father was a science-fiction fan, so Robert grew up on a voracious diet of all the top-notch sci-fi writers (there's a list below!), eventually discovering he had read the entire science-fiction section of his local library. But nowadays he writes books and runs websites. Which is fun, and nothing like work at all.

Here are some questions he's often asked (well he made them up actually, but he'd LOVE you to ask them anyway!):

What was your first job?

It was mowing the lawn for my Dad. The pay was terrible, but it was fun because I liked engines, so I revved it a lot and it sounded like I was racing around the grass.

I also used to be a golf caddy, which was funny because I don't enjoy golf.

And I sold handbags from a market stall, which is also funny because … well handbags are not really a boy-thing. But it did teach me how to sell something you don't use yourself.

Where do you live?

Right now I live in Queensland, Australia which is beautiful. The first half of my life I lived in England, which is rainy. I lived in the South of France for a little while too – that was rather nice and I'd like to do it again!

Do you play an instrument?

Ha!

I love music and used to sing and play guitar in a band. Now I don't have a guitar or a bass, but I could play one badly if asked. I'm learning to play piano (it's hard!) since I didn't do that at an early age. I think everyone should learn an instrument of some description, it's a lovely creative activity.

What do you like to read?

My dad loved Sci-Fi, so that was a big influence. I loved John Wyndham, Philip K Dick, Robert Heinlein and I have a soft spot for Isaac Asimov (who had great non-fiction books about space that I loved). So I still love Sci-Fi, but also like Fantasy; Thrillers and some Action. I also enjoy Young Adult books hugely. I mean, who doesn't like Harry Potter? (If you don't, I feel for you, I really do haha!)

What is an Entrepreneur anyway?

Hmm. Good question. I wish you hadn't asked it. (What's that you say, these are questions I wrote down to ask? Oh. Alright then, better answer it.).

Ahem. An entrepreneur is someone who looks for opportunities to help people by providing a service or a product that is not available; or could be made much better. I think having a creative or an entrepreneurial spirit is a wonderful thing, and with more of it, we could change the world for the better. (And not always with money as the reason!)

Can I get in touch with you to ask more questions?

Yes, as long as they are easy ones!
Just use the "Contact" link on my website at RobertScanlon.com/contact-robert/ and send me a message!

One last thing before you go ...

If you found this book useful, I'd love your help. Would you be willing to head over to Amazon and review this book? You'll be able to let other people know that you've made use of the material within, and I will be forever in your debt!

Thank you,

Robert

www.ingramcontent.com/pod-product-compliance
Lightning Source LLC
Chambersburg PA
CBHW050658110426
42739CB00035B/3444